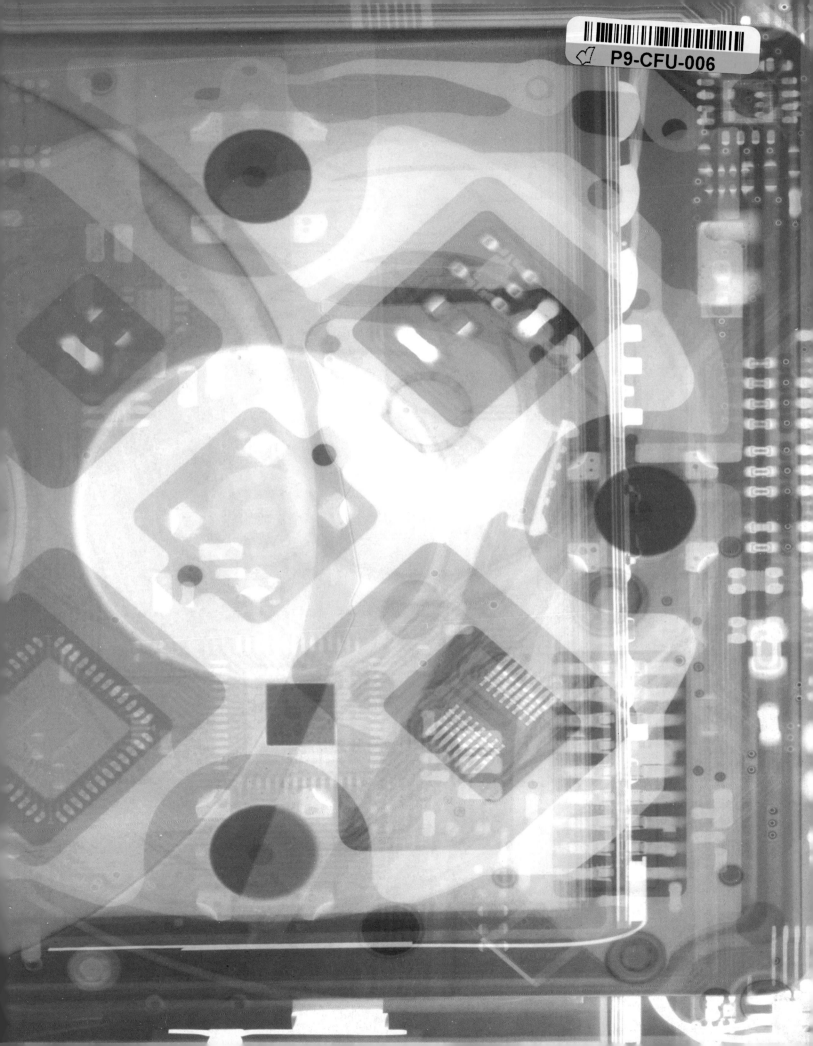

COOL STUFF
AND HOW IT WORKS

LONDON, NEW YORK, MELBOURNE,
MUNICH and DELHI

Project Editors Kate Bradshaw, Julie Ferris,
Andrea Mills, Rosie O'Neill

Art Editors Philip Letsu, Joanne Little,
Sarah Ponder, Johnny Pau

Senior Editors Carey Scott, Fran Jones, Sarah Larter
Senior Art Editor and Styling Joanne Connor

Managing Editor Camilla Hallinan
Managing Art Editor Sophia M. Tampakopoulos Turner

DTP Coordinator Siu Yin Ho

Art Director Simon Webb
Publishing Manager Andrew Macintyre
Category Publisher Jonathan Metcalf

Picture Research Louise Thomas
Production Alison Lenane
Jacket Design Bob Warner

Illustrators Kevin Jones, Andrew Kerr, Lee Gibbons

Consultants Roger Bridgman, Tom Standage,
Ian Graham, Dr. Susan Aldridge

First American Edition, 2005

Published in the United States by
DK Publishing, Inc.
375 Hudson Street
New York, New York 10014

05 06 07 08 09   10 9 8 7 6 5 4 3 2 1

Copyright © 2005 Dorling Kindersley Limited

A Catalog record for this book is available from the Library
of Congress.

ISBN 0-7566-1465-1

Color reproduction by Icon Reproduction, London
Printed and bound in China by SNP Leefung

Discover more at
www.dk.com

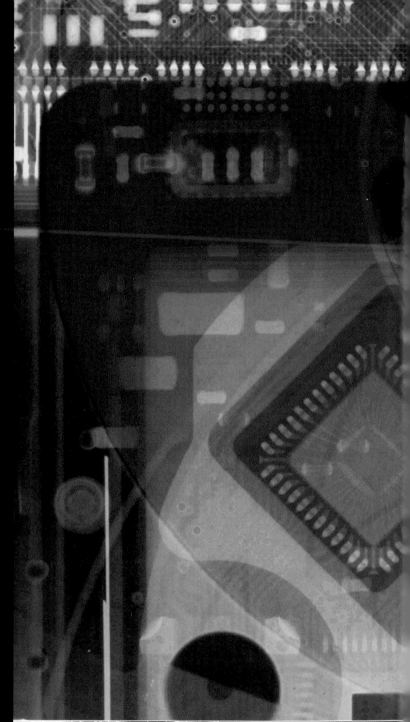

COOL STUFF
AND HOW IT WORKS

Written by Chris Woodford, and Luke Collins,
Clint Witchalls, Ben Morgan, James Flint

CONTENTS

8 Imaging techniques
10 More imaging techniques

CONNECT

14 Introduction >> **16** Microchip
18 Cell phone >> **20** Fiber optics
22 Digital radio >> **24** LCD TV
26 Toys gallery >> **28** Voice recognition
30 Pet translator >> **32** Iris scan
34 Neon >> **36** Links gallery
38 Internet >> **40** Video link
42 Satellite >> **44** What next?

PLAY

48 Introduction >>
50 Sneaker >> **52** Soccer
54 Racket >> **56** Snowboard
58 Bike >> **60** Fabric gallery
62 Camera >> **64** Games
66 Guitar >> **68** Compact disc
70 MP3 player >> **72** Arenas gallery
74 Headphones >> **76** DJ decks
78 Fireworks >> **80** What next?

LIVE

84 Introduction >>
86 Match >> **88** Light bulb
90 Mirror >> **92** Watch
94 Battery >> **96** Solar cell
98 Heat gallery >> **100** Microwave
102 Fridge >> **104** Aerogel
106 Homes gallery >> **108** Lock
110 Shaver >> **112** Aerosol
114 Washing machine >> **116** Vacuum
118 Robot helper >> **120** What next?

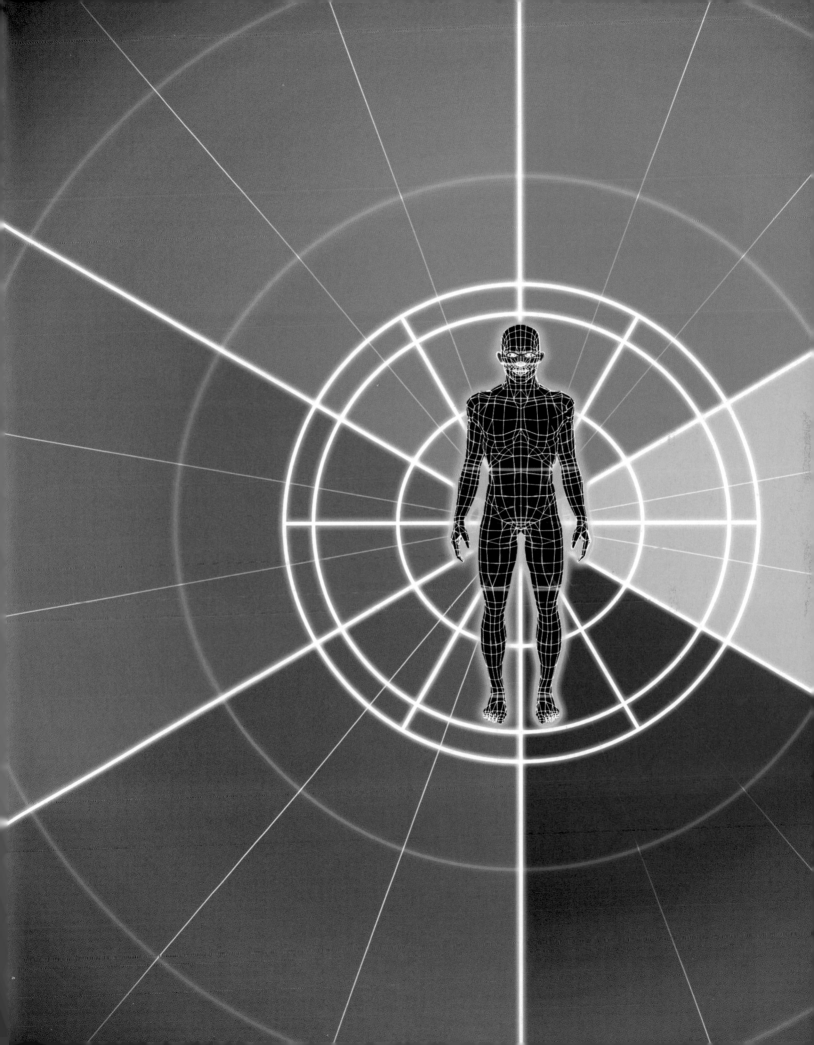

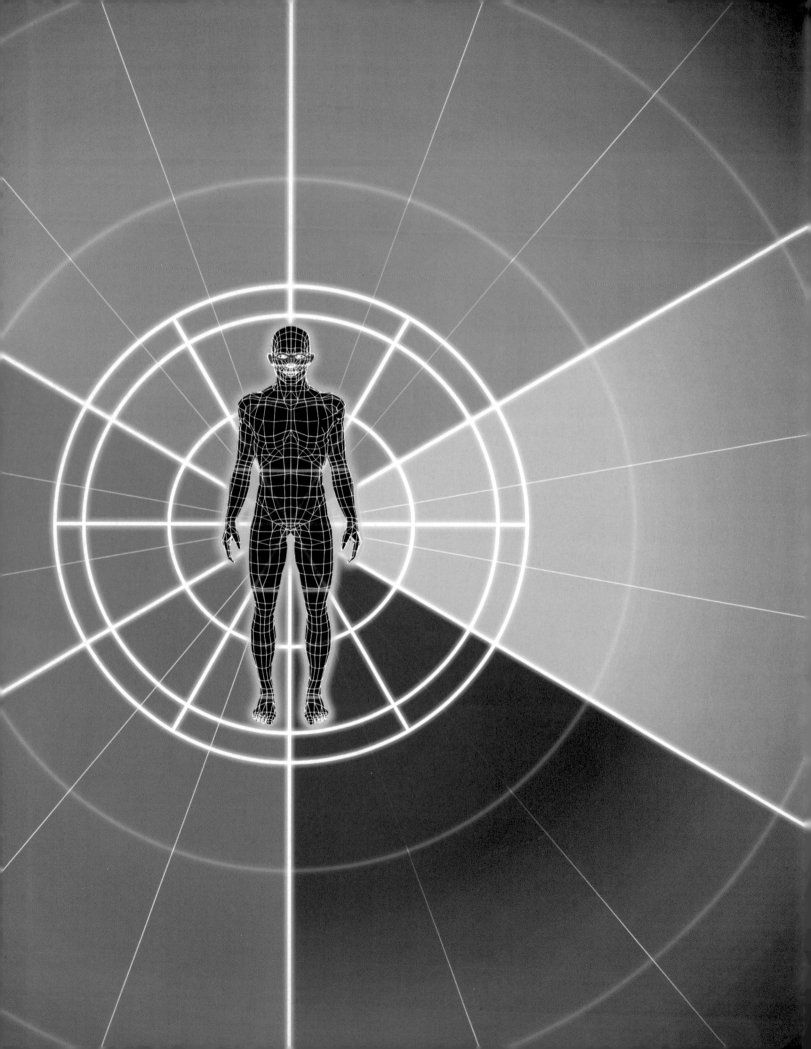

MOVE

124 Introduction »

126 Motorcycle » **128** Fuel-cell car

130 Car engine » **132** Parts gallery

134 Crash test » **136** Car tower

138 Wheelchair » **140** Elevator

142 Submersible » **144** Osprey

146 Jet engine » **148** Wind tunnel

150 Black box » **152** Routes gallery

154 Navigation » **156** Space Shuttle

158 Space probe » **160** What next?

WORK

164 Introduction »

166 Digital pen » **168** Laptop

170 Motherboard » **172** Flash stick

174 Virtual keyboard » **176** Laser printer

178 Scanner » **180** ID gallery

182 Smart card » **184** Radio ID tag

186 Robot worker » **188** Wet welding

190 Fire suit » **192** Glues gallery

194 Doppler radar » **196** What next?

SURVIVE

200 Introduction »

202 Scans gallery » **204** MRI scan

206 Laser surgery » **208** Robot surgery

210 Pacemaker » **212** Camera capsule

214 Bionic limbs » **216** Skin graft

218 Cells gallery » **220** Vaccination

222 Antibiotics » **224** IVF

226 Biochip » **228** What next?

REFERENCE

232 Timeline » **236** Groundbreakers

240 Techno terms » **252** Index

256 Acknowledgments

Imaging techniques

Over the last century, successive breakthroughs in imaging technology have transformed the way we see the objects that surround us. From medicine to engineering to weather forecasting, worlds invisible to the naked eye can now be observed. There are microscopes that can take pictures of individual atoms, the building blocks of matter. These are so small that they have to be magnified 100 million times to become visible. At the other end of the scale, the almost perfect mirrors inside the Hubble Space Telescope capture images of dying stars in distant galaxies.

▶ MACROPHOTOGRAPHY

Macrophotography makes a small subject, such as this image of a human eye on a liquid crystal display (LCD) screen, appear life-size or greater. A special camera lens with powerful magnification lets the photographer focus from just a few inches away. Macrophotography can reveal details that are very difficult, or impossible, to make out with the naked eye. It is often used to take extreme close-up pictures of plants and insects. Scientists can also attach cameras to microscopes to capture objects in even greater detail. This technique is called photomicrography.

◀ DOPPLER RADAR

Doppler radar helps meteorologists to track storms, tornadoes and, as pictured here, hurricanes. Doppler radar measures an object's speed and direction of movement. A transmitter sends out radio waves into the sky. These travel at the speed of light until they reach their target—usually water droplets in clouds—then they bounce back. By calculating the time it takes for the echoes to bounce back, a computer can work out where clouds are. It can also figure out how much water a cloud contains from the strength of the reflected echo beam. In this way, a detailed picture of weather events can be formed.

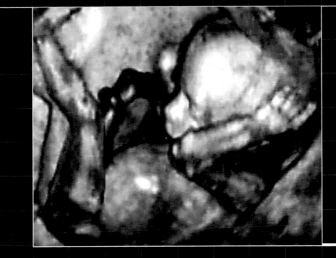

◀ULTRASOUND

Ultrasound is a medical imaging technique often used to check a baby's development in its mother's womb. A probe sends out millions of pulses of high-frequency sound waves—at least 100 times greater than those within the range of human hearing—into the body each second. By measuring the time it takes for the echoes to return to the probe, a detailed image is produced on the screen of the ultrasound machine. To produce three-dimensional (3-D) images, such as this one, many scans are taken and combined by a computer.

◀X-RAY MACHINE

This X-ray of a guitar's components has been enhanced with color. Images like this are called false-color X-rays. X-ray machines work like cameras, but instead of visible light they use X-rays, which can penetrate soft materials to reveal the hard structures inside an object. They are most commonly used to diagnose broken bones, but high doses can damage living tissue, so they must be used sparingly. They are also used by engineers to detect tiny flaws in metal structures, by astronomers to observe distant stars, and by airport security to scan luggage.

▲ MAGNETIC RESONANCE IMAGING

Magnetic Resonance Imaging (MRI) allows doctors to explore the body's structures, such as the brain's network of nerve connections, shown here. An MRI scanner bombards the body with radio waves that cause vibrations in atoms held in position by the scanner's powerful magnets. These tiny movements produce the information for a computer to build up a very detailed three-dimensional image. MRI helps doctors diagnose serious conditions, and provides clues about the workings of the brain.

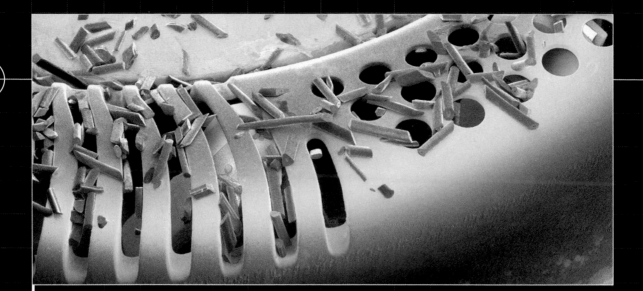

▲ SCANNING ELECTRON MICROSCOPE

A Scanning Electron Microscope (SEM) reveals tiny organisms and viruses that are invisible to the naked eye. It can also make images of objects that are difficult to see, such as these tiny hairs on an electric shaver. An SEM works by focusing a stream of electrons into a narrow beam that sweeps the object. The electrons bounce off the object and are converted into an electrical signal by a detector. The signal is used to create a photograph-like image on a TV screen that has a very high resolution, or level of detail. The image is photographed to make a black-and-white image, but can be colored digitally—false-colored—by a computer.

▲ INFRARED THERMOGRAPHY

Infrared thermography is a technique that uses a special camera to see heat. Every object, even very cold ones such as ice cubes, releases infrared, or heat, radiation. In a heat picture, or thermogram, higher temperatures show up as brighter areas. Although the images are black and white, they can be colored to provide as much information as possible. Thermography has many uses, including medical diagnosis, search-and-rescue operations, and monitoring the energy efficiency of buildings.

◀ CUTAWAY

A cutaway is an illustration technique that reveals the internal parts of an object. This technique is often used to show how something works, usually in 3-D—for example, the cushioning technology in a high-tech running shoe, or the position of an engine in a car. Cutaways were originally drawn on paper by hand, and were very time-consuming. Today, technical illustrators are more likely to create cutaways on a computer screen. With digital imaging software and 3-D graphic tools, an artist can create a realistic illustration of an object by superimposing some layers on an image and making others transparent.

▶ SCHLIEREN PHOTOGRAPHY

Schlieren photography is used to photograph the flow of air around an object—for example, an aircraft in a wind tunnel. In this image, the technique has been used to capture the shock waves caused by an exploding firecracker. Schlieren photography works because a fast-moving object disturbs the air, squashing it in some places and stretching it in others. This causes changes in air pressure and density. When light passes through the air, the differences in density make it refract (bend), causing the image to become lighter or darker where this happens. Color is added to the image with the use of filters.

◀ EXPLODED VIEW

An exploded view is a type of illustration that separates out the parts of an object—for example, the different layers of this smart card. A computer uses separate images of each different element of the object and superimposes them on a main image so that they are depicted in their correct order. This allows us to see how the parts fit together and also the way they relate to one another. Exploded views are often found in technical manuals to show the order in which the different elements need to be assembled.

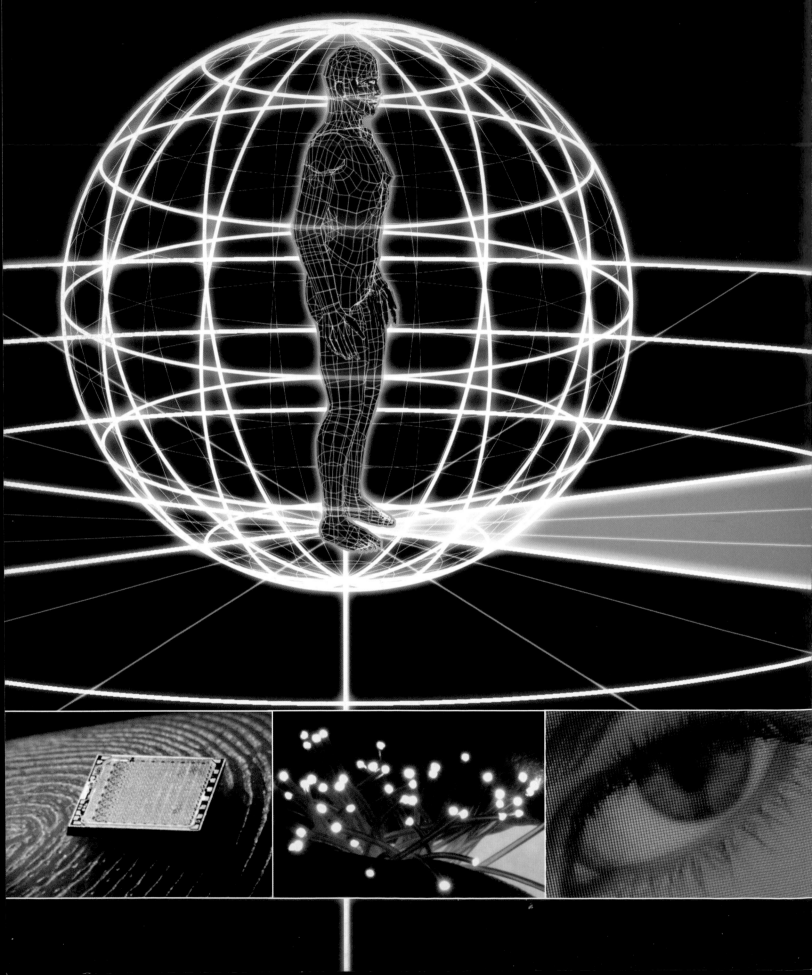

>>CONNECT

Microchip >> Cell phone >> Fiber optics >> Digital radio >>
LCD TV >> Voice recognition >> Pet translator >> Iris scan >>
Neon >> Internet >> Video link >> Satellite

Communication systems have existed for thousands of years. A postal system, with relays of riders to deliver messages, was used in ancient Persia (now Iran) as long ago as the 6th century BC. Until the 1800s, sending mail in this way was the only method of long-distance communication. The time it took for a message to be received depended on the speed of the carrier.

The electric telegraph was widely used by the mid-1800s, and this meant that, for the first time, messages made up from a special code could be sent and received without delay. With the invention of the telephone in 1876, people could have conversations with each other even if they were hundreds, and later thousands, of miles apart.

Today, digital technology has revolutionized the way we communicate. Digital means turning information—images, words, sounds, as well as text—into streams of ones and zeros that can be read by digital devices such as computers or cell phones. Digital technology allows millions of telephone calls, text messages, and emails to be sent instantly around the world. None of this would be possible without computers and fiber-optic cables, which can carry 100 billion ones and zeros per second at the speed of light.

REMOTE CONTROL

When digital computers were developed soon after World War II, they took up whole rooms and were no more powerful than a digital watch is today. This might seem puny compared to today's computers, but even so, in 1969, a computer was able to make the calculations that helped astronauts land on the Moon.

Since then, computers have become much smaller. As they have reduced in size and cost, they have also become much more powerful and user-friendly. The processing power of a computer is found in its microchip, or electronic brain. A microchip has millions of tiny switches, or transistors, made chemically on the surface of a wafer of silicon, a chemical element most commonly found in sand. These electronic switches allow computers to carry out mind-boggling numbers of calculations every single second.

> " We can share information, exchange ideas, and form online communities with people thousands of miles away. "

Two or more computers connected together form a network. From tree roots to spiderwebs to our own brains, networks are everywhere. By linking many simple units, very complex structures can be formed. The Internet connects hundreds of millions of computers together worldwide so they can access the World Wide Web—the part of the Internet that provides information in the form of websites. In 1993, there were only 50 sites. Today, there are more than eight billion. This immensely powerful network of computers gives us instant access to a vast amount of knowledge. You can also log on to email a friend on the other side of the world, book a vacation, buy or sell goods, or download music. The Internet has transformed the computer into the ultimate communications device, and shrunk the world to a global village.

▲ **A microchip** can be smaller than the nail on a little finger but operates like a tiny electronic brain. The most complex microchips, known as microprocessors, can pack the processing power of an entire computer onto a single chip.

MICROCHIP

▶▶ Microchips used in the latest computers can process about 10 billion instructions every second. Since 1971, the number of transistors that can fit on a single chip has increased from over 2,000 to a staggering 500 million. ▶▶

›› MICROCHIP: KEY FEATURES

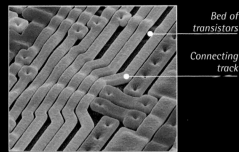

Bed of transistors

Connecting track

‹‹ 1. A microchip reveals its secrets when magnified almost 1,200 times. Transistors (purple) are built up in layers on the chip, with metallic connecting tracks positioned above them. These tiny transistors switch on and off to control electronic signals, processing thousands of pieces of information each second.

›› 2. Gold microwires— magnified here almost 300 times—link tiny electrical contact points at the edge of the chip to metal legs on its casing. Although gold is expensive, it is an excellent conductor of electricity and helps to prevent the microchip from overheating.

Gold microwire

Soldered seam

Contact point

Tweezers

Plastic casing

Metal leg

‹‹ 3. A microchip is so small and fragile that it has to be protected in a casing made of plastic or ceramic. Each of the casing's metal legs, which extend from the contact points inside the chip, can be soldered into a larger electronic circuit to connect the chip to other components.

‹BACK
In 1958, the invention of the integrated circuit—a method of shrinking entire circuits onto microchips—led to more affordable electronic goods.

Scientists are developing a microchip implant for the eye that stimulates cells around the retina. This may help blind people to see again.

FORWARD›

⌄ Making a silicon chip

▶Microchips are made from an element called silicon. They start life as crystals, which are grown from molten silicon to become cylinders over 3 ft (1 m) long and up to 1 ft (30 cm) in diameter. Each cylinder is then sliced into discs called silicon wafers.

Silicon wafers

▶The silicon wafers are heated in a furnace and etched with chemicals, which form the tiny tracks and transistors on their surface. Hundreds of chips can be made on a single wafer. Once the wafer has been tested, it is cut into individual chips, which are then mounted into protective cases.

Silicon wafer and single chip

▶▶ See also: Microprocessor p246, Motherboard p170, Smart card p182, Sneaker p50

CELL PHONE

Powerful loudspeaker can work as an earpiece or speaker-phone.

▶▶ Cell phones let you make or take calls wherever you happen to be. A quarter of the world's population now makes their phone calls this way, and around 800 million cell phones are in use worldwide. ▶▶

◀ **Screen** has a 176 x 220 pixel (color dot) display that can show photos taken by the built-in camera. A graphics accelerator chip allows it to play movies, music videos, and games.

▶ **Ultra-thin keypad** is a third of the thickness of a conventional phone keypad. Its built-in blue light glows so that numbers are visible in the dark.

▶ **This cell phone** is a handheld personal communication center, with email, Web browser, and state-of-the-art video and game player. It has a built-in camera and two color screens (one on the inside of the case and another seen when the case is closed). It weighs just 3¹/₃ oz (95 g).

◀◀BACK

The first mobile phone network, Advanced Mobile Phone System (AMPS), appeared in Chicago in 1978. It used a system of ten cells to link 2,000 customers.

All cell phones will have built-in multimedia players that can stream (simultaneously download and play) music and video from the Internet.

FORWARD▶▶

▲ **Digital camera** has a zoom lens that can magnify up to four times. Photos taken are stored in the phone's memory and can be sent to other people's phones.

Internal aerial is built into the phone's hinge.

▶ **SIM (Subscriber Identity Module)** contains a microchip that stores your personal details and can be switched from phone to phone.

ACTUAL SIZE OF PHONE

▶▶ See also: Battery p94, Digital radio p22, Internet p38, Voice recognition p28

▶▶ HOW CELL PHONES WORK

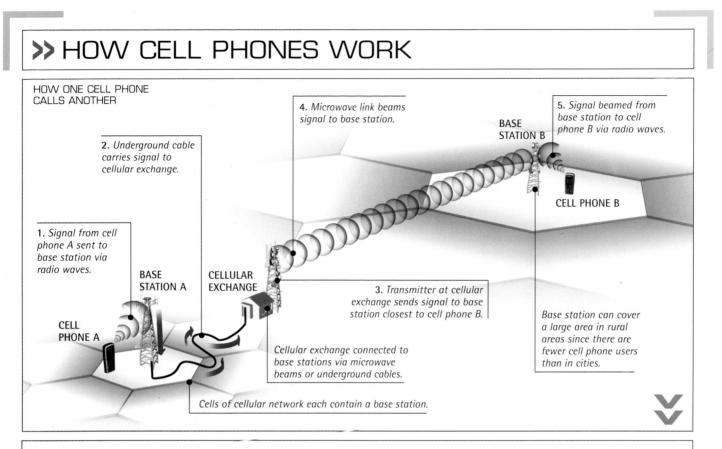

HOW ONE CELL PHONE CALLS ANOTHER

4. *Microwave link beams signal to base station.*

5. *Signal beamed from base station to cell phone B via radio waves.*

BASE STATION B

CELL PHONE B

2. *Underground cable carries signal to cellular exchange.*

1. *Signal from cell phone A sent to base station via radio waves.*

BASE STATION A

CELLULAR EXCHANGE

3. *Transmitter at cellular exchange sends signal to base station closest to cell phone B.*

CELL PHONE A

Cellular exchange connected to base stations via microwave beams or underground cables.

Base station can cover a large area in rural areas since there are fewer cell phone users than in cities.

Cells of cellular network each contain a base station.

Cell phones operate within a network of cells—areas covered by a radio transmitter mast known as a base station. Cells vary in size but overlap slightly, so that when you move from one cell to another your call can be handed off (passed without interruption) from one cell to the next. A central exchange links the cells; it also connects one cellular network (usually operated by one company) to other cellular networks and to the landline (wired-phone) network.

Cell phones send and receive calls as streams of digital data. This has many advantages over the analog technology still used in many landlines. There is less interference and better sound quality. Digital calls can be encrypted (scrambled) to prevent eavesdropping. Cell phones also send and receive voice, fax, text, and Internet data. Cellular networks can carry more digital calls than landline networks. Some send information using packet switching (known as GPRS), just like the Internet.

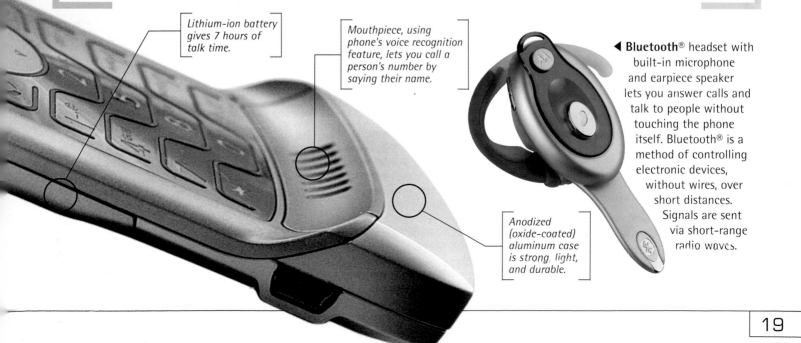

Lithium-ion battery gives 7 hours of talk time.

Mouthpiece, using phone's voice recognition feature, lets you call a person's number by saying their name.

◀ **Bluetooth®** headset with built-in microphone and earpiece speaker lets you answer calls and talk to people without touching the phone itself. Bluetooth® is a method of controlling electronic devices, without wires, over short distances. Signals are sent via short-range radio waves.

Anodized (oxide-coated) aluminum case is strong, light, and durable.

Image: macrophoto of fingers holding optical fibers

Glass core of a single fiber is less than one-tenth the thickness of a human hair.

Tiny point of light emerges from fiber's tip.

Bendable silica glass carries signals around corners.

FIBER OPTICS

▶▶ Fiber-optic cables, pulsing with light, are the traffic lanes of the information superhighway. By converting huge amounts of digital data into light signals, one tiny fiber can carry 10 million telephone calls simultaneously. ▶▶

Information transmitted by fiber optics starts out as an electric current carrying a stream of digital data. A light source, often a laser, turns the current into pulses of light and fires them into the cable. At the receiving end, a photodiode (light-detecting device) receives the light pulses and turns them back into an electric current that recreates the original stream of data. Light pulses travel down the fiber's core via different paths, known as modes, by reflecting off the surrounding cladding. In multiplexing (shown right), different streams of information are sent through the core of the fiber at the same time using a slightly different wavelength of light for each stream. Light can travel in zigzags for short-range communications, but for longer distances, much thinner fibers are used to send light signals via the more direct route, straight down the fiber's center.

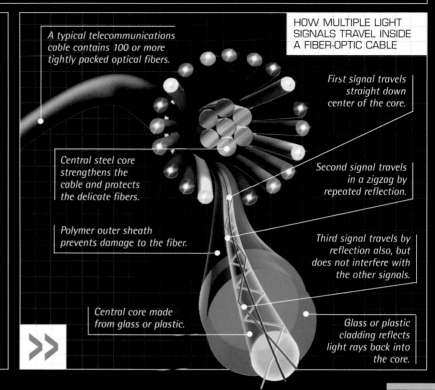

HOW MULTIPLE LIGHT SIGNALS TRAVEL INSIDE A FIBER-OPTIC CABLE

A typical telecommunications cable contains 100 or more tightly packed optical fibers.

Central steel core strengthens the cable and protects the delicate fibers.

Polymer outer sheath prevents damage to the fiber.

Central core made from glass or plastic.

First signal travels straight down center of the core.

Second signal travels in a zigzag by repeated reflection.

Third signal travels by reflection also, but does not interfere with the other signals.

Glass or plastic cladding reflects light rays back into the core.

◀ Optical fibers are hair-thin strands of glass, or sometimes plastic, that transmit digital information at the speed of light—fast enough to circle Earth seven times a second. They cost less and carry more signals than the copper wires that they are replacing. International phone calls and high-speed Internet connections are now much cheaper thanks to fiber-optic cables.

⌄ Making optical fibers

▶The glass core of an optical fiber starts as a thick, solid rod known as a preform. This is made by pumping two gases, silicon dioxide and germanium dioxide, into a hollow tube mounted on a slowly turning lathe. A burner travels up and down the tube, heating it from below until a solid glass core has completely formed inside it.

Burner heating preform in lathe

◀The preform is lowered into a tower at 3,500°F (1,900°C). As the vertically-hung glass melts, it stretches under its own weight. A machine at the base of the tower pulls and shapes the molten glass into thin cylindrical fibers. A laser measures the fibers and the machine speeds up or slows down to keep their diameter constant.

Pulling and shaping thin fibers

▶▶See also: Camera capsule p212, Mirror p90, Video link p40

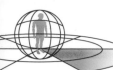
DIGITAL RADIO

▶▶ Digital radio sends programs through the air as numeric codes. Unlike analog radio, which can be affected by buildings and other obstacles, digitally coded signals deliver clear sound even if you're in a moving car or far from a transmitter. ▶▶

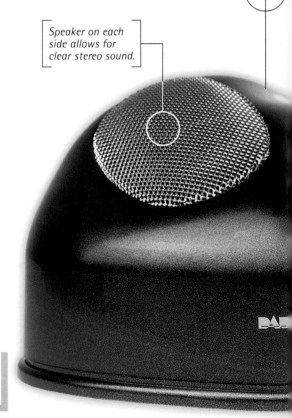

>> HOW DIGITAL RADIO WORKS

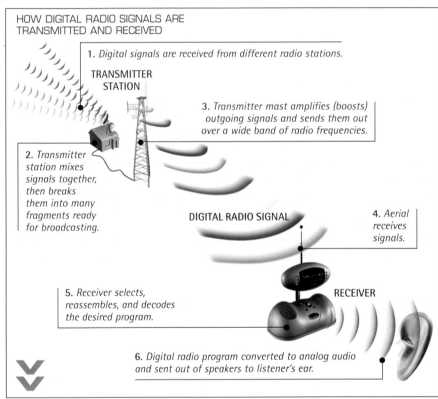

HOW DIGITAL RADIO SIGNALS ARE
TRANSMITTED AND RECEIVED

1. Digital signals are received from different radio stations.

TRANSMITTER
STATION

3. Transmitter mast amplifies (boosts) outgoing signals and sends them out over a wide band of radio frequencies.

2. Transmitter station mixes signals together, then breaks them into many fragments ready for broadcasting.

DIGITAL RADIO SIGNAL

4. Aerial receives signals.

5. Receiver selects, reassembles, and decodes the desired program.

RECEIVER

6. Digital radio program converted to analog audio and sent out of speakers to listener's ear.

▶ **This digital radio,** called The Bug, has a built-in memory chip that records incoming radio signals. At the push of a button, you can pause and even rewind live programs. Unlike an analog radio, it displays the title and singer of a song being played. The display also shows the station name, which makes it easier to tune.

Speaker on each side allows for clear stereo sound.

In analog radio, each radio station beams signals through the air on a separate, narrow band (range) of radio waves. As the signal travels, buildings, hills, and electrical equipment can interfere with it. Some radio waves never arrive, causing gaps in transmission; others are distorted, and the listener hears hiss, crackle, and stations leaking into each other's frequencies. With digital radio, programs are turned into digital codes (long strings of zeros and ones), each of which represents a fraction of a second of music or speech. The strings of numbers are broken into fragments, and then transmitted over a wide band of radio waves. Each fragment is sent more than once, at slightly different times, and over slightly different radio frequencies. Even if some fragments are lost along the way, the radio can piece together enough to form a clear and complete program.

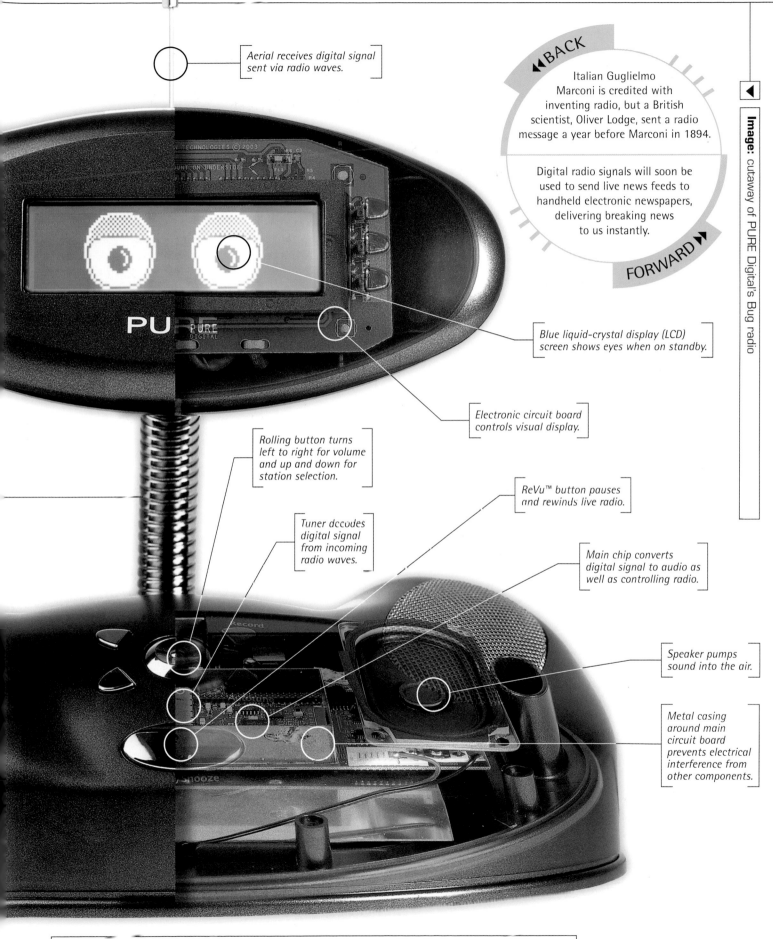

Aerial receives digital signal sent via radio waves.

◀◀BACK

Italian Guglielmo Marconi is credited with inventing radio, but a British scientist, Oliver Lodge, sent a radio message a year before Marconi in 1894.

Digital radio signals will soon be used to send live news feeds to handheld electronic newspapers, delivering breaking news to us instantly.

FORWARD▶

Image: cutaway of PURE Digital's Bug radio

Blue liquid-crystal display (LCD) screen shows eyes when on standby.

Electronic circuit board controls visual display.

Rolling button turns left to right for volume and up and down for station selection.

ReVu™ button pauses and rewinds live radio.

Tuner decodes digital signal from incoming radio waves.

Main chip converts digital signal to audio as well as controlling radio.

Speaker pumps sound into the air.

Metal casing around main circuit board prevents electrical interference from other components.

▶▶ See also: Headphones p74, LCD TV p24, MP3 player p70, Radio waves p249

▲ **Tiny colored squares** known as pixels make up the images on a TV screen. LCD (liquid-crystal display) screens, such as this one, are used in an ever-increasing number of televisions. They are also used in computer monitors, cell phones, and digital music and movie players.

LCD TV

▶▶There are an estimated 1.5 billion television sets in the world today—one for every four people on the planet. LCD TVs are now the flattest, lightest, most reliable, and energy-efficient TVs around. ▶▶

▶▶ See also: Camera p62, Games p64, Laptop p168, Light p246

≫ HOW AN LCD TELEVISION WORKS

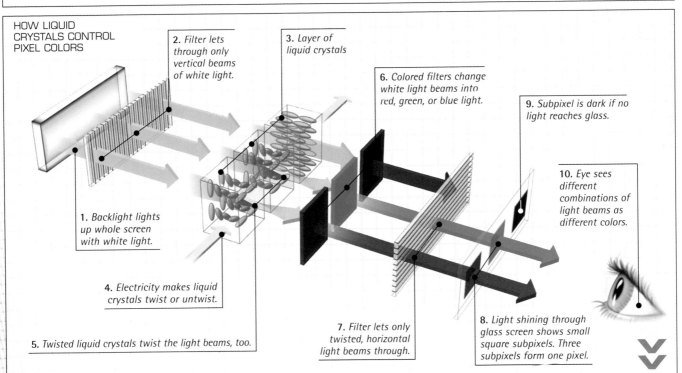

HOW LIQUID CRYSTALS CONTROL PIXEL COLORS

2. *Filter lets through only vertical beams of white light.*

3. *Layer of liquid crystals*

6. *Colored filters change white light beams into red, green, or blue light.*

9. *Subpixel is dark if no light reaches glass.*

10. *Eye sees different combinations of light beams as different colors.*

1. *Backlight lights up whole screen with white light.*

4. *Electricity makes liquid crystals twist or untwist.*

5. *Twisted liquid crystals twist the light beams, too.*

7. *Filter lets only twisted, horizontal light beams through.*

8. *Light shining through glass screen shows small square subpixels. Three subpixels form one pixel.*

An LCD screen is made up of several million tiny squares called pixels, each containing a red, green, and blue subpixel. Each subpixel is controlled by a group of microscopic liquid crystals positioned behind it. Electronic circuits inside the TV work out which pixels need to be switched on and off to make a picture. They pass tiny electric signals through the liquid crystals so that their molecules twist and untwist, acting like tiny light switches to turn each subpixel on and off.

As their name suggests, liquid crystals have certain things in common with both liquids and solids. In solids, molecules are largely fixed in place. In liquids, molecules can move more freely. When electricity flows through liquid crystals, the molecules twist or untwist, but stay in much the same place. Their twisting can be precisely controlled by adjusting how much electricity flows through them. This makes them perfect for controlling the pixels of an LCD television.

◀◀BACK

Austrian botanist Friedrich Reinitzer discovered liquid crystals in 1888. LCD screens were first used in the early 1970s for wristwatches and calculators.

Liquid-crystal displays may soon be added to windows to replace blinds or curtains. At the flick of a switch they will block light to darken a room.

FORWARD▶▶

≫ Mixing light

▶ It is possible to make any color by mixing together red, blue, and green light. Red and blue mix to form a bright purple called magenta. Blue and green lights combine to make a bright blue known as cyan. Yellow is made where red and green overlap. When all three colors shine equally, they make white light or shades of gray (depending on their brightness). Black occurs if no light shines.

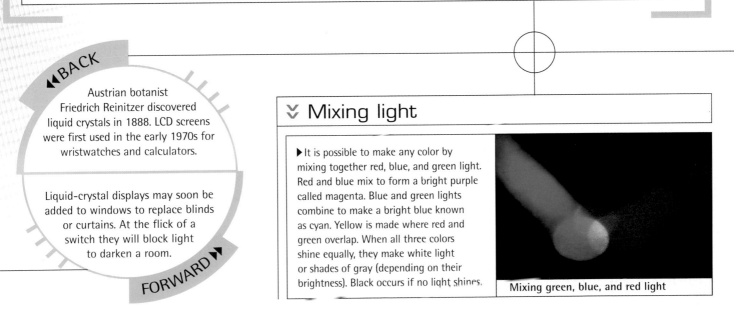

Mixing green, blue, and red light

TOYS

Electronic toys are being developed to make our lives easier and more fun. People can communicate while on the move, talk face-to-face over the Internet, and watch TV programs where and when they want.

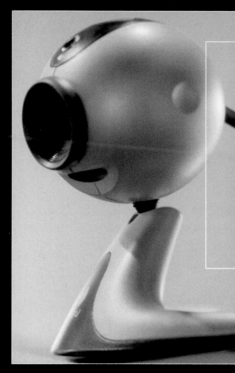

◀◀ Webcam

Computers can become videophones using a camera the size of a golf ball. A webcam is a digital camera that plugs into a computer, captures around 30 still pictures every second, and sends them across the Internet so that they play like a video on another person's computer screen. If two computer users have webcams, they can see each other while talking.

▶▶ Wi-Fi card

Wireless Fidelity, or Wi-Fi, connects a computer to the Internet using invisible radio waves instead of cables. Plugging this credit-card-sized circuit board into a laptop computer allows Internet access at Wi-Fi hot spots—places with equipment to send and receive radio signals from a Wi-Fi computer.

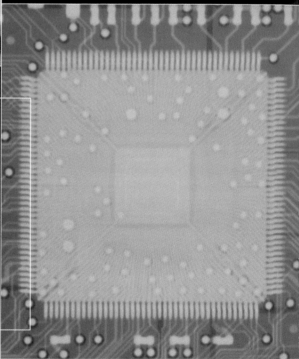

ARCHOS

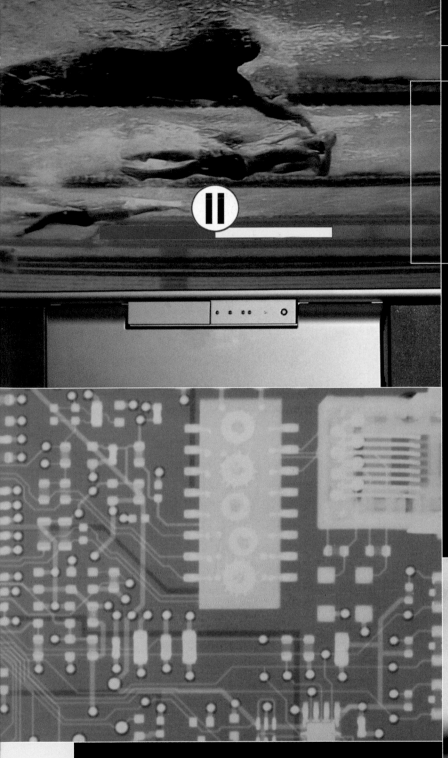

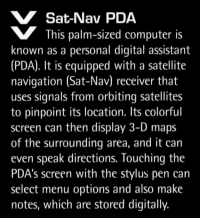

◀◀ Digital television

With interactive features and access to more channels, digital televisions are gradually replacing older analog TV sets. Some digital TVs contain hard-drive memories similar to those in a computer. They can record, store, and play back hours of TV programs and can also pause live television so not a second is missed.

▼▼ Sat-Nav PDA

This palm-sized computer is known as a personal digital assistant (PDA). It is equipped with a satellite navigation (Sat-Nav) receiver that uses signals from orbiting satellites to pinpoint its location. Its colorful screen can then display 3-D maps of the surrounding area, and it can even speak directions. Touching the PDA's screen with the stylus pen can select menu options and also make notes, which are stored digitally.

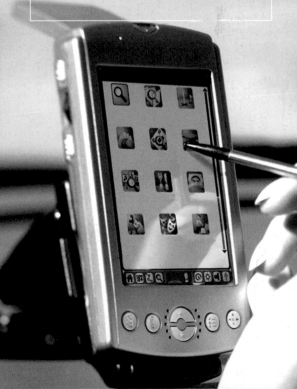

◀◀ MP4 player

Millions of people already own handheld digital music players that store and play tunes in a computer file format called MP3. But MP4 players take digital technology a step further—they make movies portable, too. This MP4 player stores up to 16 hours of movies on its 20-GB hard drive and plays them on a crystal-clear 3.5-in (9-cm) LCD TV screen.

▶▶ See also: Laptop p168, LCD TV p24, MP3 player p70, Navigation p154

VOICE RECOGNITION

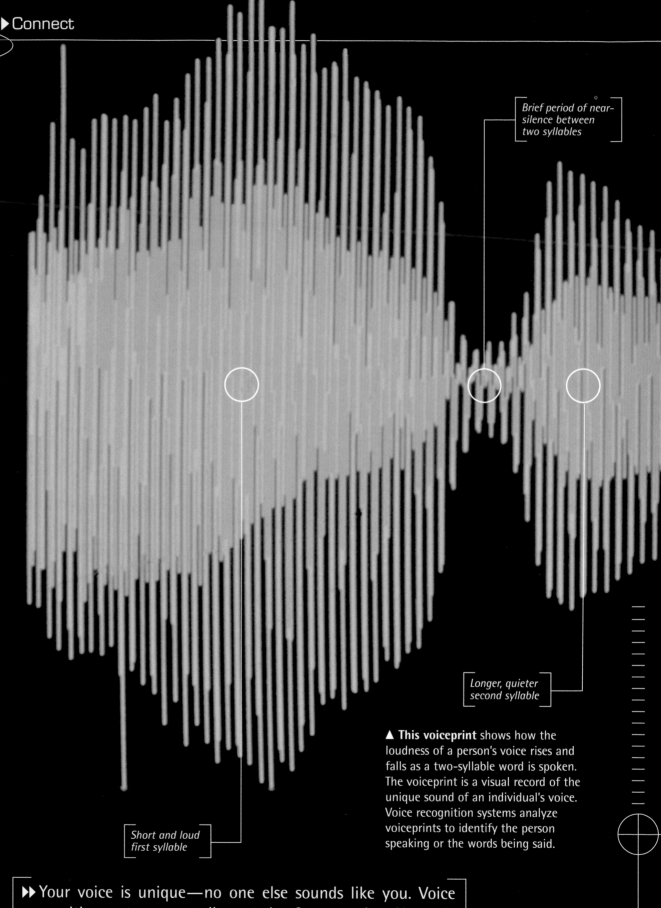

Brief period of near-silence between two syllables

Longer, quieter second syllable

▲ **This voiceprint** shows how the loudness of a person's voice rises and falls as a two-syllable word is spoken. The voiceprint is a visual record of the unique sound of an individual's voice. Voice recognition systems analyze voiceprints to identify the person speaking or the words being said.

Short and loud first syllable

▶▶ Your voice is unique—no one else sounds like you. Voice recognition systems can tell one voice from another. Not only that, they can identify up to 50,000 different spoken words. ▶▶

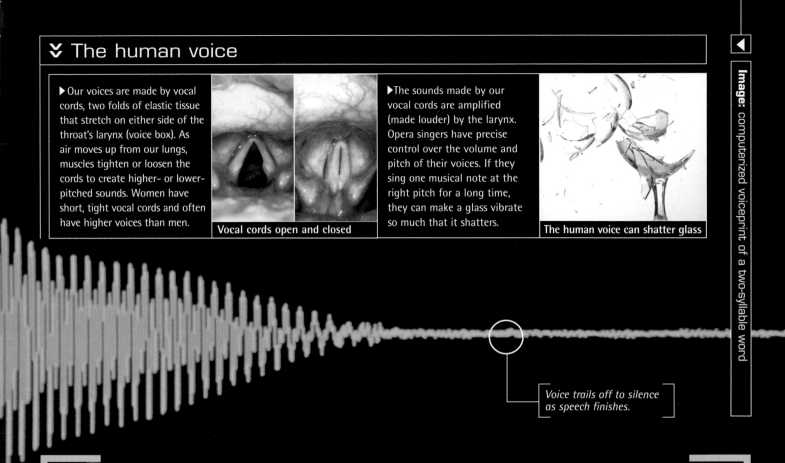

❯ The human voice

▶ Our voices are made by vocal cords, two folds of elastic tissue that stretch on either side of the throat's larynx (voice box). As air moves up from our lungs, muscles tighten or loosen the cords to create higher- or lower-pitched sounds. Women have short, tight vocal cords and often have higher voices than men.

Vocal cords open and closed

▶The sounds made by our vocal cords are amplified (made louder) by the larynx. Opera singers have precise control over the volume and pitch of their voices. If they sing one musical note at the right pitch for a long time, they can make a glass vibrate so much that it shatters.

The human voice can shatter glass

Image: computerized voiceprint of a two-syllable word

Voice trails off to silence as speech finishes.

❯❯ HOW VOICE RECOGNITION WORKS

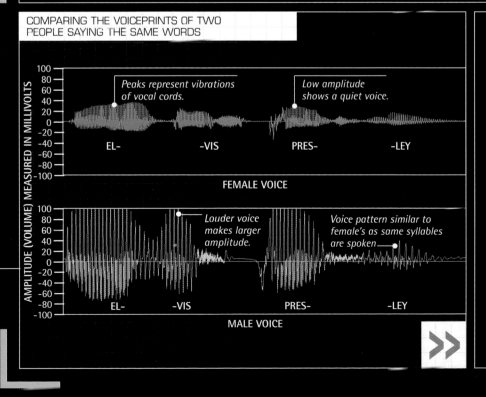

COMPARING THE VOICEPRINTS OF TWO PEOPLE SAYING THE SAME WORDS

AMPLITUDE (VOLUME) MEASURED IN MILLIVOLTS

Peaks represent vibrations of vocal cords.

Low amplitude shows a quiet voice.

EL-　　　-VIS　　　PRES-　　　-LEY

FEMALE VOICE

Louder voice makes larger amplitude.

Voice pattern similar to female's as same syllables are spoken

EL-　　　-VIS　　　PRES-　　　-LEY

MALE VOICE

Although everyone's voice sounds different, all voices make similar patterns of sound energy when they say the same words. These simple graphs show how amplitude (volume) changes in the voices of two people, a female and a male, in the few seconds it takes to say two words. Speech patterns like this are used in computer voice-recognition systems, where people speak words or commands into a microphone instead of typing them into a keyboard. Before the computer can recognize words, it has to be trained by listening to the voices of hundreds of different people saying many different words. Then, when it hears an unfamiliar voice saying one of these words, it matches the pattern of sound energy to the voice patterns in its memory to find out what the person has said.

▶▶ See also: MP3 player p70, Pet translator p30, Sound wave p250

Image: close-up of Takara's Meowlingual pet translator handset

PET TRANSLATOR

Sound wave formed by cat's meow travels toward handset's built-in microphone.

Liquid-crystal display (LCD) screen shows translations as picture icons and words.

◀BACK

Dr. Matsumi Suzuki helped to invent pet translation after matching the sounds made by dogs, cats, and dolphins to the behavior he observed.

One day, all pets may be implanted with a satellite-navigation tracking chip to help their owners locate them if they get lost.

FORWARD▶▶

▲ **A pet translator,** such as this Meowlingual for cats or Bowlingual for dogs, reveals an animal's moods in many different ways. Apart from translating basic noises, it can monitor changes in an animal's behavior, help with training, and even reveal the early signs of illnesses.

▶▶ Handheld pet translators capture meows and barks and translate them into picture icons and words. They use voiceprint technology to reveal the secret thoughts of cats and dogs. ▶▶

⌄ Neural networks

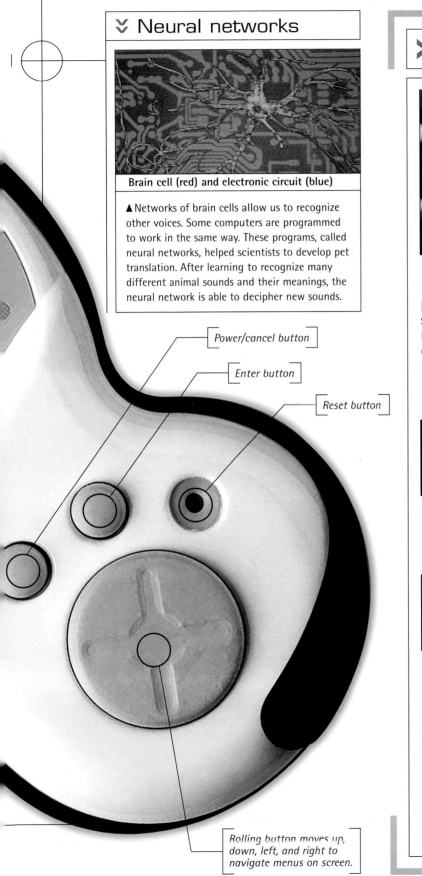

Brain cell (red) and electronic circuit (blue)

▲ Networks of brain cells allow us to recognize other voices. Some computers are programmed to work in the same way. These programs, called neural networks, helped scientists to develop pet translation. After learning to recognize many different animal sounds and their meanings, the neural network is able to decipher new sounds.

Power/cancel button

Enter button

Reset button

Rolling button moves up, down, left, and right to navigate menus on screen.

≫ PET TRANSLATIONS

⋀ **Bowlingual's** collar and handset work together to capture a dog's bark. A microphone on the collar picks up the bark, which is then turned into a digital signal and beamed through the air via radio waves to the handset. The handset then matches distinctive features of the digital bark to patterns stored in its database.

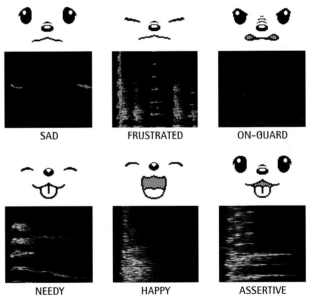

SAD   FRUSTRATED   ON-GUARD

NEEDY   HAPPY   ASSERTIVE

⋀ **Dogs can produce** many different barks and sounds, which all look very different when viewed as digital voiceprints. Bowlingual's handset stores details of 200 different barks, in the form of voiceprints, in a way similar to a human voice recognition system. Although different breeds make different sounds, the translator can usually match a bark to one of six moods. A sad bark involves brief, high-pitched noises, while an angry (on-guard) bark is a mixture of lower-pitched, growling noises that last up to five times longer. Once matched, the handset displays the appropriate face and word translation of the bark.

▶▶ See also: Digital radio p22, LCD TV p24, Voice recognition p28

IRIS SCAN

▶▶ Iris recognition systems are the quickest, most reliable method of identifying individuals so far devised. ▶▶

≫ HOW IRIS SCANNING WORKS

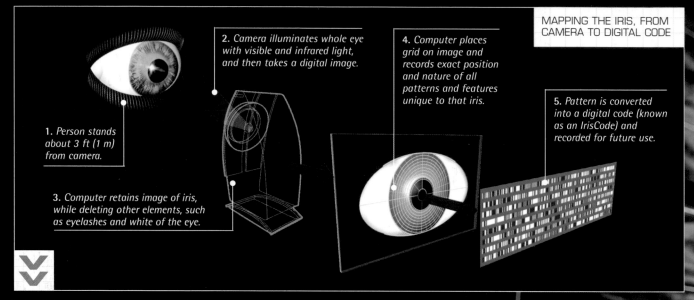

MAPPING THE IRIS, FROM CAMERA TO DIGITAL CODE

1. Person stands about 3 ft (1 m) from camera.

2. Camera illuminates whole eye with visible and infrared light, and then takes a digital image.

3. Computer retains image of iris, while deleting other elements, such as eyelashes and white of the eye.

4. Computer places grid on image and records exact position and nature of all patterns and features unique to that iris.

5. Pattern is converted into a digital code (known as an IrisCode) and recorded for future use.

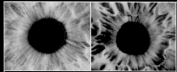

Iris colors, like skin tones, depend on a pigment (coloring) called melanin. Lots of pigment gives a brown iris; less means eyes are blue, green, or gray.

Swirling, colored iris patterns make all eyes unique—even identical twins have different patterns. A computerized system that recognizes people by their iris patterns is the latest and most accurate method of biometric identification—the science of identifying people by recording their unique biological features. Iris recognition systems are already in use in high-security buildings, such as airports.

The first time a person uses the system, there is a two-minute process in which their eyes are photographed. The resulting image is converted into a digital IrisCode and stored in a database. The next time the individual passes through the system, their iris is scanned again. The system searches for a match on its database of IrisCodes. Within two seconds a match can be found and the person identified.

≫ Fingerprint ID

▶ In this picture, a computer has outlined the central area of a fingerprint in green and highlighted key ridges with red dots. By measuring the dots and the angle of the ridges, the computer turns the fingerprint pattern into a digital code that can be compared with other stored codes. Although fingerprinting is an effective method of identification, the iris recognition system is 1,000 times more accurate.

Computerized fingerprint analysis

◀◀BACK

In 1994, British computer scientist John Daugman invented the mathematical process for turning iris patterns into digital codes.

Iris recognition is so reliable that it might completely replace passports and credit-card PINs at ATMs in the future.

FORWARD▶▶

▶▶ See also: Camera p62, ID p180, Laser surgery p206, Smart card p182

Image: computerized biometric iris scan

Iris is a ring of muscle that opens and closes to control light.

Pupil looks black but is a round hole that lets light enter eye.

Radiating lines help to measure unique features of iris.

▲ **Iris recognition systems** place a grid of coordinates on an image of the iris, like lines of latitude and longitude placed on maps and globes. These coordinates precisely locate unique iris features, such as colors, shades, and markings.

NEON

▶▶ Vibrant neon advertisements fill our cities with color. The city of Las Vegas has an estimated 15,000 miles (25,000 km) of neon lighting—enough to stretch more than halfway around the world. ▶▶

◀ **Neon lights** do not necessarily use neon gas. Each light is made of a series of glass tubes containing any of the noble gases: helium, neon, argon, krypton, xenon, and radon. Each of these gases glows a specific color when electricity passes through it. When combined, the gases produce still more colors.

Normally colorless, neon glows red when electricity passes through it.

A mixture of argon and neon gases creates this green light.

▶▶ See also: Fireworks p78, Light bulb p88, Noble gases p247

≫ HOW A NEON LIGHT WORKS

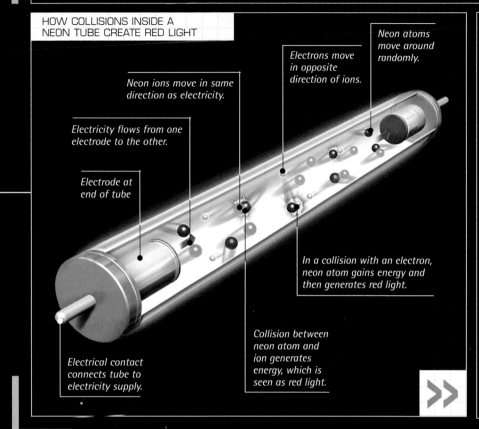

HOW COLLISIONS INSIDE A
NEON TUBE CREATE RED LIGHT

Neon atoms move around randomly.

Electrons move in opposite direction of ions.

Neon ions move in same direction as electricity.

Electricity flows from one electrode to the other.

Electrode at end of tube

In a collision with an electron, neon atom gains energy and then generates red light.

Collision between neon atom and ion generates energy, which is seen as red light.

Electrical contact connects tube to electricity supply.

A **neon light** is a sealed tube filled with neon gas at low pressure. The gas consists of millions of neon atoms, whizzing around randomly. When a high electric voltage (up to 15,000 volts) is applied to the metal electrodes at either end of the tube, it ionizes the gas: some neon atoms lose electrons and become ions. The atoms, ions, and electrons hurtle around the tube in different directions. All these moving particles have kinetic energy (energy of movement). If an atom or ion is involved in a collision, it can absorb some of the kinetic energy. This makes it unstable, however, so it quickly tries to get rid of the energy by giving off particles of light called photons. With neon gas, the light produced appears red. With other noble gases, the photons appear as light of other colors. The noble gases in these tubes also exist in the air around us. They make up about one percent of every breath we take.

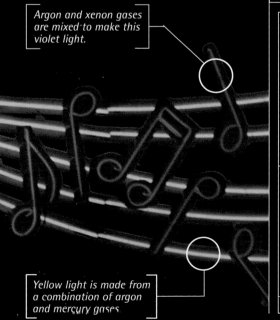

Argon and xenon gases are mixed to make this violet light.

Yellow light is made from a combination of argon and mercury gases.

≫ Bioluminescence

▶Living creatures that glow produce light inside their bodies through a process called bioluminescence. This firefly is making bright yellow flashes in its tail through a reaction that turns chemical energy into light. The reaction takes place in its lower body, where a protein called luciferin reacts with oxygen from the air. Fireflies glow to attract mates or to warn off predators.

Nighttime flight of a firefly

Warning flash of a jellyfish

◀Jellyfish make light in different ways for different reasons. Some scare off predators with bright warning flashes. Others release thousands of glowing particles to distract enemies. Some even make a luminous slime that sticks to predators to make them visible to other attackers. In the deepest, darkest parts of the ocean, over 90 percent of marine creatures are bioluminescent.

LINKS

Complex communication
networks across Earth and
in space are evolving and
expanding all the time.
These links allow people
to contact one another
in many different ways,
quicker than ever before.

⌃ Television links
Every television station
has a master control room.
This uses computers to
combine signals from many
live and recorded programs
to provide a continuous
broadcast. These signals are
then sent along cables or
transmitted via radio waves
to reach our television sets.

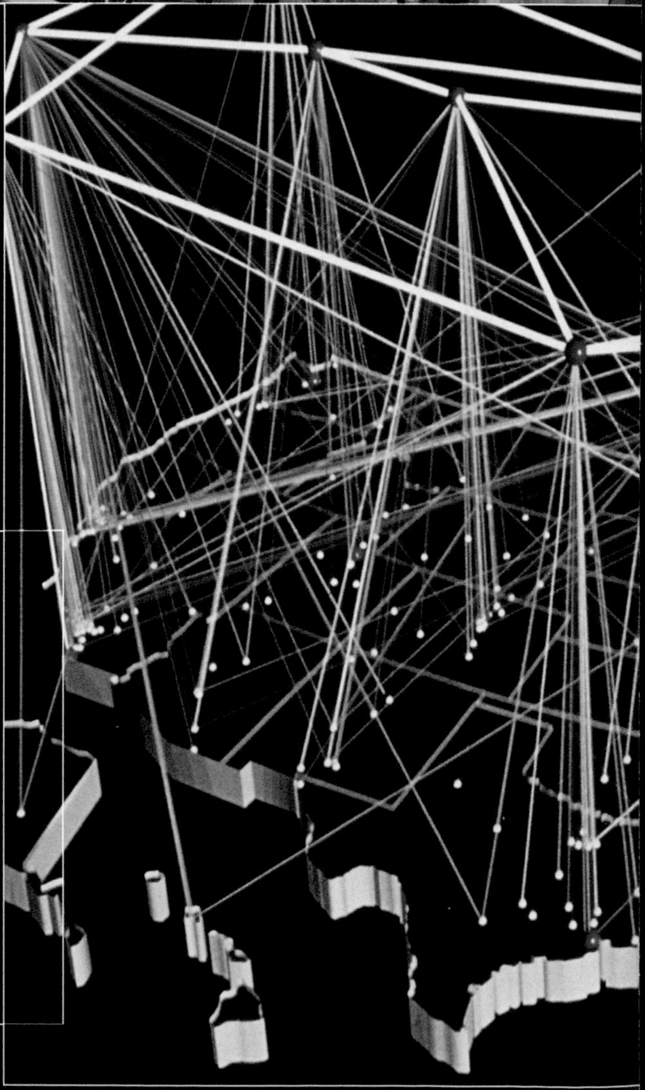

≫ Computer networks
This diagram shows the US
National Science Foundation's
computer network. It links
scientists' computers throughout
the US, but is just one of the
many networks that can link one
computer to another. Computer
networks can be internal links
within private companies, public
systems that span entire nations,
or the global web of the Internet.

↦ See also: Cell phone p18, Internet p38, Satellite p42

≫ Satellites

From their position high above Earth, communication satellites work together to bounce TV and radio signals around the world. Satellite phones can also enable people in remote areas without land-line or cell-phone networks to make calls, putting people on opposite sides of the globe in touch.

∨ Telephone cables

Lifting a handset or pressing the call button causes an electrical signal to be sent from your phone to a local telephone exchange. These local exchanges use circuits and wires, such as these, to route the signal to its destination and connect the call. Telephone signals can be transmitted via copper or fiber-optic cables, or by radio waves, and may be relayed by satellites.

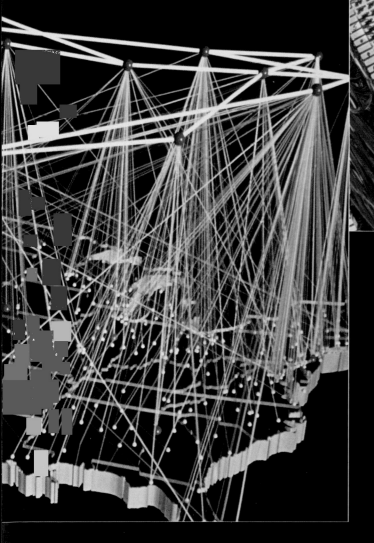

≫ Microwave mast

These tall towers, with transmitter and receiver dishes mounted on them, are microwave relay stations. They receive signals sent through the air via microwaves (a type of radio wave), and then route them to the next relay station. Microwaves can carry TV and radio signals, telephone calls, images, and fax-machine data almost instantaneously.

INTERNET

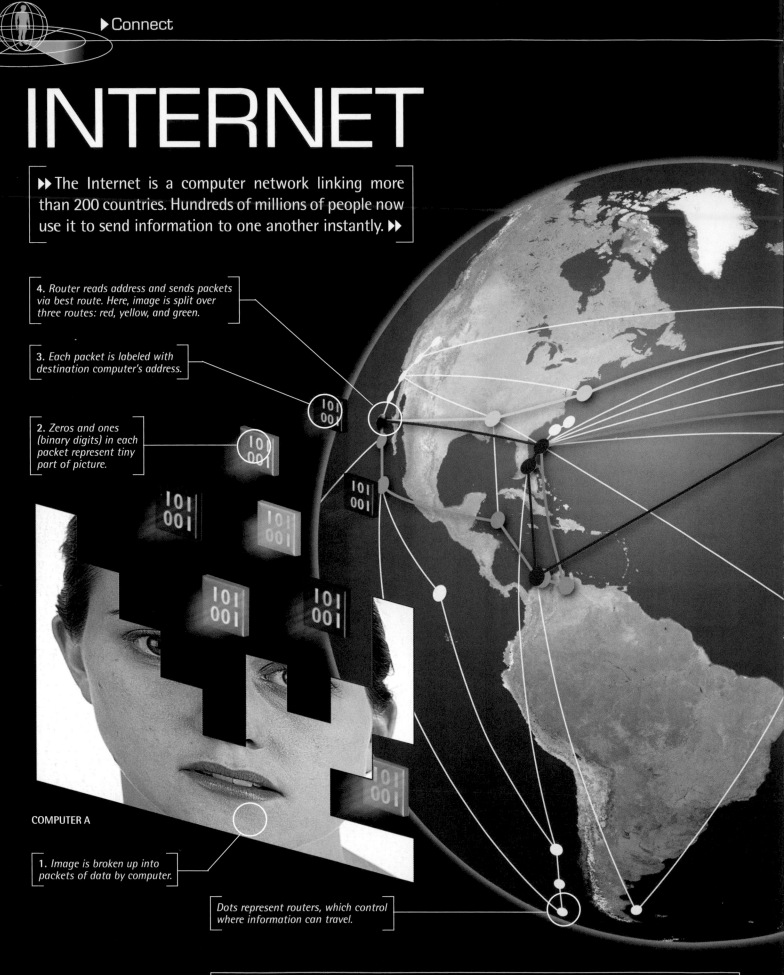

▶▶ The Internet is a computer network linking more than 200 countries. Hundreds of millions of people now use it to send information to one another instantly. ▶▶

4. *Router reads address and sends packets via best route. Here, image is split over three routes: red, yellow, and green.*

3. *Each packet is labeled with destination computer's address.*

2. *Zeros and ones (binary digits) in each packet represent tiny part of picture.*

COMPUTER A

1. *Image is broken up into packets of data by computer.*

Dots represent routers, which control where information can travel.

▶▶ See also: Laptop p168, Links p36, Packet p248, Toys p26

6. *Packets are sorted and put back together by destination computer.*

5. *Packets reach destination by avoiding busy or broken links.*

COMPUTER B

◀ **The Internet** began in the 1960s when a group of academics launched a project to link together large computer systems at four US universities. Now it has grown into a global network that links millions of home computers and LANs (local-area computer networks) in schools, corporations, and governments. Most people use the Internet for sending email, but it can carry other information, too, including music files, TV and radio programs, instant messages, and phone calls. Information travels across the Internet in packets of data by a method called packet switching. A user-friendly Internet application known as the World Wide Web lets us view pages of information and create our own. We can now share information, exchange ideas, and form online communities with people thousands of miles away, thanks to the Internet's global village.

Networks in nature

Strands of a spider's web

◀ A spiderweb is a dense framework of silky strands linking at many points. The Internet's World Wide Web is also highly interconnected. Its pages are connected by electronic cross-references called links. Using links, people can explore Web pages in different ways and different orders to follow their own interests.

▶When moles make underground burrows, they build many different entrances and exits and a complex network of paths in between. If part of the burrow collapses, the animals can still travel down other routes. The Internet can survive failures in the same way. In computing, this idea is known as redundancy.

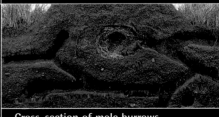

Cross-section of mole burrows

Lines represent paths information can travel across the Internet.

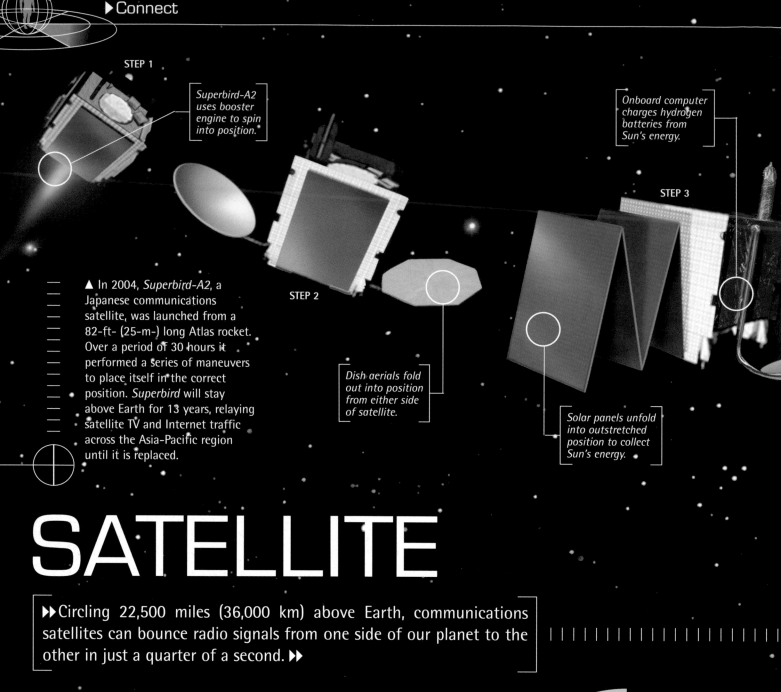

STEP 1

Superbird-A2 uses booster engine to spin into position.

Onboard computer charges hydrogen batteries from Sun's energy.

STEP 3

STEP 2

▲ In 2004, *Superbird-A2*, a Japanese communications satellite, was launched from a 82-ft- (25-m-) long Atlas rocket. Over a period of 30 hours it performed a series of maneuvers to place itself in the correct position. *Superbird* will stay above Earth for 13 years, relaying satellite TV and Internet traffic across the Asia-Pacific region until it is replaced.

Dish aerials fold out into position from either side of satellite.

Solar panels unfold into outstretched position to collect Sun's energy.

SATELLITE

▶▶ Circling 22,500 miles (36,000 km) above Earth, communications satellites can bounce radio signals from one side of our planet to the other in just a quarter of a second. ▶▶

⌄ Launching satellites

▶ Most satellites travel into space on rockets, but some are launched from the Space Shuttle. Large craft are hoisted into position using a long robotic arm. Smaller satellites are launched from a rotating turntable inside the cargo bay, as shown here. The turntable spins the satellite before springs push it into orbit. The spinning motion (known as gyroscopic stability) makes the satellite follow a steady path. When it has cleared the Shuttle, its rocket boosters fire to set its orbiting speed.

Launch in space

◀◀BACK

Writer Arthur C. Clarke dreamed up the idea of communications satellites in 1945. The first such satellite, *Echo I*, was launched 13 years later.

Scientists are worried that obsolete satellites and other space junk could cause a catastrophic collision with rockets or space stations.

FORWARD▶▶

STEP 4

Satellite spins over Earth
in geostationary orbit.

>> HOW A COMMUNICATIONS SATELLITE WORKS

HOW A COMMUNICATIONS SATELLITE
TRANSMITS A SIGNAL FROM ONE
POINT ON EARTH TO ANOTHER

*4. Electrical device called a transponder
boosts radio signal so that it is strong
enough to return to Earth.*

*3. Receiving aerial
collects incoming
radio signal.*

*5. Transmitting aerial
directs signal back to Earth.
It can transmit to multiple
destinations, including
other satellites if necessary.*

*2. Uplink radio
signal travels
from Earth
to satellite.*

*6. Downlink radio
signal beams
back to Earth.*

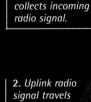

*1. Ground station A
uses huge dish
antenna to beam
radio signal to satellite.*

*7. Ground station
B receives signal
from satellite.*

A communications satellite
has to send and receive, or
relay, thousands of phone
calls and TV programs across
Earth simultaneously. It
does so by catching and
relaying microwave (high-
energy radio wave) signals
that are transmitted from
the ground. These signals
travel through space at the
speed of light in narrowly
focused beams.

Most communications
satellites orbit the Earth
in the same direction and at
the same speed as the Earth
rotates. They are always over
the same point on the Earth,
making them appear
stationary. This is called
geostationary orbit (GEO).
Several hundred of these
communications satellites
are in geostationary orbit.

>> See also: Cell phone p26, Links p36, Radio waves p249, Space Shuttle p156

Today, computers and communication devices are light enough for us to carry around wherever we go. The next phase will see them getting smaller still. In the long term, the development of quantum and DNA computing technology will result in machines that work a billion times faster than current silicon-based computers.

In the next decade, most electronic devices will become connected to the World Wide Web by high-bandwidth fiber optics. When you are on the move, computers built into your clothing will be able to link with navigational satellite systems to tell you your precise location, and enable you to download information on local services.

"Computers that harness the incredible storage power of human DNA will perform calculations at unimaginable speed."

Invisible sensors embedded in public spaces, from parking ramps to art galleries, will recognize and respond to your presence. These areas, called "intelligent environments," will be able to provide information according to your needs and preferences, such as showing the way to a parking space or directing you to an artwork that particularly interests you. The technology may also be used to sell products: as you pass by a digital billboard, the display might change automatically to show items tailored to your own lifestyle.

Sensors will play a central role in the development of "affective computing." This technology will enable computers to gauge moods and respond to them. Cars will be able to detect when you are stressed or angry and slow down automatically to reduce the risk of accidents. Chairs will know when you are bored, tired, or frustrated and shift their position to make you feel more relaxed or alert. Phones will be able to register whether you are happy or

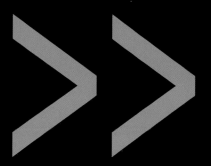

sad while you are speaking, and create emotions or color feedback patterns to communicate this to the person at the other end of the line.

Future generations of computers may not even use silicon-based technology. Computers that harness the incredible storage capacity of human DNA, found in our genes, could one day perform calculations at speeds unimaginable today. Quantum computing will use atoms and molecules to perform vast numbers of calculations simultaneously.

Communication technologies will bring new benefits, and past obstacles will disappear. For example, instant translation technology will allow you to speak in English into your cell phone and be heard in Japanese by the person you are calling in Tokyo. On the other hand, with our cell phones and computers constantly communicating with one another, satellites surveying our positions from space, and sensors monitoring us on the ground, privacy may become impossible. Some people fear that this problem outweighs the benefits that better communications will bring. But the information age is here to stay, and it will continue to make the world feel like a smaller place, and to be one in which everyone takes part in the free exchange of ideas and information.

FIBRE OPTICS

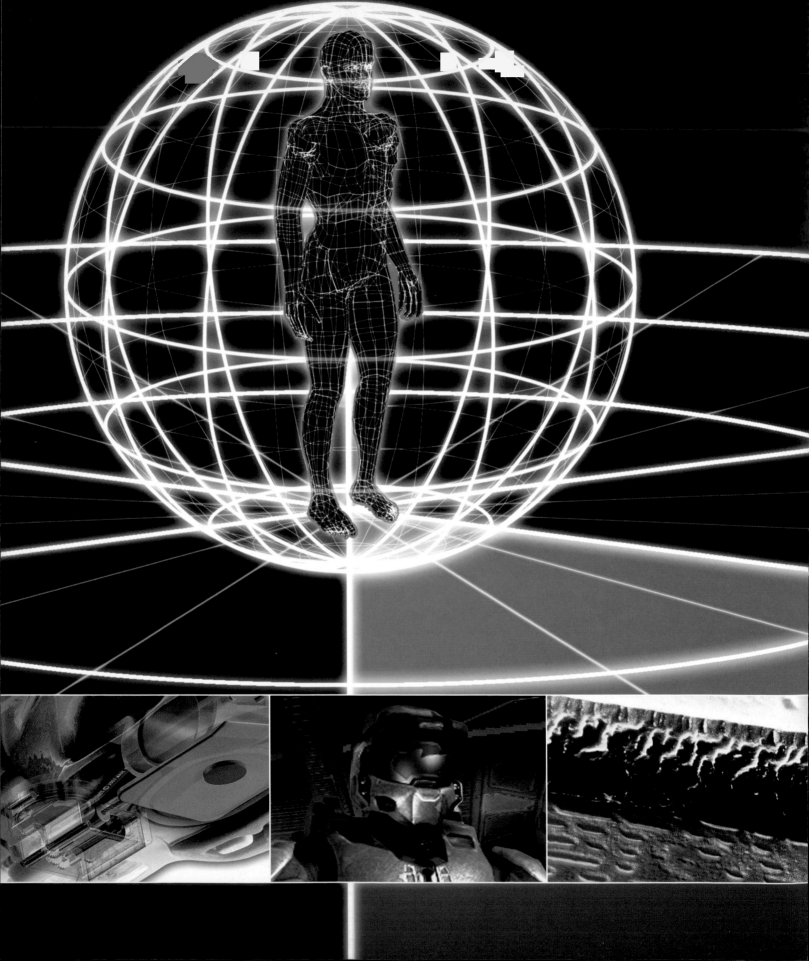

>>PLAY

Sneaker >> Soccer >> Racket >> Snowboard >> Bike >> Camera >> Games >> Guitar >> Compact disc >> MP3 player >> Headphones >> DJ decks >> Fireworks

Games and sports are ways of making play more organized. Throughout history, people have invented thousands of different kinds of activities, ranging from ancient board games such as chess to athletics and "extreme" sports such as snowboarding and skateboarding. Over the last few decades, digital technology has added another dimension to the way we choose to spend our leisure time.

In a world where sports have become increasingly competitive, technology can make all the difference between winning and losing. With the help of computer-aided design and modeling, the equipment used for many sports is constantly improving. Tennis rackets are becoming more responsive and powerful, soccer balls lighter and more effective, and running shoes more supportive and better at absorbing impact.

Advances in fabric technology have led to the development of high-performance sportswear. Swimmers, for example, can wear swimsuits with special streamlining that can save vital fractions of a second. Breathable fabrics' special venting systems help keep athletes cool and dry. Skiers and mountaineers can stay warm with lightweight but extremely well insulated jackets.

SEM OF GUITAR STRING

Sports, of course, are not the only way we play. Computer games have had a global impact and are familiar to millions of people. The first video game was invented in 1958. It was called Tennis for Two, and it was played on an oscilloscope—a device for measuring sound waves. The first video game that you could play on a television was called Pong and was introduced in 1975. It involved two players hitting a "ball" back and forth across the screen—another tennis game! Today's console games are both far more sophisticated in their design and more challenging to play. From building and running imaginary cities to recreating realistic battle scenes, the games are so complex that they can cost as much to make as a movie.

> " In 2004, the Athens Olympics was seen on TV by four billion people—two-thirds of the planet's population. "

Digital technology has also opened up a world of creative opportunities. Before the advent of affordable digital video cameras and simple-to-use film editing software, filmmaking was a specialized activity. Now that the technology is so widely available, creating a movie is within everyone's reach. It is a similar story with making music. Just as the introduction of the electric guitar in the 1950s revolutionized popular music, digital technology is now having a similar impact. You do not need special training to compose music—computer-aided composition tools can provide most of the necessary skills.

The way our entertainment is delivered to us is also changing. Most homes have a range of devices including televisions, audio systems, DVD players or video recorders. But now it is possible to have all these devices in one unit. Thanks to wireless communication and high-speed Internet connections, the personal computer is becoming a digital center, or hub, for the many different forms of entertainment that are available.

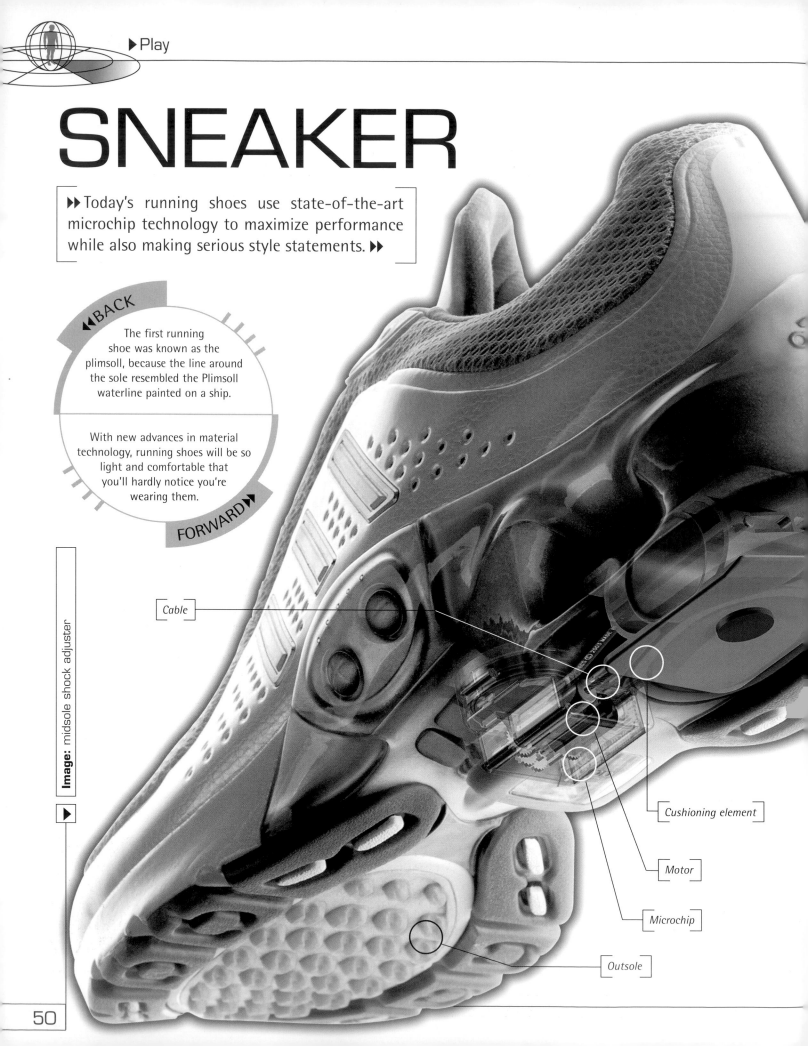

SNEAKER

▶▶ Today's running shoes use state-of-the-art microchip technology to maximize performance while also making serious style statements. ▶▶

◀◀BACK

The first running shoe was known as the plimsoll, because the line around the sole resembled the Plimsoll waterline painted on a ship.

With new advances in material technology, running shoes will be so light and comfortable that you'll hardly notice you're wearing them.

FORWARD▶▶

Image: midsole shock adjuster

Cable

Cushioning element

Motor

Microchip

Outsole

◀ **This high-tech** running shoe has an automatically adjusting cushioning system in its midsole. This allows it to adapt continually to changing running surfaces and individual running styles, giving optimum performance during a run.

>> HOW THE SENSOR WORKS

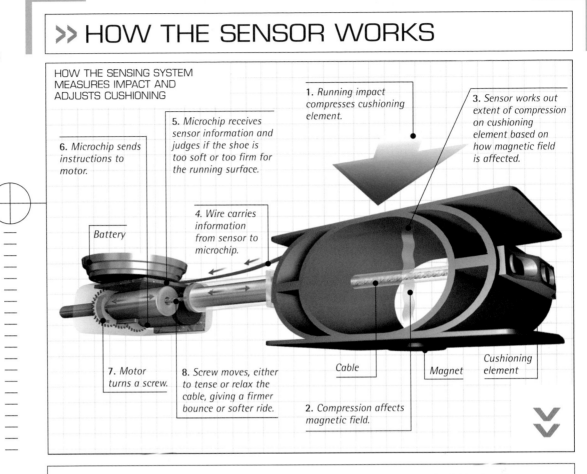

HOW THE SENSING SYSTEM MEASURES IMPACT AND ADJUSTS CUSHIONING

1. *Running impact compresses cushioning element.*

3. *Sensor works out extent of compression on cushioning element based on how magnetic field is affected.*

5. *Microchip receives sensor information and judges if the shoe is too soft or too firm for the running surface.*

6. *Microchip sends instructions to motor.*

4. *Wire carries information from sensor to microchip.*

Battery

7. *Motor turns a screw.*

8. *Screw moves, either to tense or relax the cable, giving a firmer bounce or softer ride.*

Cable

Magnet

Cushioning element

2. *Compression affects magnetic field.*

Midsole

Every owner of a pair of running shoes has an individual running style and body weight. In addition, running conditions are never the same—soft grass, gravel, and hard pavements are all very different surfaces to run on. This remarkable running shoe has a microchip and an adjustable cushioning element in its midsole that adjusts the shoe to give optimum performance for each individual and on any running surface. Once the person has started running, a sensor takes one thousand readings every second. The information it receives triggers continual changes to the shoe's cushioning. These changes happen in such a subtle way that all the runner notices throughout the run is how comfortable the shoes are.

⌄ Shock absorption

▶When people run, their bodies absorb four times their weight with each step. This image is color-coded to show areas of pressure: red indicates the most pressure, followed by yellow, green, and blue. Shoes help protect the feet by absorbing shock in all these areas.

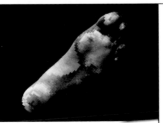

Imprint of bare foot

▶In a running shoe, the job of the midsole is to provide shock absorption and stability. The outsole, on the undersurface, provides traction, or grip. This treaded layer has a studded design that enhances traction on different surfaces.

X-ray of outsole

▶▶ See also: Fabric p60, Microchip p16, p246, Sensor p250

▶▶ See also: Arenas p72, Racket p54, Sneaker p50

SOCCER

▶▶ Soccer is a multi-million-dollar industry with millions of fans. Better equipment means better games, so Nike tested fifteen prototypes before introducing the Total 90 Aerow Hi-Vis Ball. ▶▶

Image: player swerves ball

◀BACK

The first modern soccer ball was patented in 1855. It consisted of an inflatable rubber bladder surrounded by a leather coating.

Future balls may have radio tags inside, helping referees to be certain whether or not the ball has crossed the line in a goal mouth scramble.

FORWARD▶

Angle of kick spins the ball, determining how it will fly through air.

>> HOW A BALL GETS ITS SWERVE

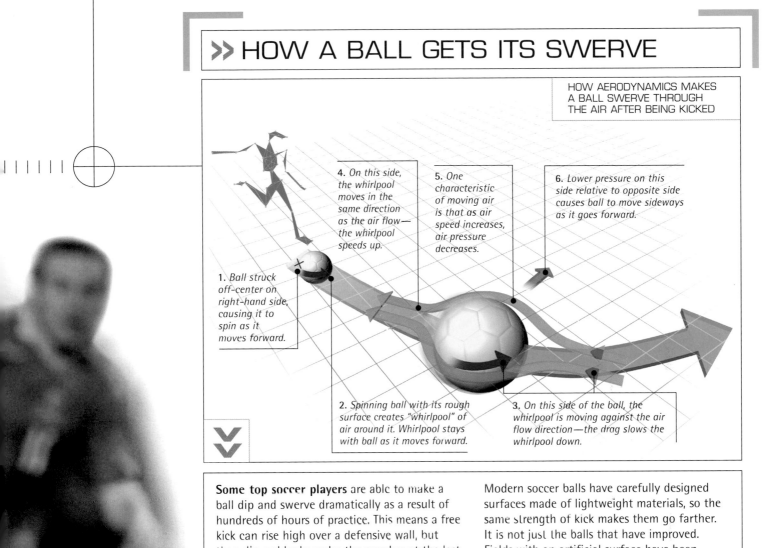

HOW AERODYNAMICS MAKES
A BALL SWERVE THROUGH
THE AIR AFTER BEING KICKED

1. *Ball struck off-center on right-hand side, causing it to spin as it moves forward.*

4. *On this side, the whirlpool moves in the same direction as the air flow—the whirlpool speeds up.*

5. *One characteristic of moving air is that as air speed increases, air pressure decreases.*

6. *Lower pressure on this side relative to opposite side causes ball to move sideways as it goes forward.*

2. *Spinning ball with its rough surface creates "whirlpool" of air around it. Whirlpool stays with ball as it moves forward.*

3. *On this side of the ball, the whirlpool is moving against the air flow direction—the drag slows the whirlpool down.*

Some top soccer players are able to make a ball dip and swerve dramatically as a result of hundreds of hours of practice. This means a free kick can rise high over a defensive wall, but then dip suddenly under the crossbar at the last second. Spinning the ball has become easier as lighter, more sophisticated soccer balls have been produced. The original leather balls were heavy to kick and became heavier still when they absorbed moisture from a wet field.

Modern soccer balls have carefully designed surfaces made of lightweight materials, so the same strength of kick makes them go farther. It is not just the balls that have improved. Fields with an artificial surface have been developed. They are most useful in winter, when it is often too wet to play on real grass. The first artificial fields were very bouncy, making ball control difficult, but recent artificial fields act much more like the real thing.

◀ **Player Marco Bresciano** kicks the Nike Total 90 Aerow Hi-Vis, a soccer ball that has been designed to fly more quickly and accurately than other balls on the market. It uses a six-layer casing to make it durable and quick to react to a kick, and a special pattern and coating to make it fly accurately over long distances.

⌄ Changing shape

▶ A soccer ball deforms when kicked because it is not rigid, although it is impossible to see in the actual instance of a kick. In this image, we see a depression in the ball's lower left side caused by impact pressure from the kicking foot. When a ball deforms, the air inside it acts like a spring. The ball and the air inside it absorb some of the energy from the kick. They then release this energy to create the ball's bounce.

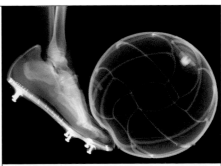

False-color X-ray of foot and soccer ball

Wiring carries electrical energy between microchip and fibers.

Piezoelectric fibers create electrical energy.

◀BACK

First introduced in 1874, tennis was known as Sphairistike. Fortunately, this was soon replaced with the more pronounceable name of Lawn Tennis.

The fastest serve in a championship match reached 153 mph (246.2 km/h), in 2004. The HEAD® Intelligence™ racket may help beat this record.

FORWARD▶▶

▶ The key to playing tennis is hitting the ball with power and control. This racket helps achieve that by ensuring that as much of the energy from the player's stroke is transferred to the ball as possible, and in a controlled way. This means that the player can make the ball move faster and position it more accurately, so that it is harder to return.

Microchip stores electrical energy.

RACKET

▶▶ Tennis has evolved from a game played in long pants or heavy skirts to a fast and furious competition in which players use the latest technology to gain the edge. ▶▶

▶▶ See also: Crash test p134, Guitar, p66, Piezoelectricity p248

≫ HOW THE RACKET WORKS

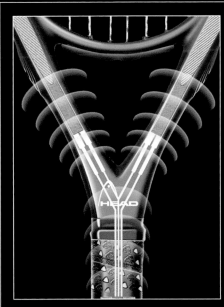

2. The vibrations stretch piezoelectric fibers in the racket's throat (shown below). The fibers convert the mechanical energy into electrical energy. This travels in the form of an electrical current to a microchip in the handle of the racket, which stores it up and then sends it back to the fibers. The fibers stiffen enough to stifle the vibrations and return the original mechanical energy to the ball.

1. When a racket hits a ball, the racket bends, absorbing some of the energy. Ideally, all that energy would flow back into the ball as the racket straightens out. With a standard racket, the energy is wasted through vibrations in the racket head and the player's arm. This intelligent racket has a way of harnessing the energy of these vibrations, shown here traveling from the racket's head to its throat.

3. When the racket stiffens as a result of the piezoelectric fibers, the ball is propelled back sooner than it would otherwise be. A standard racket—here superimposed in red—is still being bent backward when the stiffened one has already straightened. The faster return gives the player a greater advantage over his or her opponent, who will need to move very quickly to reach the ball.

≫ What is the piezoelectric effect?

Close-up of quartz crystals

◀When you squeeze a piezoelectric material such as quartz, it gives out a spark. This is how the racket's fibers produce electricity when they receive vibrations from the racket head. The piezoelectric effect also works the other way around, so if you apply electricity to a piezoelectric material, it changes shape. This is how the racket's fibers stiffen the racket head when they receive electricity from the microchip.

Image: snowboarder performing jump

◀BACK

The earliest snowboards were marketed as Snurfers. They had ropes for steering and looked like a cross between a sled and a ski.

There could be more people riding snowboards than using skis by 2015, according to some market forecasts.

FORWARD▶▶

▲ A boarder "catches air" as he performs an impressive jump. Board shapes have evolved to match different terrains and riding styles. Boarders can compete in cross-country, downhill, and trick-riding contests to test their strength, skill, stamina, and speed.

Tail

SNOWBOARD

▶▶ What started as an alternative to skiing and sledding is now one of the fastest-growing of alpine sports. Snowboarders can compete in competitions held on the slopes or in snow parks. ▶▶

▶▶ See also: Arenas p72, Bike p58

» HOW A SNOWBOARD WORKS

Freestyle
The short, wide, symmetrical shape of freestyle boards allow riders to perform tricks and to ski with either foot in front.

Freeride
These boards are often used by beginners, since they work in most conditions, but with practice they can also be used for jumps and tricks.

Freecarving
Also known as alpine, or racing, boards, these are long and narrow for making high-speed turns on a zigzagging slalom track.

HOW THE FOUR LAYERS OF A SNOWBOARD MAKE IT STRONG AND FAST

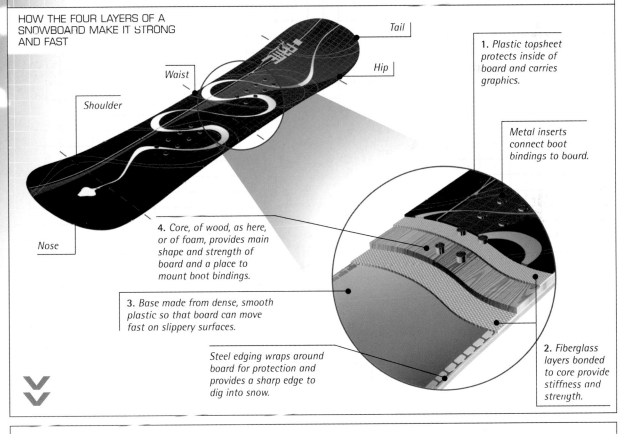

Nose

Tail

Waist

Hip

Shoulder

Nose

1. *Plastic topsheet protects inside of board and carries graphics.*

Metal inserts connect boot bindings to board.

4. *Core, of wood, as here, or of foam, provides main shape and strength of board and a place to mount boot bindings.*

3. *Base made from dense, smooth plastic so that board can move fast on slippery surfaces.*

Steel edging wraps around board for protection and provides a sharp edge to dig into snow.

2. *Fiberglass layers bonded to core provide stiffness and strength.*

First, surfboards started the craze for surfing on waves, then skateboards made urban surfing on sidewalks possible. Now surfers ride on snow with a snowboard. The most popular snowboarding competitions are freeriding events, where riders tackle downhill slopes as fast and with as much style as possible, and freestyle events, where they can show off their tricks using ramps to twist and turn in the air.

Snowboarders wear soft boots strapped into plastic connecting straps called bindings, which are mounted diagonally across the board. Riders control the board as gravity pulls them downhill by shifting their weight between heel and toe and from one foot to the other. This makes the edges of the board dig into the snow, causing it to turn. Pushing down hard on both heels or toes turns the board sharply so that it stops.

BIKE

▶▶ Olympic cyclists need to ride as fast as possible against the clock or each other. So their bicycles are lighter and more aerodynamic than normal bicycles, often with only one gear and no brakes. ▶▶

Tapering helmet reduces air resistance and protects the rider.

Breathable, flexible Lycra® clothing reduces muscle fatigue.

Built-in air channels on elbow rests keep rider's arms cool.

Front forks made from strong, stiff carbon composites.

Front wheel has flattened blades instead of spokes.

Airstream hardly disturbed by rider's body

>> OLYMPIC BIKE: KEY FEATURES

<< **The front** of a moving object usually creates the most drag. On a normal bicycle, wide handlebars force the rider to sit with arms apart, creating lots of drag. To solve this, an Olympic time-trial bicycle has two sets of handlebars positioned side by side. The narrow pair in the center can be gripped to reduce drag when the bicycle is traveling straight; the wider pair on the outside is used only for steering and braking.

◀ An Olympic bicycle is tested in a wind tunnel to improve its aerodynamic design and minimize drag (air resistance). Because the rider's body is wider than the bicycle, it creates almost twice as much drag. To minimize this, riders wear streamlined clothing and crouch to work with the bike as a single, aerodynamic unit.

>> **The bicycle frame** has to withstand huge stresses from the rider's weight as well as twisting forces when turning corners. An Olympic superbike has a frame made from a single piece of tough, carbon-composite material. This spreads forces evenly throughout and is reinforced in key places with super-strong titanium. The frame's sides are curved like the surface of an airplane wing so that air travels smoothly around it to reduce drag.

<< **Wheels** move faster than other bicycle parts, so they can create drag. To avoid this, the front wheel has flattened, aerodynamic blades that can be easily steered into a moving airstream. A bladed wheel is weaker than an ordinary bicycle wheel with spokes, so it is strengthened with a thick rim. The rear wheel does not need to steer, so it is an even more aerodynamic solid disc. These bicycles are often made without brakes. At the end of a race, the rider pedals more slowly to gradually stop the bike.

Wheel's smooth carbon skin covers a tough but lightweight honeycomb structure.

Back wheel powers bike at speeds up to 35 mph (56 km/h).

❯❯ Computer-aided design

▶Instead of using wind tunnels, engineers can use lasers to scan the shape of the bicycle and rider to create a 3D computer model. They can then test different aerodynamic bicycle and helmet designs to find those that create the least drag. This pointed aerodynamic helmet, designed by computer, allows air to flow smoothly around it.

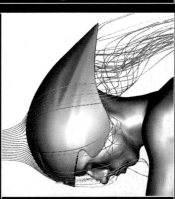

3D computer model of helmet

FABRIC

New technology has helped to create fabrics that keep us warm in winter and cool in summer, absorb perspiration, and keep us dry when it rains. Here is how a few of these fabrics work.

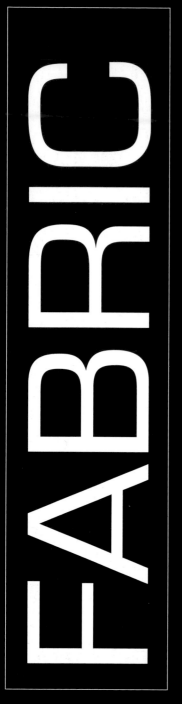

Λ Aqua shift

As soon as swimmers hit the water, they create drag—resistance caused by the turbulence from their movements. They have to use up energy to swim against it. To combat drag, swimsuits are made of clinging fabric that helps streamline the body. This swimsuit's horizontal bands redirect the flow of water around the body, further reducing drag.

≫ Breathable fabrics

These are used to make wet-weather clothing. Breathable fabrics combine more than one layer of nylon (seen here, in pink) with a porous inner layer (yellow). The inner layer contains tiny holes—smaller than raindrops but bigger than individual water molecules. This lets sweat out but prevents rain from getting in. The outer layers are wind-resistant, keeping the wearer warm.

▶▶ See also: Bike p58, Parts p132

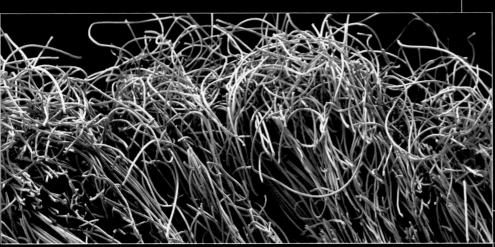

◀◀ Fleece
This is a soft material valued for its light weight and excellent insulating properties. It is used for outdoor clothing. Fleece is made from long, feltlike fibers, closely interwoven with one another. Air is trapped between the fibers and is heated by the body.

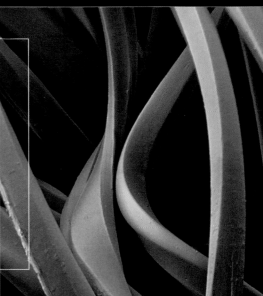

▶▶ Sweat absorbers
Fabrics that absorb sweat can help make clothes more comfortable. These fibers are coated with two different substances that stop the fabric from becoming wet during wear. One of the substances absorbs the body's moisture and the other transfers the moisture to the outside.

▼▼ Lycra®
Lycra® is a strong, highly elastic fiber that is often used to make close-fitting but flexible clothing such as sportswear. This magnified image shows Lycra® and nylon fibers in a pair of cycling shorts: the thin, crisscrossing red and yellow lines are Lycra® and the other parts of the weave are layers of nylon.

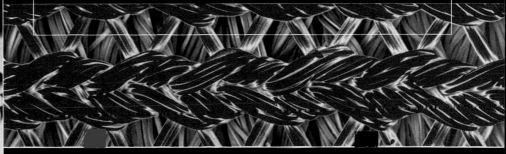

CAMERA

▶▶A digital camera allows you to see your pictures moments after they have been taken, and makes it easy to store, share, and print them. ▶▶

Image: exploded view of Fuji S5000

▶

6. *Screen allows users to check pictures instantly.*

7. *Removable memory card stores images.*

FinePix

FUJIFILM XD 128MB

5. *Circuit processes output from sensor into digital form, so it can be viewed, deleted, or stored.*

▶ **Digital photographs** record information as numbers, rather than chemical changes in a piece of film. This means that there is no need for developing, so you can see your pictures moments after they have been taken, and simply delete them if they are not right. Unlike film, there is no gradual decay of stored images over time, so you can make perfect copies of your pictures many years later.

4. *Sensor is made of millions of pixels. Each measures brightness and color of one tiny part of image.*

▶▶ See also: Digital technology p243, Iris scan p32, LCD TV p24, Microchip p16, Sensor p250

>> HOW THE SENSOR WORKS

Digital cameras use lenses to focus the image onto an electronic sensor instead of a strip of film. When a picture is taken, the sensor converts the light striking it into an electrical charge. The charge is then sent to a circuit inside the camera, which measures it and gives it a digital value. Computer chips process the data to construct the image, which is then stored on a memory card.

The images in the card can be taken to a professional developer for high-quality prints, or downloaded to your computer. This is done either by connecting the camera to a computer with a cable, or by removing the memory card and putting it into the computer's card reader. The images can be printed, emailed, and manipulated using computer software, or uploaded to the Web. The speed with which images can be retrieved, and the creative possibilities that follow, have revolutionized photography.

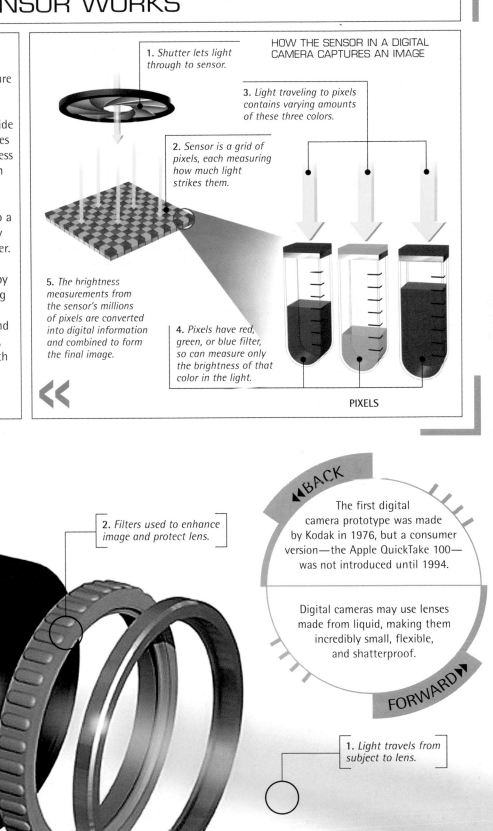

HOW THE SENSOR IN A DIGITAL CAMERA CAPTURES AN IMAGE

1. Shutter lets light through to sensor.

3. Light traveling to pixels contains varying amounts of these three colors.

2. Sensor is a grid of pixels, each measuring how much light strikes them.

5. The brightness measurements from the sensor's millions of pixels are converted into digital information and combined to form the final image.

4. Pixels have red, green, or blue filter, so can measure only the brightness of that color in the light.

PIXELS

3. Autofocus system ensures sharp image.

2. Filters used to enhance image and protect lens.

◀BACK

The first digital camera prototype was made by Kodak in 1976, but a consumer version—the Apple QuickTake 100—was not introduced until 1994.

Digital cameras may use lenses made from liquid, making them incredibly small, flexible, and shatterproof.

FORWARD▶

1. Light travels from subject to lens.

⌄ Powerful processors

▶Games have become more elaborate since the first basic computer games. Today's game consoles are powerful computers that use a microprocessor chip and a 3-D graphics controller to run the game. The microprocessor works out where the characters are and what they are doing, and tells the 3-D graphics controller. The graphics chip inside the controller calculates what those characters should look like on screen. Both chips do billions of calculations each second to produce a realistic-looking game.

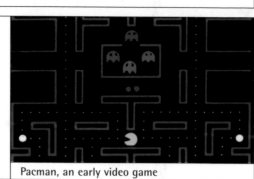
Pacman, an early video game

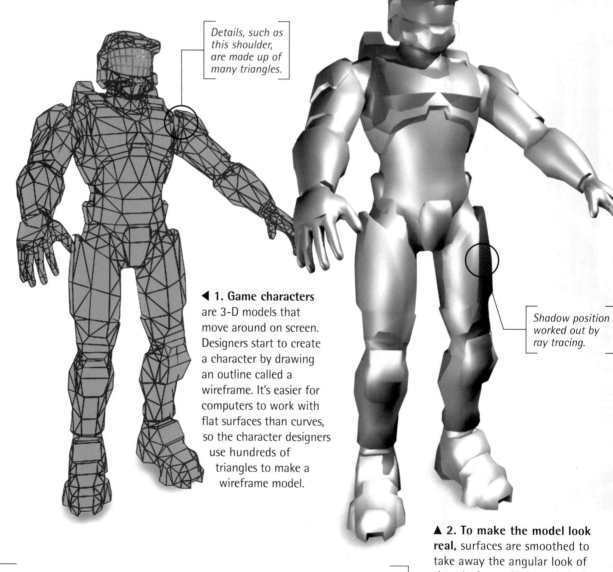

Details, such as this shoulder, are made up of many triangles.

◀ **1. Game characters** are 3-D models that move around on screen. Designers start to create a character by drawing an outline called a wireframe. It's easier for computers to work with flat surfaces than curves, so the character designers use hundreds of triangles to make a wireframe model.

Shadow position worked out by ray tracing.

▲ **2. To make the model look real,** surfaces are smoothed to take away the angular look of the wireframe. Light and shadow are added in a process called ray tracing, which works out how light would be reflected off the character at different angles.

GAMES

▶▶ Games consoles can put you in the driving seat of a race car, let you pilot a 747, or allow you to become a fantastic creature moving through a mythical world. ▶▶

▶ **4. Final color detail** is added, then the last step is to put the model into its environment. Since the figure may move quickly around the scene, each change of position and view of the background must be calculated separately.

Visor color is applied in layers to give depth.

Detail is added to leg.

◀**BACK**

The first video game console, the Magnavox Odyssey, was produced in 1971. Plastic sheets were placed over the screen to provide background graphics.

Sony, Toshiba, and IBM have developed a new chip called Cell. Its designers predict it will make game consoles run ten times faster.

FORWARD▶

▲ **3. Surface detail** is applied to the model. In this case, the computer mimics the way that metal armor reflects light and applies this to the figure.

▶▶ See also: Arenas p72, Microchip p16, Microprocessor p246, Toys p26

GUITAR

▶▶ The electric guitar started out as a way of making an ordinary guitar sound much louder, but has now become an established instrument with its own place in history. ▶▶

≫ HOW AN ELECTRIC GUITAR WORKS

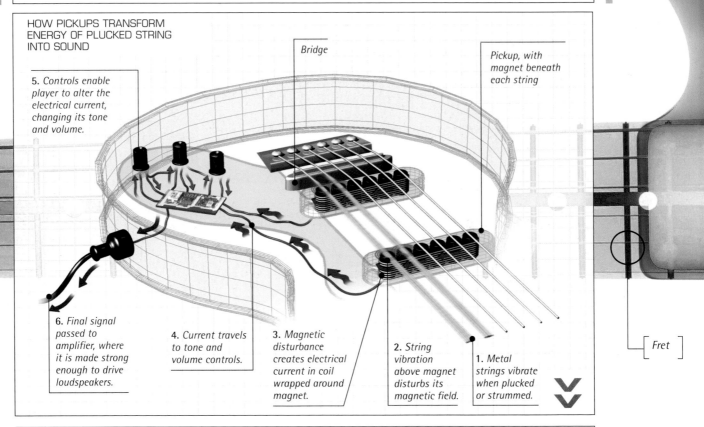

HOW PICKUPS TRANSFORM ENERGY OF PLUCKED STRING INTO SOUND

Bridge

Pickup, with magnet beneath each string

5. Controls enable player to alter the electrical current, changing its tone and volume.

6. Final signal passed to amplifier, where it is made strong enough to drive loudspeakers.

4. Current travels to tone and volume controls.

3. Magnetic disturbance creates electrical current in coil wrapped around magnet.

2. String vibration above magnet disturbs its magnetic field.

1. Metal strings vibrate when plucked or strummed.

Fret

Guitars use a set of six strings of different thicknesses and stretched to different tensions. When played together, they produce a set of notes, known as a chord. The strings don't make much sound on their own, so they need to be amplified. In an acoustic guitar, the vibration of the strings sets the air in the guitar's hollow body vibrating as well, making the sound louder. However, an electric guitar amplifies the sound in a different way. The vibration of the strings is converted by a device called a pickup into an electrical signal.

Loudspeakers then turn this electrical energy back into sound waves. The first electric guitar, called the Vivi-tone, was invented in 1933, but it was not a success. It was not until the rise of popular music in the 1950s that guitars became widely used. Since then, guitars such as the Gibson® Les Paul and the Fender Stratocaster® have become mass-selling classics, each renowned for producing a very particular sound. Some modern guitars are now used to control electronic synthesizers, giving guitarists access to a new palette of sounds.

▶▶ See also: Headphones p74, Racket p54, Sound wave p250, Vibration p251

⌄ Thickness and vibration

▶When a string is plucked, it vibrates very fast. The speed of this vibration is called its frequency. Different frequencies produce different musical notes, and are determined by the length, thickness, and tension of the plucked string. The thicker the wire, the slower the vibration, and the lower the note that is produced.

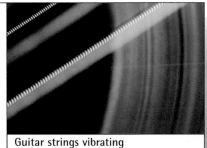

Guitar strings vibrating

▼ **All guitars rely** for their sound on controlling how strings vibrate. The guitar is tuned by changing the tension in each string. Different notes can be played on a string by pressing it against frets on the guitar's neck, shortening its effective length and so playing a higher note.

Image: false-color X-ray of electric guitar

Pickup

Volume and tone controls

COMPACT DISC

▶▶ CDs spin around hundreds of times a minute while a glowing beam of laser light reads their data. The spiral track that holds all the information is almost 3 miles (5 km) long. ▶▶

Image: false-color SEM of CD's surface

Protective plastic layer covers data layer below.

Bumps spiral out from center of CD in continuous line.

Space between bumps is highly reflective.

▶▶ See also: Binary p241, Digital radio p22, DJ decks p76, Laser p246, Microchip p16

›› HOW A COMPACT DISC IS READ

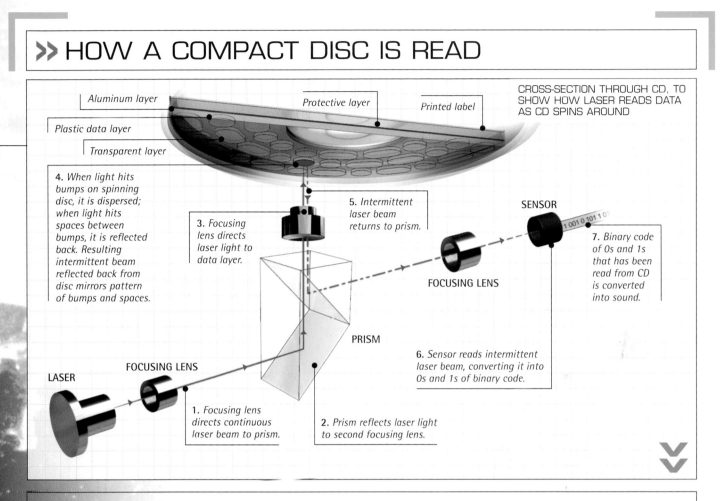

CROSS-SECTION THROUGH CD, TO SHOW HOW LASER READS DATA AS CD SPINS AROUND

Aluminum layer

Protective layer

Printed label

Plastic data layer

Transparent layer

4. *When light hits bumps on spinning disc, it is dispersed; when light hits spaces between bumps, it is reflected back. Resulting intermittent beam reflected back from disc mirrors pattern of bumps and spaces.*

3. *Focusing lens directs laser light to data layer.*

5. *Intermittent laser beam returns to prism.*

SENSOR

1 001 0 101 1 0

7. *Binary code of 0s and 1s that has been read from CD is converted into sound.*

FOCUSING LENS

PRISM

6. *Sensor reads intermittent laser beam, converting it into 0s and 1s of binary code.*

LASER

FOCUSING LENS

1. *Focusing lens directs continuous laser beam to prism.*

2. *Prism reflects laser light to second focusing lens.*

In a digital recording, sound is converted into a long series of 0s and 1s—binary code. These are then represented as bumps and spaces on a tiny spiral track under a CD's surface. A CD is made up of layers. The bottom layer is transparent and carries the data layer where the information is stored. The data layer is covered with a layer of shiny aluminum, and topped with a layer of plastic that protects it, gives the CD strength, and carries the label. Music information is read from the CD using a laser beam focused through the transparent layer onto the spinning spiral track. Bumps disperse the laser light, but if there is no bump, the laser hits the shiny aluminum and is reflected back strongly. A sensor picks up the intermittent reflections from the disc as it spins and turns the signal back into 0s and 1s, which in turn are converted back into sound.

◀ **The tiny bumps** that can be seen in this SEM of a CD's surface are no more than 500 nm wide ("nm" stands for nanometer, which is just one thousand-millionth of a meter). Their minuscule size means that a CD contains millions of bumps. These bumps are how a CD stores its digital data—0s and 1s—that a CD player converts back into sound.

⌄ Master disc

▶CDs can be made cheaply by stamping them out using a mold. The master mold is made of metal, because it has to be extremely accurate and durable. The master carries the opposite pattern of that needed on the final CD, so a bump on the master forms a pit on the CD. One very expensive master can stamp out thousands of low-cost plastic copies.

Manufacture of a master compact disc

MP3 PLAYER

▶▶ MP3 players are portable music machines that can store and play thousands of songs. Most will fit in your pocket; some are small enough to be built into cell phones and even sunglasses. ▶▶

▶ **This MP3 player** is the size of a deck of cards. It consists of just three main elements: a hard disk, a circuit board, and a battery. The hard disk stores thousands of tracks as digital data, the circuit board translates data into sound, and the battery provides power.

➤➤ HOW MP3 COMPRESSION WORKS

FOUR WAYS THAT RECORDED MUSIC IS COMPRESSED INTO MP3 FORMAT

VOLUME

PITCH

TIME

Very high tones which vary more than 20,000 times per second (20,000 Hz) cannot be heard by humans. These sounds are not stored.

Bats can hear these high tones.

RANGE OF HUMAN HEARING

Whales can hear these low tones.

Loud sounds at one pitch block out quieter sounds at other pitches, which therefore do not need to be stored (crosshatched front and behind).

Repetitive sounds are recognized and recorded once. Next time they appear (hatched), earlier recording is reused.

Very low tones which vary less than 20 times per second (20 Hz) cannot be heard by humans. These sounds are not stored.

Just as the size of a book depends on how many words are in it, the more information a digital file contains, the larger it is. MP3 players can be small because their software records only the sounds that we can hear, saving valuable storage space. The software identifies four ways it can avoid recording certain sounds, detailed above. In addition, it only records the left and right channels when they are actually different.

Together, these techniques reduce, by ten or twelve times, the amount of information that needs to be stored when music is recorded. Similar data compression techniques are used in all digital media. They are used to squeeze multiple phone calls down international telephone lines, to shrink the size of picture files so that they are easier to email, and to make digital television and radio possible by squashing lots of information into a very limited section of the airwaves.

▶▶ See also: Compact disc p68, DJ decks p76, Headphones p74, Toys p26

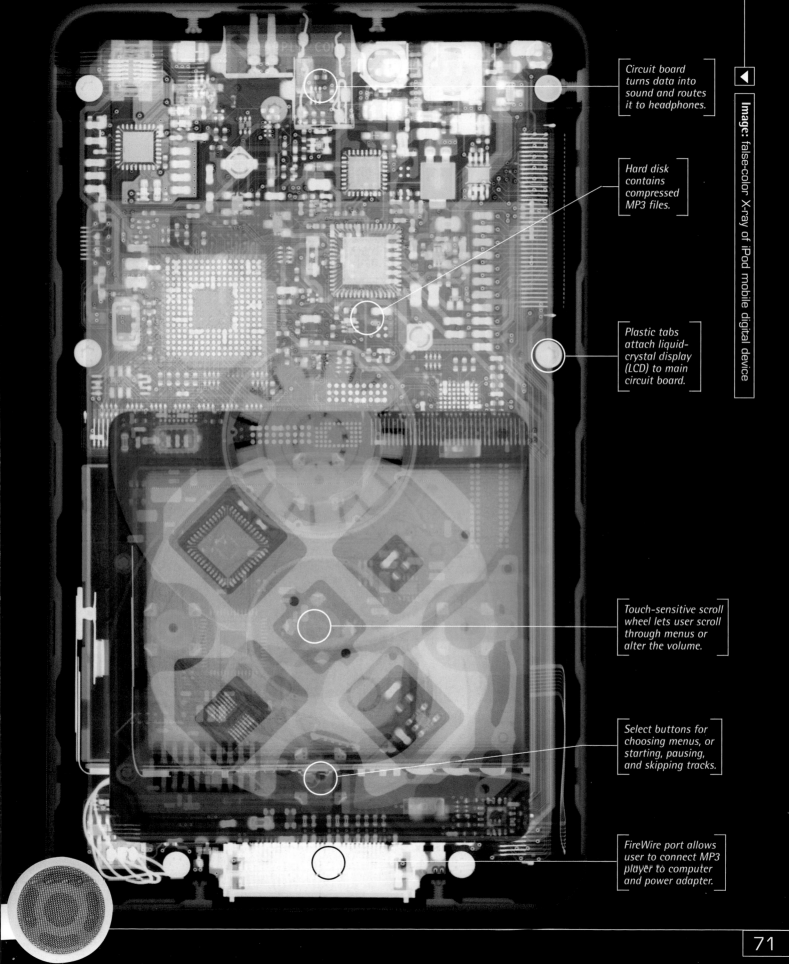

Circuit board turns data into sound and routes it to headphones.

Hard disk contains compressed MP3 files.

Plastic tabs attach liquid-crystal display (LCD) to main circuit board.

Touch-sensitive scroll wheel lets user scroll through menus or alter the volume.

Select buttons for choosing menus, or starting, pausing, and skipping tracks.

FireWire port allows user to connect MP3 player to computer and power adapter.

ARENAS

Arenas enable climbers, surfers, cyclists, and other sports enthusiasts to train year-round. Technology creates outdoor conditions, such as snow and waves, even where they do not occur naturally.

◄◄ Wave simulator
Surfers can spend hours waiting in the water for the perfect wave to ride in to shore. Indoor wave pools provide a sequence of waves so that they can practice without the wait. Wave pools can be programmed to simulate the wave types found in different parts of the world.

►► Artificial turf
Golf courses take up a lot of land and are expensive in built-up areas. But putting greens, on which players practice their putts (rolling the ball into the hole), can be small. Here, artificial turf has been laid on a skyscraper's roof, allowing golfers to practice their putts downtown.

◀◀ Climbing wall
Using indoor climbing walls, climbers can work on their skills, strength, and stamina in the comfort and safety of a sports center, whatever the weather. Then, when the summer climbing season comes around, they're fit and ready to go. Climbing walls are made of concrete, embedded with a combination of real rocks and artificial handholds and footholds. Climbers use a harness attached to a rope so that they can try out daring moves without risk of injury.

▼ Velodrome
How do you make a long-distance event like cycling into a spectator sport? Wrap the long track into an oval and put it indoors. Velodromes (named after velocipedes, an early name for bicycles) have banked tracks and a staggered start so each rider cycles the same distance, whether they are on the inside or outside of the oval. Riders use the banking to gain position and attack the race leaders, creating a game of tactics and cunning.

◀◀ Inside a snowdome
Skiing and snowboarding do not have to be winter sports. Snowdomes contain slopes of different heights so that beginners can learn the basics, and the more experienced can brush up on their skills, before heading for the real slopes. Snowdomes are kept very cold and manufacture their own snow to create a true alpine experience, even at the height of summer.

▶▶ See also: Bike p58, Snowboard p56

HEADPHONES

▶▶ Headphones allow you to enjoy music without disturbing anyone else. Some headphones are pads that cover the ear; others are buds worn inside it. ▶▶

⌄ Sound and the ear

▶The outer ear directs sound waves into the ear canal, where they meet the eardrum. There, sound waves are turned into vibrations, and transmitted to the cochlea, a curled tube filled with fluid. The vibrations make the fluid move. This movement is sensed by tiny hairs within the cochlea, which turn it into electrical signals that are sent to the brain.

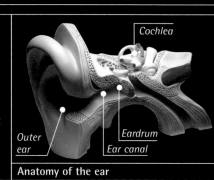

Cochlea

Outer ear

Eardrum

Ear canal

Anatomy of the ear

◀BACK

The first stereo headphones were launched in 1958 by the American company Koss and were designed to be used with a record player.

Some companies are developing wireless headphones that can be linked to portable music players, so you can listen without a tangle of wires.

FORWARD▶

>> HOW HEADPHONES WORK

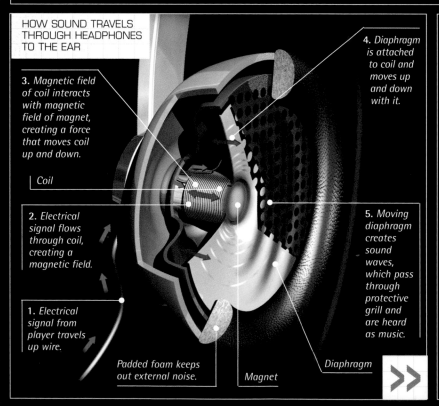

HOW SOUND TRAVELS THROUGH HEADPHONES TO THE EAR

3. *Magnetic field of coil interacts with magnetic field of magnet, creating a force that moves coil up and down.*

Coil

2. *Electrical signal flows through coil, creating a magnetic field.*

1. *Electrical signal from player travels up wire.*

Padded foam keeps out external noise.

4. *Diaphragm is attached to coil and moves up and down with it.*

5. *Moving diaphragm creates sound waves, which pass through protective grill and are heard as music.*

Magnet

Diaphragm

>>

Headphones channel sound to both ears, and each earpiece is connected to the source by a wire. A signal is transferred through the wire to a coil wrapped around a tube that encloses a cylindrical magnet. When the signal flows through the coil, it creates a changing electromagnetic field. This interacts with the magnet's own field to create a force that moves the coiled tube up and down. This in turn moves the diaphragm. The sound waves are created by the diaphragm, which pushes the air in front of it, reproducing the sound from the source.

Pilots need to hear information and instructions over the roar of airplane and helicopter engines. Headphones have been developed that can cancel out a lot of this external noise, so only the sound fed to the headphones is heard.

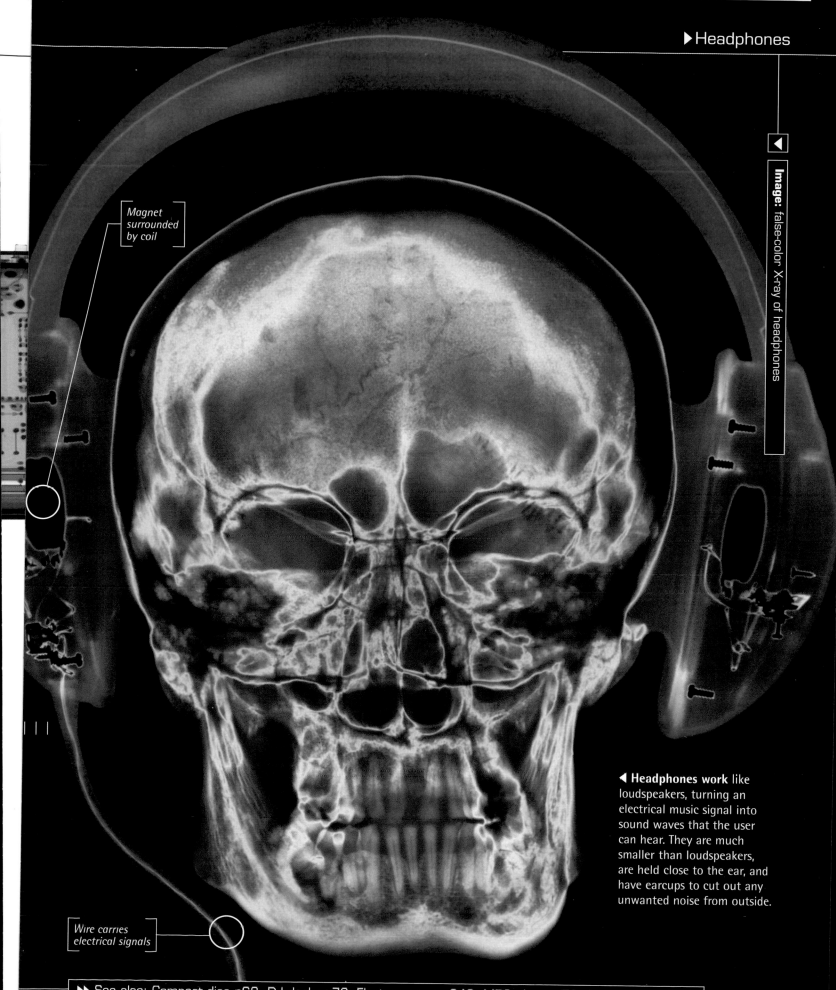

Image: false-color X-ray of headphones

Magnet surrounded by coil

◀ **Headphones work** like loudspeakers, turning an electrical music signal into sound waves that the user can hear. They are much smaller than loudspeakers, are held close to the ear, and have earcups to cut out any unwanted noise from outside.

Wire carries electrical signals

▶▶ See also: Compact disc p68, DJ decks p76, Electromagnet p243, MP3 player p70, Sound wave p250

FIREWORKS

≫ HOW FIREWORKS EXPLODE

HOW A MULTIBREAK SHELL FIREWORK EXPLODES

7. Careful arrangement of stars in second section means they can be made to spread out in a pattern.

5. The burning fuse ignites stars in still-burning second section.

6. Stars in second section ignite and begin to explode.

4. Second section of firework continues with fuse still burning.

3. After ignition, stars blast away from firework and explode spectacularly.

2. As rocket rises, fuse continues to burn and ignites "stars" contained in lower section of firework.

Fuse

1. Lit fuse ignites the lifting charge— gunpowder—at base of firework.

Fireworks were developed in the second century BC by the ancient Chinese for use in religious ceremonies. From this peaceful beginning, they were turned into weapons of war. In the Middle Ages, rockets were used to set fire to opponents' camps. Later, rockets were built to deliver packets of gunpowder, exploding on impact. In 1605, a group of conspirators led by Guy Fawkes made an attempt to blow up London's Houses of Parliament with gunpowder. In Great Britain, their failure is celebrated with annual fireworks displays. Today, fireworks displays around the world use sophisticated blends of explosive and color chemistry to produce cascades of color and sound. They are coordinated by automatic firing mechanisms.

The brilliant colors that fireworks make are produced by a mixture of chemicals. Magnesium and aluminum burn to produce white light, sodium salts produce yellow, strontium nitrate or carbonate produces red, and barium nitrate produces green. Copper salts produce blue, and various forms of carbon, including charcoal, produce orange.

≫

▶▶ A firework is a device in which gunpowder and other chemicals explode to produce color, sparks, smoke, and sound. Fireworks displays can paint the sky with multicolored designs in time to music. ▶▶

Image: Schlieren photograph of firecracker explosion

◄◄ BACK

The earliest rockets were probably made by stuffing bamboo poles with an explosive mixture of chemicals and then lighting them.

The latest fireworks use compressed air to blast fireworks into the sky, so that their displays are not blotted out by the smoke from lifting charges.

FORWARD ▶▶

Expanding shock wave

Hot combustion gases at center of explosion

Firecracker debris being flung apart by force of explosion

◄ **Explosions occur** when chemicals react with one another very quickly and release energy as heat, light, movement, and sound. This image, taken using a technique called Schlieren photography, shows shock waves in the air around a firecracker as it explodes. These shock waves can be harnessed to lift a firework into the sky.

▶▶ See also: Chemical reaction p241, Combustion p242, Jet engine p146, Match p86, Space Shuttle p156

Computer games will increasingly become a more shared experience with other people. Wireless communications and high-speed connections will result in more networked games, which will allow you to play against players who may be located anywhere on the planet, rather than just pitting you against computer-generated opponents. There will also be exciting developments in the way we control and interact with computer games. Control buttons and joysticks will disappear, to be replaced with sensors and cameras that read your body movements and facial expressions. Advanced speech recognition will instantly react to voice commands.

> **A head-mounted display will allow you to superimpose computer-generated images and sounds onto the real world.**

The explosive growth in computer power could mean that by 2010 it will be difficult to distinguish between digitally created images and what is real. New display technologies will narrow the gap even further. In the 1990s, the advent of virtual reality gave people the opportunity to immerse themselves in a virtual world by putting on a pair of goggles with computer images projected on the inside. The next step is likely to be head-mounted displays that beam images directly onto the retina inside the eye. Augmented reality will blur the boundaries even further by allowing you to see the real world through your head-mounted display and superimposing computer-generated images, sounds, and even smells.

While some of these worlds will remain strictly in the realms of fantasy, others will immerse you in role-playing experiences much closer to home. So-called epistemic games will enable you

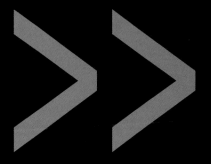

to act out the challenges facing a real-life person such as a surgeon, architect, pilot, or soldier. These games already form part of the training for people who intend to follow these careers, and will become increasingly detailed and realistic.

Back in the real world, spectators attending sporting events, from track meets to football games, will be able to have a much more interactive experience from their seats. Wireless handheld devices will provide fans with on-demand instant action replays from different cameras positioned around the stadium. There will also be access to all kinds of information, from complex rules to statistics about individual players or teams.

As space flight becomes more accessible, people dream of playing zero-gravity sports beyond Earth's atmosphere. Lunar golf was first played in 1971, when astronaut Alan Shepard hit a golf ball on the Moon. In years to come, we may be able to race spacecraft equipped with solar sails. These giant mirrored sails will be pushed through space by light energy from the Sun. Because the spacecraft do not have to carry their own fuel supplies, they can travel at much greater speeds. So who knows—maybe the sky is no longer the limit.

WATERPROOF SPORTS FABRIC

>>LIVE

Match >> Light bulb >> Mirror >> Watch >> Battery >> Solar cell >>
Microwave >> Fridge >> Aerogel >> Lock >> Shaver >> Aerosol >>
Washing machine >> Vacuum >> Robot helper

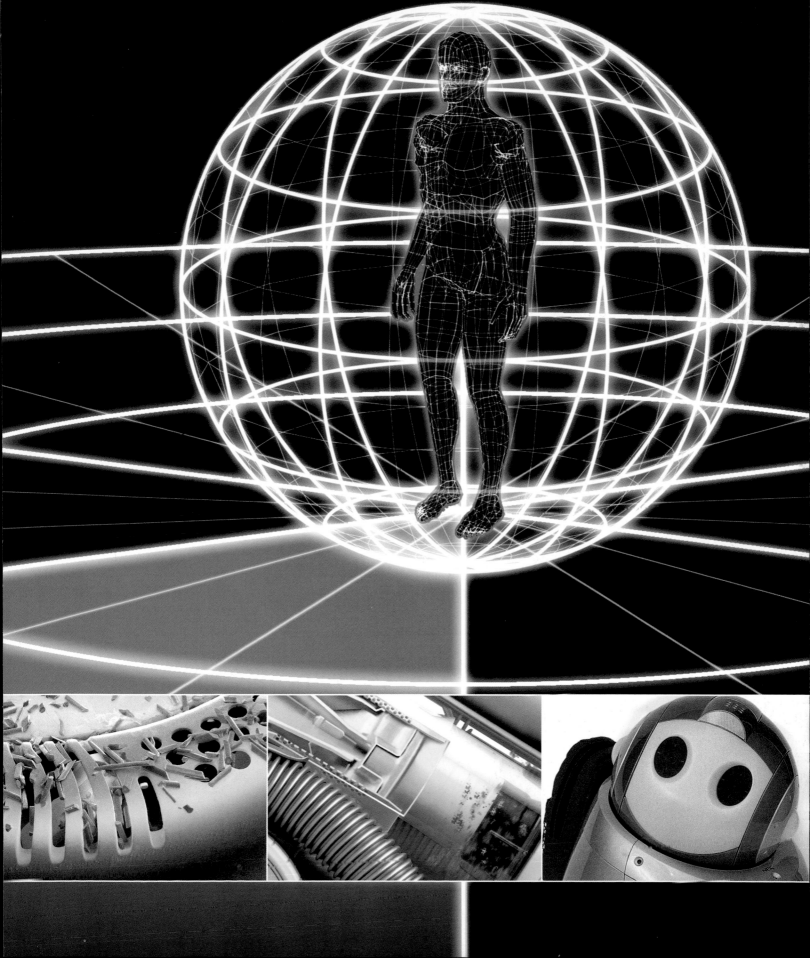

Today, most of us in the industrialized world can cook a meal in minutes using a microwave oven, or program a washing machine to clean and dry our clothes and a dishwasher to wash our kitchen utensils while we are out of the home. Just 150 years ago, there were very few labor-saving devices of any kind.

Without gas or electricity, household tasks had to be done by hand and were very time-consuming. To wash dirty laundry, for example, wood had to be chopped, a fire lit to heat the water, and clothes scrubbed and wrung out by hand. Each day of the week was usually reserved for a particular chore, such as laundry, ironing, baking, or cleaning the house. Most of the work involved was physically very demanding and left little time for other activities.

The arrival of electricity in homes during the late 19th and early 20th centuries resulted in the invention of a range of domestic devices designed to make life easier, from the electric shaver to the electric toaster. Small, high-speed electric motors made the development of effective washing machines, refrigerators, and lightweight vacuum cleaners possible. Housework became less of a daily struggle and homes became cleaner, healthier environments.

CLOSE-UP OF AIR VENT

In the second half of the 20th century, new technologies continued to have a big impact on the domestic scene. The magnetron, a vacuum tube used in radar systems, led to the development of the microwave oven. By the end of the century, many household appliances, including ovens and dishwashers, had timers and programming devices controlled by microprocessors. Food could be prepared quickly and easily. Many tasks could now be carried out automatically and simultaneously, simply at the push of a button or two.

The way we live has been revolutionized by domestic appliances. The time needed for household chores has been dramatically reduced and leisure time has increased. But it has come at a cost. Older refrigerators contain chemicals called chlorofluorocarbons (CFCs), which damage the ozone layer, the planet's natural defense system against harmful radiation from the Sun. Most of the electricity that powers our household appliances comes from burning oil, coal, or gas in power stations. Burning these fuels, however, releases gases into the atmosphere that are responsible for climate change—one of the main threats facing our planet during the 21st century.

> "Previously time-consuming and physically demanding tasks can today be carried out at the push of a button."

One of the ways to cut down on the amount of electricity that we consume is to make our homes and household devices more energy-efficient. By making washing machines that use less water and houses that retain heat effectively, we can cut down on the amount of power that we use. Technologies that harness alternative sources of power, such as solar cells and wind turbines, are being developed, too. Coupling energy-efficient devices with clean power will make a real difference to the planet's future.

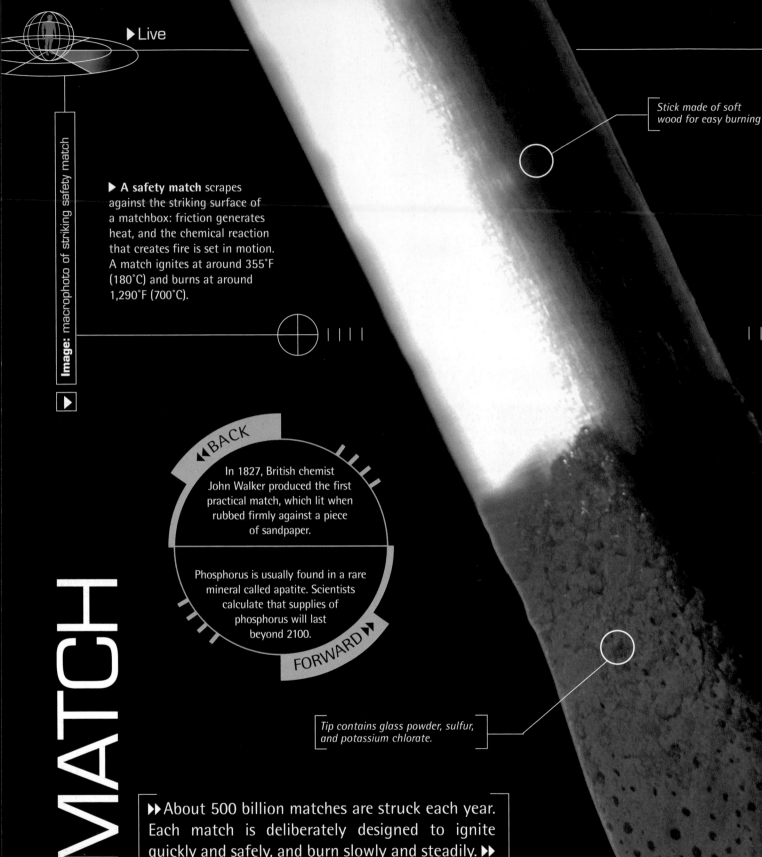

Image: macrophoto of striking safety match

Stick made of soft
wood for easy burning

▶ **A safety match** scrapes
against the striking surface of
a matchbox: friction generates
heat, and the chemical reaction
that creates fire is set in motion.
A match ignites at around 355˚F
(180˚C) and burns at around
1,290˚F (700˚C).

◀◀BACK

In 1827, British chemist
John Walker produced the first
practical match, which lit when
rubbed firmly against a piece
of sandpaper.

Phosphorus is usually found in a rare
mineral called apatite. Scientists
calculate that supplies of
phosphorus will last
beyond 2100.

FORWARD▶▶

MATCH

Tip contains glass powder, sulfur,
and potassium chlorate.

▶▶About 500 billion matches are struck each year.
Each match is deliberately designed to ignite
quickly and safely, and burn slowly and steadily. ▶▶

▶▶ See also: Combustion p242, Fire suit p190, Friction p244, Heat p98

>> HOW A MATCH WORKS

When a match is struck, friction between glass powder in the match tip and the striker on the box produces a small amount of heat. This converts the red phosphorus on the box striker into a cloud of white phosphorus gas. The white phosphorus ignites in air and makes the potassium chlorate and sulfur in the match tip react together. This reaction happens at a high enough temperature to set fire to the wood.

BEFORE

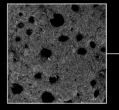

The match tip contains potassium chlorate and sulfur.

AFTER

Most of this easily burned material has been consumed by the fire.

BEFORE

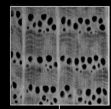

Wood is made from compounds that contain carbon, hydrogen, and oxygen.

AFTER

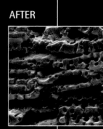

Carbon does not burn easily. It is left behind and makes the match-stick dark and crumbly.

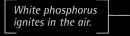

White phosphorus ignites in the air.

❯ Making fire

A natural fire in a forest

▶ Fire needs three key ingredients: fuel, heat, and oxygen. When fuel, such as wood, is heated to a high enough temperature, a chemical reaction takes place—it catches fire. Carbon-based molecules in the wood react with oxygen in the air. We see the reaction as flame, and its products as charred wood and smoke. The fire will continue until either it is extinguished or the available fuel runs out.

LIGHT BULB

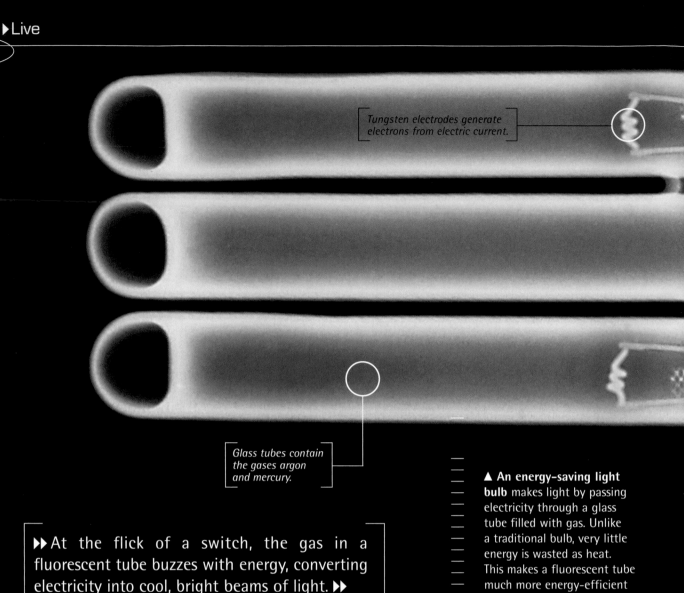

Tungsten electrodes generate electrons from electric current.

Glass tubes contain the gases argon and mercury.

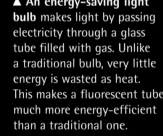

▶▶ At the flick of a switch, the gas in a fluorescent tube buzzes with energy, converting electricity into cool, bright beams of light. ▶▶

▲ **An energy-saving light bulb** makes light by passing electricity through a glass tube filled with gas. Unlike a traditional bulb, very little energy is wasted as heat. This makes a fluorescent tube much more energy-efficient than a traditional one.

⦙ Incandescence and fluorescence

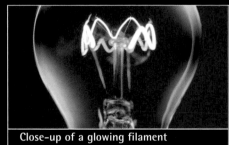

Close-up of a glowing filament

◀Ordinary light bulbs work by incandescence: they make light by creating heat. They pass electricity through a thin coil of wire known as a filament, which heats up to around 4,500°F (2,500°C). The filament glows white-hot and gives off light. Around 90 percent of the energy it emits is wasted as heat.

▶Energy-saving light bulbs work by fluorescence: they make light at a much lower temperature than incandescence without using heat. Glowworms, luminous watches, and light-sticks used by climbers all make light by fluorescence: they glow when chemicals inside them absorb or make energy, then give off that energy as light.

Test tube containing fluorescent chemical

◀BACK

The modern fluorescent bulb was patented in 1936 by George E. Inman. The best-selling model was made for industry, and was a massive 48 in (122 cm) long.

Future bulbs may use high-power light-emitting diodes (LEDS), like the lights used on electrical equipment. They last five times longer than fluorescent bulbs.

FORWARD▶

▶▶ See also: Fluorescence p244, Heat p98, Incandescence p245, Neon p34

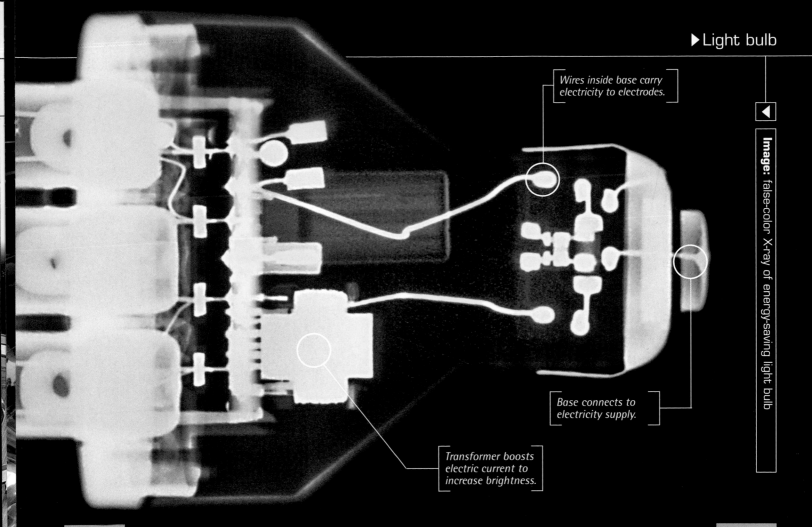

Wires inside base carry electricity to electrodes.

Image: false-color X-ray of energy-saving light bulb

Base connects to electricity supply.

Transformer boosts electric current to increase brightness.

>> HOW AN ENERGY-SAVING LIGHT BULB WORKS

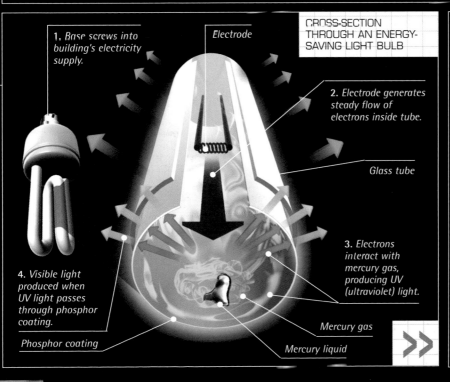

1. Base screws into building's electricity supply.

Electrode

CROSS-SECTION THROUGH AN ENERGY-SAVING LIGHT BULB

2. Electrode generates steady flow of electrons inside tube.

Glass tube

3. Electrons interact with mercury gas, producing UV (ultraviolet) light.

4. Visible light produced when UV light passes through phosphor coating.

Mercury gas

Mercury liquid

Phosphor coating

Modern, energy-saving light bulbs are a big improvement on the traditional incandescent light bulbs. Incandescent light bulbs have a white-hot filament that gives off light, but they lose a lot of energy through heat radiation. Energy-saving light bulbs pass electricity through gases in their tubes to create fluorescence with virtually no heat loss. Energy-saving light bulbs are also an improvement on traditional fluorescent strip lights because they are more compact. A device called a transformer boosts the electrical voltage to a higher level than in normal fluorescent lights, maximizing the light that is created. Compact, energy-saving bulbs also flicker less than older fluorescent lights because their electrical circuits increase the speed by which current pulses from the electrical wiring to the bulb.

Yellow represents two inner electrons at many points in their orbit

Blue represents one outer electron at many points in its orbit

BATTERY

▶▶ A rechargeable battery is a portable chemical power pack that you can use again and again. An average rechargeable battery lasts around 10 years and can be reused 1,000 times. ▶▶

▲ **The latest rechargeable batteries** contain a chemical called lithium. This image shows the structure of one lithium atom. The center of the atom, its nucleus (red), is orbited by two inner electrons (yellow) and one outer electron (blue). When lithium is used in a battery, the blue electron is removed from each lithium atom, creating something called a lithium ion. Lithium ions can store an electric charge in a battery.

>> HOW A RECHARGEABLE BATTERY WORKS

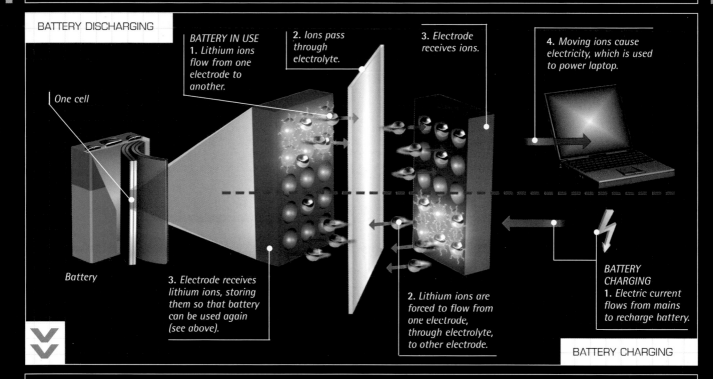

BATTERY DISCHARGING

BATTERY IN USE
1. Lithium ions flow from one electrode to another.

2. Ions pass through electrolyte.

3. Electrode receives ions.

4. Moving ions cause electricity, which is used to power laptop.

One cell

Battery

3. Electrode receives lithium ions, storing them so that battery can be used again (see above).

2. Lithium ions are forced to flow from one electrode, through electrolyte, to other electrode.

BATTERY CHARGING
1. Electric current flows from mains to recharge battery.

BATTERY CHARGING

The battery inside a laptop contains one or more separate power-generating compartments, called cells. Each cell contains two electrodes separated by an electrolyte. During charging, lithium ions are forced from one electrode to the other, where they are stored. When the battery is connected to a circuit—when the laptop is switched on—the ions immediately begin to move back to the other electrode. This movement is electricity. As the ions flow

through each cell, the battery gradually loses power. In batteries that are not rechargeable, this process happens only once. When all the ions have flowed from one electrode to the other, the battery is dead. In a rechargeable battery, the charging and recharging process can happen over and over again. Once all the ions have flowed from one electrode to the other, the battery can be recharged, forcing the ions back to the electrode they came from, thereby storing up power again.

◀ BACK

The first battery, made in 1800, was called a voltaic pile. It was made from a sandwich of paper, soaked in salt water, and pieces of metal.

Batteries may be replaced by environmentally friendly fuel cells, which convert hydrogen and oxygen into water to produce electricity.

FORWARD ▶▶

⌄ Battery graveyard

Collection of disposable batteries

◀ More than 5 billion disposable batteries are thrown away every year. They are a major cause of environmental pollution: some contain extremely toxic chemicals such as mercury and cadmium, which leak in landfills, polluting land and watercourses. Although some rechargeable batteries contain harmful chemicals, they last much longer, so far fewer are thrown away.

▶▶ See also: Electrode p243, Fuel-cell car p128, Ions p245, Laptop p168, Solar cell p96

▶▶ See also: Fuel-cell car p128, Homes p106

SOLAR CELL

▶▶ One second of the Sun's energy, if it could be harnessed, would power the world for a thousand years. Solar cells tap this massive energy source to give us clean, free power. ▶▶

| | | | | | | | | | |

≫ HOW A SOLAR CELL WORKS

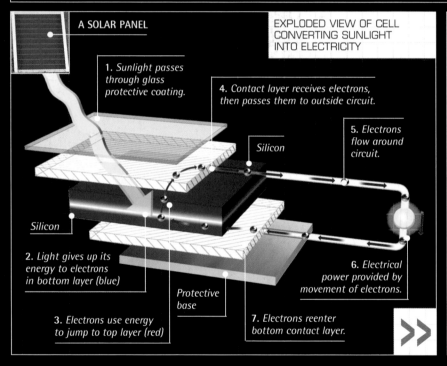

A SOLAR PANEL

EXPLODED VIEW OF CELL CONVERTING SUNLIGHT INTO ELECTRICITY

1. *Sunlight passes through glass protective coating.*

4. *Contact layer receives electrons, then passes them to outside circuit.*

Silicon

5. *Electrons flow around circuit.*

Silicon

2. *Light gives up its energy to electrons in bottom layer (blue)*

6. *Electrical power provided by movement of electrons.*

Protective base

3. *Electrons use energy to jump to top layer (red)*

7. *Electrons reenter bottom contact layer.*

≫

There are two types of solar power. Solar thermal power means collecting the Sun's heat through roof panels that have water pumped through them, providing the house with hot water. Solar electric power means converting the sunlight into electricity using a solar (or photovoltaic) cell. This is made from two layers of silicon, a chemical element extracted from sand. The bottom layer (blue) is chemically treated so that it has slightly too few electrons; the top layer (red) is treated to have slightly too many. When light falls on the cell, the energy it contains energizes the electrons in the lower layer. This causes them to jump up to the top layer, and then continue around as a steady flow of electrons—electricity—until they return to the bottom layer; an electrical circuit has been created.

⌄ Where photovoltaic cells are used

▶One tiny solar cell can power a pocket calculator. When solar cells are joined to form solar panels, they can help power a house. Photovoltaic panels like these are colored blue to absorb as much light as possible. They feed their energy into rechargeable batteries, which charge up during the day and release their power at night.

Photovoltaic panels on house roof

▶ **A solar cell** is chemically treated silicon that converts sunlight into electricity. A solar panel is made of many circular cells like this one, each the size of a compact disc. A typical panel on the roof of a house would be made up of around 36—100 cells.

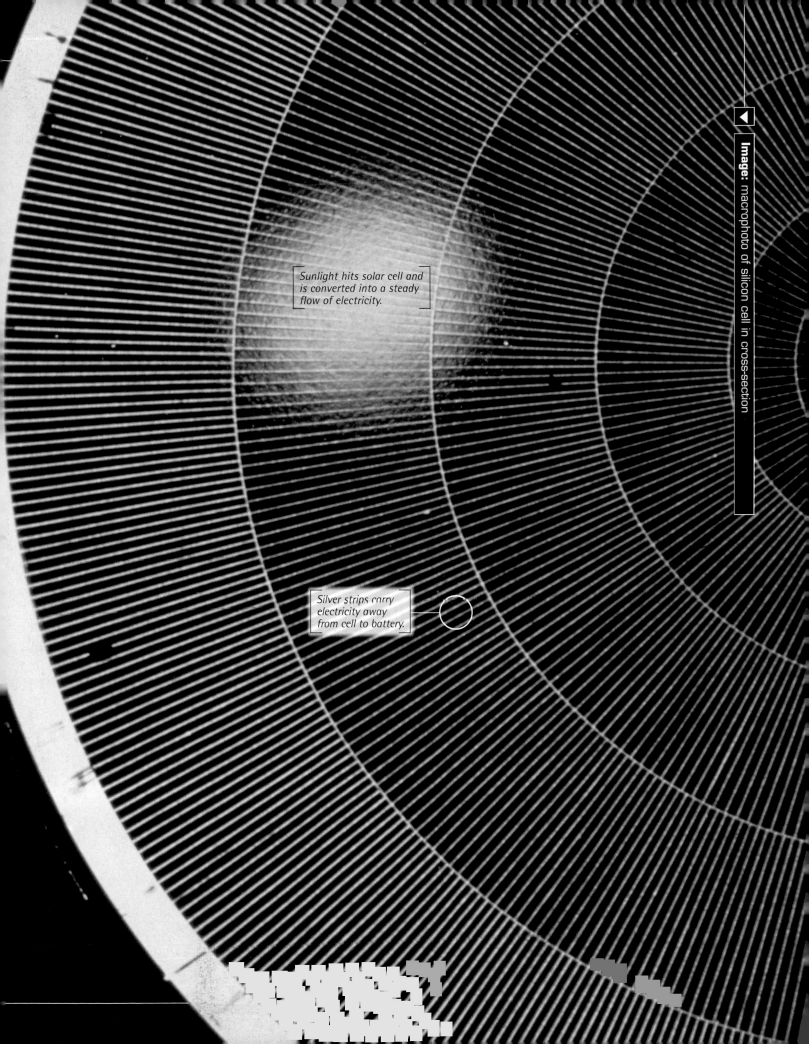

Sunlight hits solar cell and is converted into a steady flow of electricity.

Silver strips carry electricity away from cell to battery.

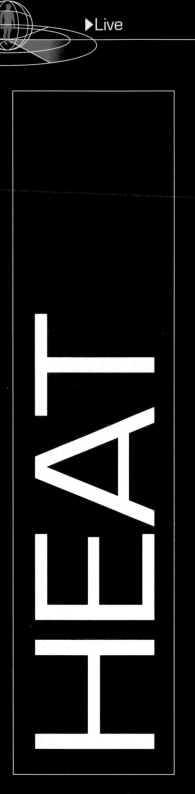

HEAT

Heat is essential for our warmth, comfort, and well-being. The images on this page show how household objects, and even our homes, gain, lose, and transfer heat.

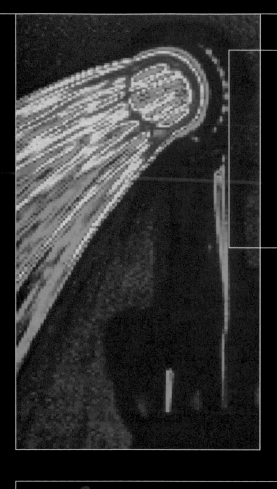

◄◄ Thermogram
A detailed temperature pattern called a thermogram records the infrared light that all objects give out. This thermogram shows a hot shower's water changing from red (hot) through yellow and green to blue (coldest) as it hits the cold air.

∨∨ Heating up
Here we can see heat transferred through different materials. The burning gas is the hottest (white). It heats the metal pan, and the pan heats the soup to the same temperature (blue). The wooden spoon remains cool.

>> Converting electricity to heat

The toaster in this X-ray works by changing electrical energy to heat energy. Elements made of thin metal wire are heated by the electrical current until they glow orange. Once the selected time has elapsed—enough to brown your toast—a switch turns off the element and releases a spring to pop up the toast.

<< Heat loss

This thermogram shows how heat leaks out of an older house. The roof and the windows (yellow) are poorly insulated and are losing the most heat. The solid walls (red, purple, and green), which have the greatest insulation, are losing the least heat. Typically, up to 25 percent of the heat generated in a house is lost through poor insulation.

∨ Hair-dryer

This colored X-ray shows the heated element inside a hair-dryer. An electric fan at the back of the device blows air over the filament, which heats it and blows the hot air out through the nozzle. The element is made of nichrome, which does not rust when heated to high temperatures.

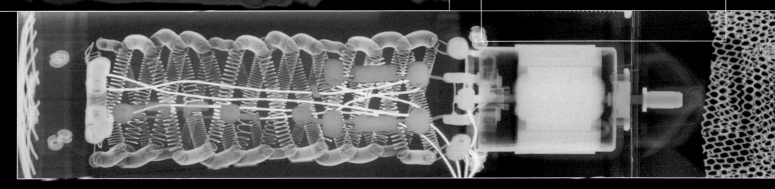

▶▶ See also: Conduction p242, Fridge p102, Light bulb p88, Microwave p100

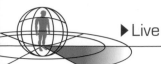

MICROWAVE

▶▶Invisible rays of microwave energy, zapping through the air, can heat food in a matter of minutes. A microwave oven can cook a meat roast six times faster than a normal oven. ▶▶

▼ **A microwave oven** cooks much more quickly than a conventional oven, but is much noisier. The humming noise of the oven is the sound of the transformer vibrating as it converts power, and the whirring noise is the sound of the fan cooling the electronic components.

Special cooking bag makes chicken skin brown and crisp.

Metal grill on door and metal seal stop microwave leakage.

Image: false-color X-ray of microwave oven

Turntable

▶▶ See also: Cell phone p18, Electromagnetic spectrum p250, Heat p98, Microwaves p247

≫ HOW A MICROWAVE WORKS

HOW A MICROWAVE
OVEN COOKS FOOD

4. *Rotating paddle scatters microwaves around oven.*

3. *Aerial sends beam of microwaves along tube called a wave guide.*

2. *Magnetron generates microwaves.*

5. *Microwave hits oven wall and is reflected back into food.*

6. *Microwave penetrates through food and makes water molecules rotate.*

Aerial sends microwaves into oven.

7. *Water molecule movement generates heat, which warms food from within.*

8. *Turntable rotates food slowly, ensuring even heating.*

1. *Transformer boosts domestic electricity.*

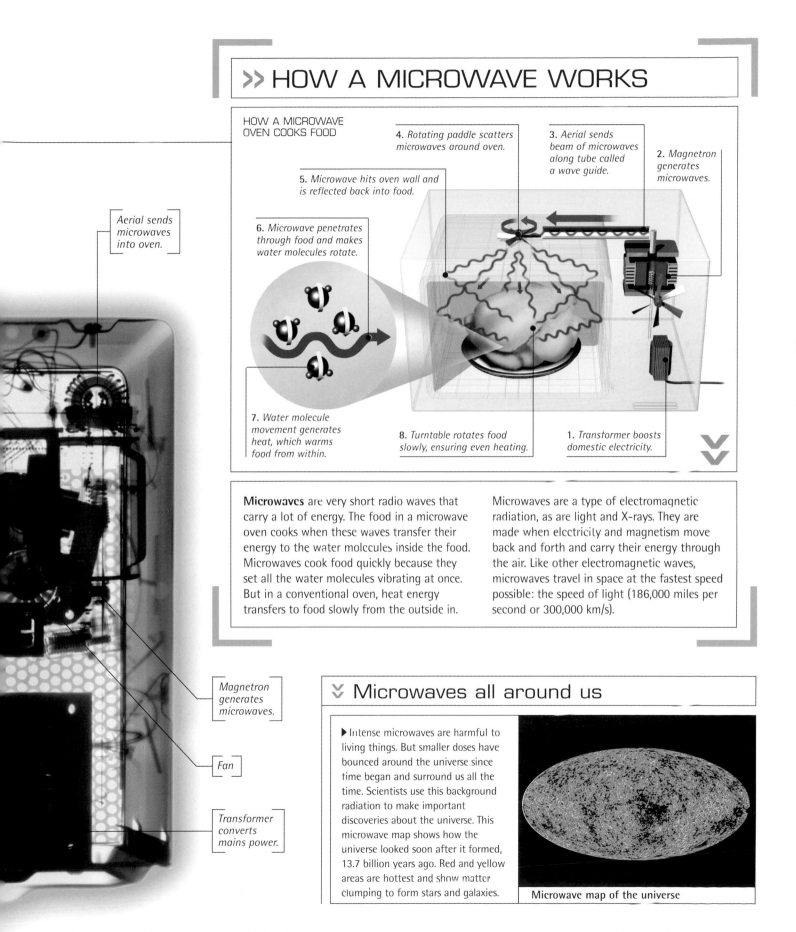

Magnetron generates microwaves.

Fan

Transformer converts mains power.

Microwaves are very short radio waves that carry a lot of energy. The food in a microwave oven cooks when these waves transfer their energy to the water molecules inside the food. Microwaves cook food quickly because they set all the water molecules vibrating at once. But in a conventional oven, heat energy transfers to food slowly from the outside in.

Microwaves are a type of electromagnetic radiation, as are light and X-rays. They are made when electricity and magnetism move back and forth and carry their energy through the air. Like other electromagnetic waves, microwaves travel in space at the fastest speed possible: the speed of light (186,000 miles per second or 300,000 km/s).

≥ Microwaves all around us

▶ Intense microwaves are harmful to living things. But smaller doses have bounced around the universe since time began and surround us all the time. Scientists use this background radiation to make important discoveries about the universe. This microwave map shows how the universe looked soon after it formed, 13.7 billion years ago. Red and yellow areas are hottest and show matter clumping to form stars and galaxies.

Microwave map of the universe

FRIDGE

▶▶A refrigerator is a heat extraction machine that keeps food fresh. The latest models use an Internet connection to reorder food when supplies get low.▶▶

Eggs stored at safe temperature

Chilled lettuce stays fresh for around one week.

≫ HOW A REFRIGERATOR WORKS

The clever part of a refrigerator is a small length of pipe called an expansion valve, fixed to the outside of the plastic food compartment. The coolant—the chemical that circulates around the refrigerator in coils—enters the narrow opening at one end of the expansion valve as a high-pressure liquid. The expansion valve becomes wider along its length, so the pressure of the coolant falls as it travels through. The drop in pressure causes the coolant to evaporate and become a cold, low-pressure gas, which is pumped into the evaporator coils inside the refrigerator. The cold gas in the coils now absorbs heat from inside the refrigerator, causing the gas to warm up and the inside of the refrigerator to cool down. The warmed-up gas then flows to the condenser coil outside the refrigerator, where the heat is lost into the air of the room.

HOW COOLANT FLOWS AROUND A REFRIGERATOR

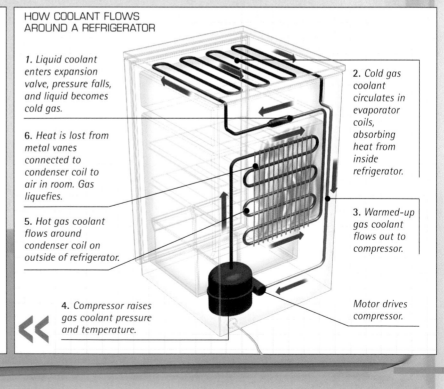

1. Liquid coolant enters expansion valve, pressure falls, and liquid becomes cold gas.

6. Heat is lost from metal vanes connected to condenser coil to air in room. Gas liquefies.

5. Hot gas coolant flows around condenser coil on outside of refrigerator.

4. Compressor raises gas coolant pressure and temperature.

2. Cold gas coolant circulates in evaporator coils, absorbing heat from inside refrigerator.

3. Warmed-up gas coolant flows out to compressor.

Motor drives compressor.

≪

▶▶ See also: Heat p245, Homes p106, Internet p38

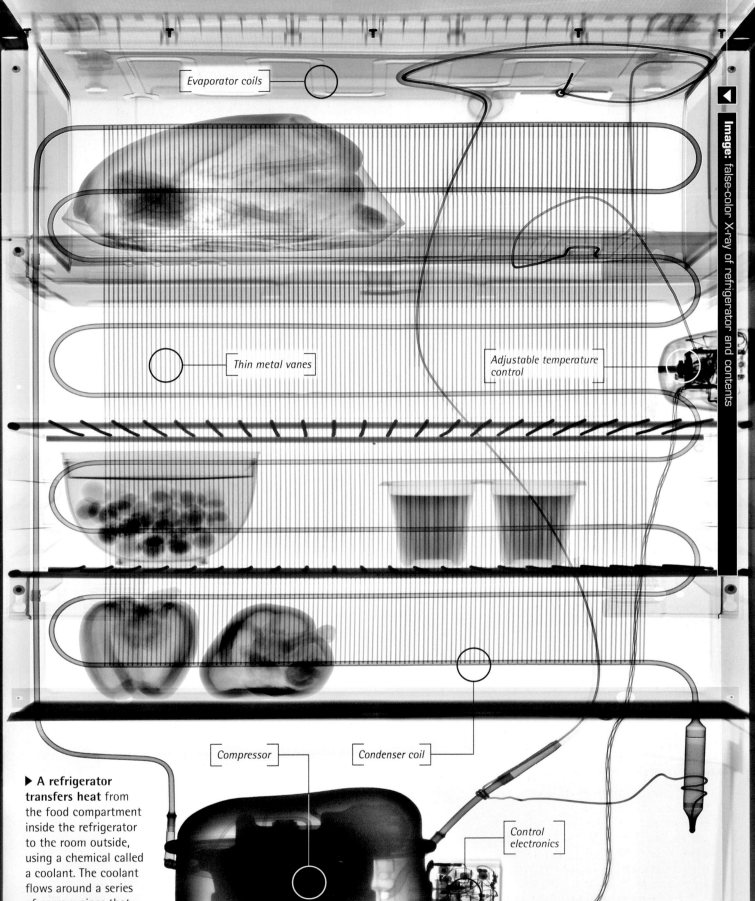

Evaporator coils

Thin metal vanes

Adjustable temperature control

Compressor

Condenser coil

Control electronics

▶ **A refrigerator transfers heat** from the food compartment inside the refrigerator to the room outside, using a chemical called a coolant. The coolant flows around a series of narrow pipes that make up a kind of heat-carrying conveyor belt.

AEROGEL

▶▶ A ghostly substance called aerogel is the lightest solid known. It is also incredibly strong. A piece of aerogel the size of a man weighs less than 2¹/₄ lb (1 kg), but it can still support the weight of a car. ▶▶

▶▶ USES AND APPLICATIONS

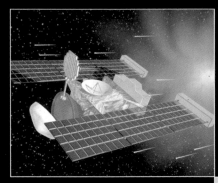

◀◀ **The Stardust space probe** collects cosmic dust (minute specks of matter from space) with a tennis-racket-shaped arm packed with aerogel. Passing dust zooms into the aerogel at vast speed, forming a trail, which reveals where it came from. This dust may reveal much about the formation of the universe.

▶▶ **Oil is transported** through very long pipelines from rigs at sea to refineries on land. When it leaves the seabed, the oil is hot and fluid. But chilly temperatures in oil-rich places, such as the North Sea, cause the oil to thicken, making it harder to pipe ashore. Aerogel is now wrapped around the pipes to insulate them, so that oil stays warm.

▲ **Packed with fuel** for long journeys, airplanes are at risk of catching fire. Because aerogel is fire-resistant, it is used to line the passenger compartments of planes to help stop a potential fire from spreading. Aerogel is also used to insulate plane engines so that they give off less heat, and helps to make engines less noisy.

◀◀ **Clothing made with aerogel** is excellent at keeping people warm. This insulated jacket is made from Spaceloft™, a fabric with a built-in layer of aerogel. A jacket only ¹/₁₀ in (3 mm) thick keeps people warm in temperatures as low as −58°F (−50°C).

Aerogel is transparent and ▶▶ lets little heat pass through it, so it is perfect for making windows. It is also very fragile, so the aerogel has to be protected in a sandwich of ordinary glass.

▶▶ See also: Fabric p60, Fire suit p190, Heat p98, Insulator p245, Space probe p158

Aerogel is such a good insulator that wax crayons don't melt when fierce heat is applied underneath.

green

Melting point of aerogel is over 2,200°F (1,200°C).

Gas flame concentrates intense heat on aerogel.

▲ **Aerogel** is made from a silica-based gel, from which the liquid is taken out. The resulting substance is mostly empty space. Its structure is stiff and will shatter if dropped. However, it is light, porous, almost transparent, and a very good insulator. A house lined with aerogel would be so well insulated that you could heat it with a candle and it would still be too hot to live in. New uses for aerogel are emerging all the time.

≫ Making aerogel

Technician analyzing material using microprobe

▲ American chemist Steven Kistler made the first aerogel in 1931. The complicated process for making the solid involves very high temperatures and pressures. The first production plant for making aerogel was based in Sweden. Today, it is manufactured throughout the world.

HOMES

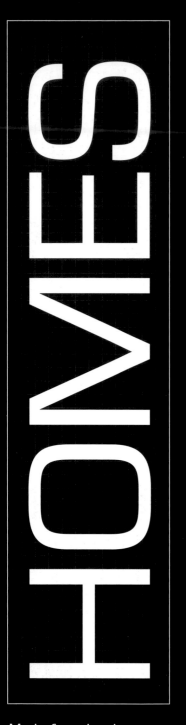

Made from local or recycled materials, generating their own power, and using resources wisely, eco-friendly buildings help protect the environment.

◄◄ Ice homes

Ice is a traditional Arctic building material. It is free, easy to shape, and melts away when summer comes. Ice is used most famously for igloos, the historic homes of the Arctic peoples. This ice hotel in Lapland is made from thousands of tons of ice and snow. Even the beds are made from blocks of ice, with soft mattresses and reindeer hides piled on top.

▶▶ Straw insulation

The walls of this eco-home are made from a cheap, natural material: straw. The heavy straw bales are stacked like gigantic bricks, and strengthened by a wood-and-steel framework coated outside with plaster. The bales are packed tightly to make the walls sufficiently fireproof. The thick walls cut heating costs by up to a quarter.

▶▶ Recycled materials

Each day, millions of tons of building materials are dug out of quarries, and millions of tons of household garbage are buried in landfills. Building eco-homes from recycled materials helps tackle both these environmental problems. This wall is made from beverage cans and car tires embedded in plaster, and will last a long time because the materials are weather-resistant.

◀◀ Solar collectors

This is the world's biggest solar furnace, at a solar research center in the French Pyrenees. The two-story mirror focuses sunlight on the small tower in front, making useful energy that is carried away by hot water pipes. Some eco-homes generate electricity and heat water using the Sun's energy collected from solar panels. Solar energy is free and does not pollute the environment. One day, every home may have its own solar panel.

▲ Sod roof

Grass roofs are good insulators. In winter, the thick mat of grass, roots, and soil traps heat inside the building. In summer, the growing grass absorbs sunlight and keeps the building cool. A plastic sheet under the sod keeps the roof waterproof. Roofs like this last more than 50 years.

107

LOCK

▶▶ Gold, money, and jewels are often kept safe by nothing more than the intricate metal mechanisms inside locks. A typical bank safe has around 10 billion combinations. ▶▶

≫ HOW COMBINATION LOCKS WORK

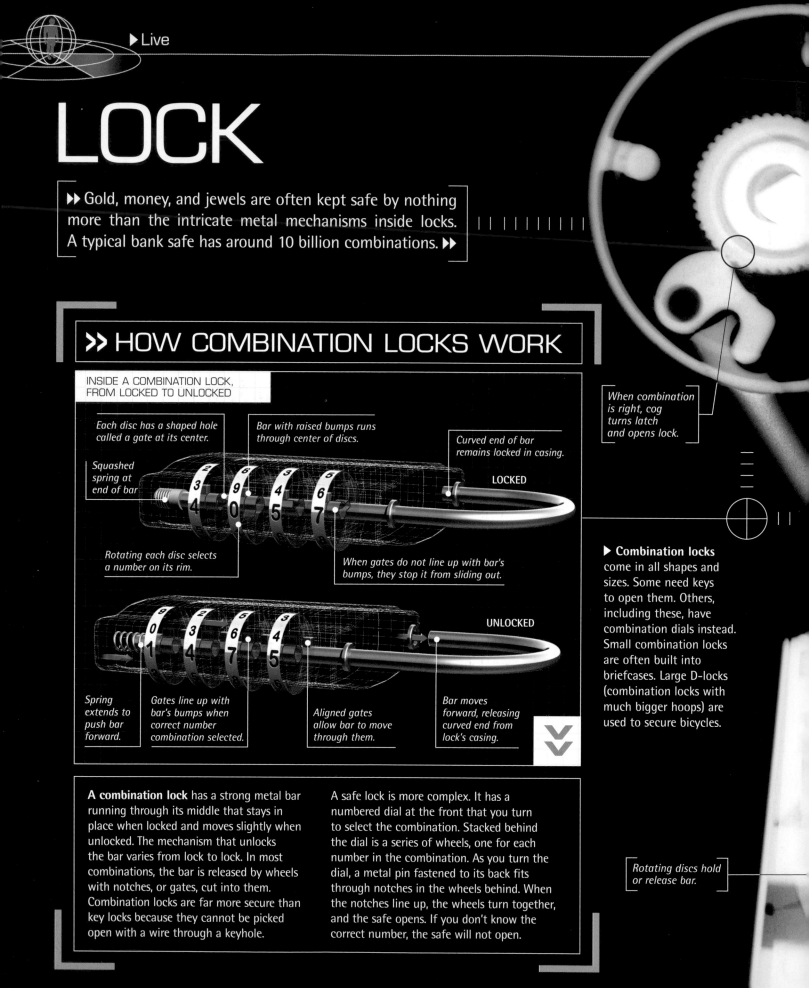

INSIDE A COMBINATION LOCK, FROM LOCKED TO UNLOCKED

Each disc has a shaped hole called a gate at its center.

Bar with raised bumps runs through center of discs.

Curved end of bar remains locked in casing.

Squashed spring at end of bar

LOCKED

Rotating each disc selects a number on its rim.

When gates do not line up with bar's bumps, they stop it from sliding out.

UNLOCKED

Spring extends to push bar forward.

Gates line up with bar's bumps when correct number combination selected.

Aligned gates allow bar to move through them.

Bar moves forward, releasing curved end from lock's casing.

When combination is right, cog turns latch and opens lock.

▶ **Combination locks** come in all shapes and sizes. Some need keys to open them. Others, including these, have combination dials instead. Small combination locks are often built into briefcases. Large D-locks (combination locks with much bigger hoops) are used to secure bicycles.

Rotating discs hold or release bar.

A combination lock has a strong metal bar running through its middle that stays in place when locked and moves slightly when unlocked. The mechanism that unlocks the bar varies from lock to lock. In most combinations, the bar is released by wheels with notches, or gates, cut into them. Combination locks are far more secure than key locks because they cannot be picked open with a wire through a keyhole.

A safe lock is more complex. It has a numbered dial at the front that you turn to select the combination. Stacked behind the dial is a series of wheels, one for each number in the combination. As you turn the dial, a metal pin fastened to its back fits through notches in the wheels behind. When the notches line up, the wheels turn together, and the safe opens. If you don't know the correct number, the safe will not open.

▶▶ See also: Radio ID tag p184, Smart card p182

Metal plate prevents U-shaped bar from coming completely out of lock.

Central dial used to enter combination and release bar.

⌄ Microscopic locks

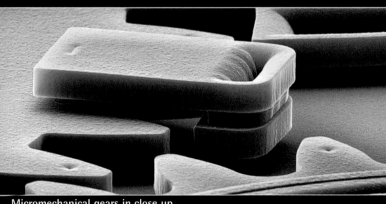

Micromechanical gears in close up

▲ The best locks are very large and intricate. In the future, micromechanisms (extremely small moving parts) could make locks more compact and much easier to manufacture. These micromechanical gears, magnified 2,200 times by an electron microscope, could be used to make a high-tech lock smaller than a fingernail. The mechanism would be so tiny that it would be almost impossible to tamper with and so much more secure than a normal-sized lock.

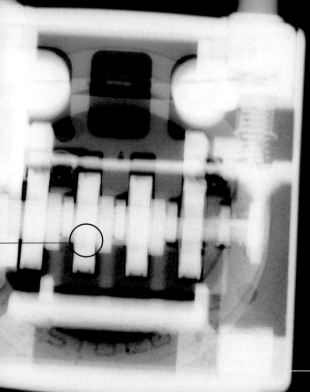

SHAVER

▶▶ The average man grows 30 ft (9 m) of beard in his lifetime. Many use electric shavers. These tiny motor mowers are driven across the face, chopping hairs quickly and painlessly. ▶▶

>> HOW A SHAVER WORKS

THE LIFT AND CUT MECHANISM
IN AN ELECTRIC SHAVER

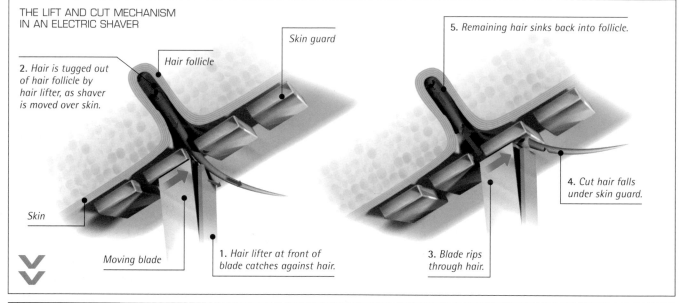

Skin guard

Hair follicle

2. *Hair is tugged out of hair follicle by hair lifter, as shaver is moved over skin.*

Skin

Moving blade

1. *Hair lifter at front of blade catches against hair.*

5. *Remaining hair sinks back into follicle.*

4. *Cut hair falls under skin guard.*

3. *Blade rips through hair.*

Hair is made of keratin, a strong protein that is also found in nails and the outer layer of skin. The metal blade of a razor is strong enough to chop through the structure of hair. Electric shavers have blades that are mounted on wheels and spin around under skin guards. As the blades whizz along, they rip through the hairs, but do not touch the skin.

This makes them quick and safe to use. They were also designed to work on a dry face with no soap. A manual shaver works much like a knife blade. Wetting the face and using soap makes the hairs softer, so the sharp blade of a manual razor can slice through hairs easily. However, this process takes much longer and does not protect the skin from cuts.

Skin guard provides barrier between blades and skin.

❯❯ Why razor blades wear out

▶ Blades and cutting instruments are made from strong, hard materials—for example, diamonds and metals. These can cut through softer materials, like hair. But even hard materials, such as this steel razor blade, eventually become blunt. Each time the blade shaves, hairs leave tiny scratches on its surface. A rough, old blade is less able to slice through hair than a smooth, new one, so it cuts less well.

Worn edge of a steel razor blade

▼ **This working electric shaver** reveals why it is safer to use than a manual razor blade. The metal skin guard on its surface acts like a sieve. As the shaver presses against the skin, hairs poke down through the slits in the guard and are cut by the spinning blades beneath it. Skin stays safely out of reach of the blades and cannot be cut accidentally.

One of the blades rotating under skin guard

Image: magnified image of an electric shaver

Holes in metal skin guard allow cut hair to fall through.

◀◀BACK

An American, Colonel Jacob Shick, patented the electric shaver in 1928. His invention was inspired by the rotating mechanisms in machine guns.

Shavers of the future may have no blades at all. Using tiny laser beams, they will heat and seal up hair follicles, permanently stopping hair from growing.

FORWARD▶▶

▶▶ See also: Laser eye surgery p206

AEROSOL CAN

▶▶ At the press of a button, an aerosol can releases a burst of pressurized liquid and sprays it evenly over a wide area. Aerosol cans hold many things, including air fresheners and hairspray. ▶▶

Image: Schlieren photograph of aerosol stream

Aerosol spreads out as it gets farther from can.

Hairspray consists of drops of liquid suspended in volume of gas.

⌄ How aerosols depleted the ozone layer

▶A layer of ozone gas in Earth's upper atmosphere (the stratosphere) acts like a natural sunblock, screening out harmful ultraviolet radiation. From the 1930s to the 1980s, chemical propellants used in aerosol cans reacted with ozone gas and caused some of it to disappear. This left an enormous hole in the ozone layer over Antarctica. Those chemicals are now banned, but the hole will not be filled for many decades.

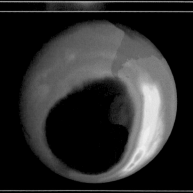

Ozone hole over Antarctica (in blue)

◀◀ BACK

The potential of aerosol cans was not fully realized until World War II, when the US military introduced a device for dispensing insecticide.

Aerosol cans containing medicines will have an electronic counter, so that patients know they've used the correct dose, and when to re-order their prescription.

FORWARD ▶▶

▶▶ See also: Fridge p102, Gas p244, Neon p34, Pressure p249

>> HOW AN AEROSOL CAN WORKS

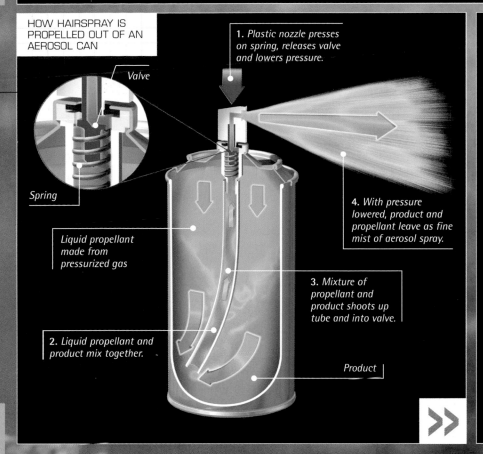

HOW HAIRSPRAY IS PROPELLED OUT OF AN AEROSOL CAN

Valve

Spring

1. *Plastic nozzle presses on spring, releases valve and lowers pressure.*

Liquid propellant made from pressurized gas

4. *With pressure lowered, product and propellant leave as fine mist of aerosol spray.*

3. *Mixture of propellant and product shoots up tube and into valve.*

2. *Liquid propellant and product mix together.*

Product

An aerosol can contains two different elements: a propellant, which is normally a gas, such as butane or propane, and a liquid product, such as hairspray. The propellant is pumped into a can under pressure, becomes a liquid, and mixes with the product. When the nozzle of the can is pressed and the valve opens, the propellant shoots out, turning back into a gas, which expands in the air. It takes with it droplets or particles of the product. This cloud of gas and product is an aerosol.

Some aerosols are made another way, using a trigger-handle that you squeeze repeatedly. As you pump the handle, the air above the liquid is pressurized, which forces the liquid up a small tube and out through a nozzle to form a spray. This type of product is safer and more environmentally friendly than an aerosol can, since it makes a spray without using propellants.

Aerosol expands outward when it is released from pressurized container.

Aerosol released through tiny opening on nozzle.

▲ **This expanding cloud** of hairspray is an aerosol: a collection of liquid droplets that are finely spread out within a gas. To create an aerosol, both the gas and liquid are squeezed into a contained area—in this case, a can— and released under pressure through a tiny opening in the can's nozzle. The particles of the liquid are dispersed through the air with the released gas. Aerosols are not just manufactured, but can be found in the natural world; for example, clouds, fog, and smog are all aerosols.

WASHING MACHINE

▶▶ Pile in your laundry, add detergent, choose a program, and the washing machine does the dirty work. In its final spin, the inner drum races around at up to 80 mph (130 km/h). ▶▶

≫ HOW A WASHING MACHINE WORKS

HOW WATER AND DETERGENT CIRCULATE INSIDE A WASHING MACHINE

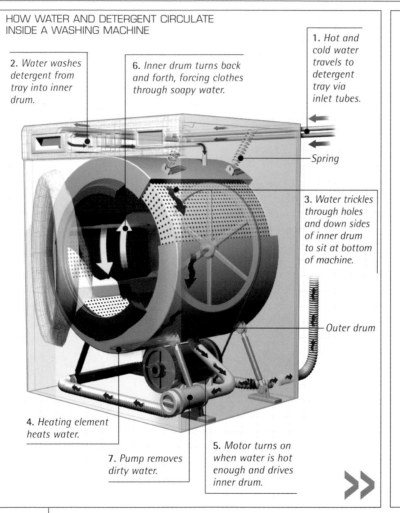

1. Hot and cold water travels to detergent tray via inlet tubes.

2. Water washes detergent from tray into inner drum.

6. Inner drum turns back and forth, forcing clothes through soapy water.

Spring

3. Water trickles through holes and down sides of inner drum to sit at bottom of machine.

Outer drum

4. Heating element heats water.

7. Pump removes dirty water.

5. Motor turns on when water is hot enough and drives inner drum.

The very latest washing machines are designed to be environmentally friendly, using as little water and energy as possible. Before beginning a wash, the machine weighs the load, and calculates how much water is needed. Using less water means less electricity is required to heat it. It also means the drum is lighter, so less energy is needed to turn it. Some machines are designed to use less detergent, too. As the drum turns, paddles built into the sides scoop up the water and detergent and sprinkle it over the clothes to increase cleaning power.

After the load has been rinsed, the drum spins up to 1,400 times per minute (23 times per second) to drain it. The drum has hundreds of tiny holes around its rim. As it spins, the water flies out through the holes. Some machines can remove two-thirds of the water during spinning, so less energy is needed to dry the load.

⌄ Top-loaders

▶ Top-loading washing machines have an upright tub rather than a horizontal drum. Clothes and detergent are loaded at the top, and the clothes are stirred in the water by a paddle called an agitator. Front-loading machines are more energy-efficient than top-loaders because they spin at faster speeds and use less energy for drying. Front loaders are also better for the environment, using around 5 percent less water.

Top loaders on production line

▶▶ See also: Detergent p242, Robot helper p118, Vacuum p116

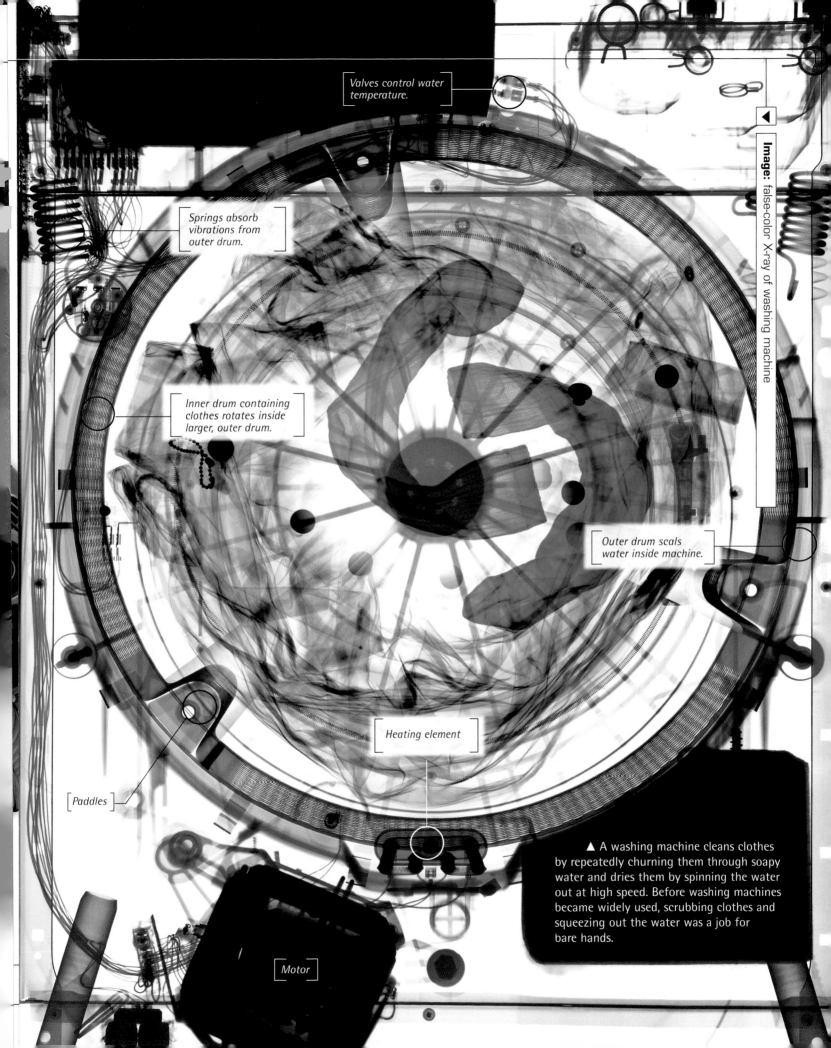

Valves control water temperature.

Springs absorb vibrations from outer drum.

Inner drum containing clothes rotates inside larger, outer drum.

Outer drum seals water inside machine.

Heating element

[Paddles]

▲ A washing machine cleans clothes by repeatedly churning them through soapy water and dries them by spinning the water out at high speed. Before washing machines became widely used, scrubbing clothes and squeezing out the water was a job for bare hands.

Motor

Within the next few years, we are likely to be wearing clothes with computers, communications devices, and heating systems built into them. New kinds of synthetic fibers, as well as ways of combining traditional fabrics with high-tech materials such as aerogel, are making clothes lighter, more in tune with our bodies, and easier to clean.

The development of new materials will also have a big impact on our homes. Walls and windows could be insulated with aerogel, a lightweight but incredibly efficient insulating material. Less power will be needed to keep us warm, cutting down fossil fuel usage. Millions of houses might be able to source their energy from solar panels. These will be made from an infrared sensitive film, capable of being sprayed onto any surface. Even on cloudy days, they will convert the Sun's energy into electricity, making them much more efficient than current solar cell technology.

> A new science called biomimicry is looking to nature's own ingenious design solutions to solve human problems.

A new science called biomimicry is looking to nature to solve human problems. After 3.8 billion years of evolution, nature has worked out some ingenious and effective design solutions. Architects, designers, and engineers are becoming inspired by biomimicry, and new technologies could be developed as a result. For example, outside walls that copy the surface of lotus leaves will be cleaned by rainwater, rather than made more dirty by it. Colors of objects, such as cars, clothing, or the walls in your home, could alter according to how much natural light bounces off them, just as a peacock's feathers change color by reacting to light. And adhesive tape could mimic the way the hairs on a gecko's foot produce static electricity, allowing it to climb up walls.

Our homes will become responsive to our needs. Almost any household object or appliance can be made smarter with sensors and microchips. These tiny devices will be found in every room, working away invisibly. This is called "ubiquitous computing." Washing machines will know when their parts are faulty or worn and contact a service engineer with a status report. Bathroom cabinets could alert you when medicines are close to their expiration dates. When you are about to run out of milk, your refrigerator could automatically order another carton from the supermarket. Smart homes could also help the elderly and ill. Sensors in the floor, for example, could detect if you have fallen and alert a care-giver or the emergency services.

By the end of the century, many of the everyday items we use may be produced not in big industrial plants, but in our own homes. Replicating machines, already in development, will "print out" parts made of resin, using a set of instructions stored on a computer. The parts could then be assembled into various objects, such as pieces of furniture, kitchen utensils, plates and cups, or even other replicating machines. These machines will become cheap enough for most of us to own or access, in much the same way that computers have become commonplace today.

AEROGEL

>>MOVE

Motorcycle >> Fuel-cell car >> Car engine >> Crash test >>
Car tower >> Wheelchair >> Elevator >> Submersible >> Osprey >>
Jet engine >> Wind tunnel >> Black box >> Navigation >>
Space Shuttle >> Space probe

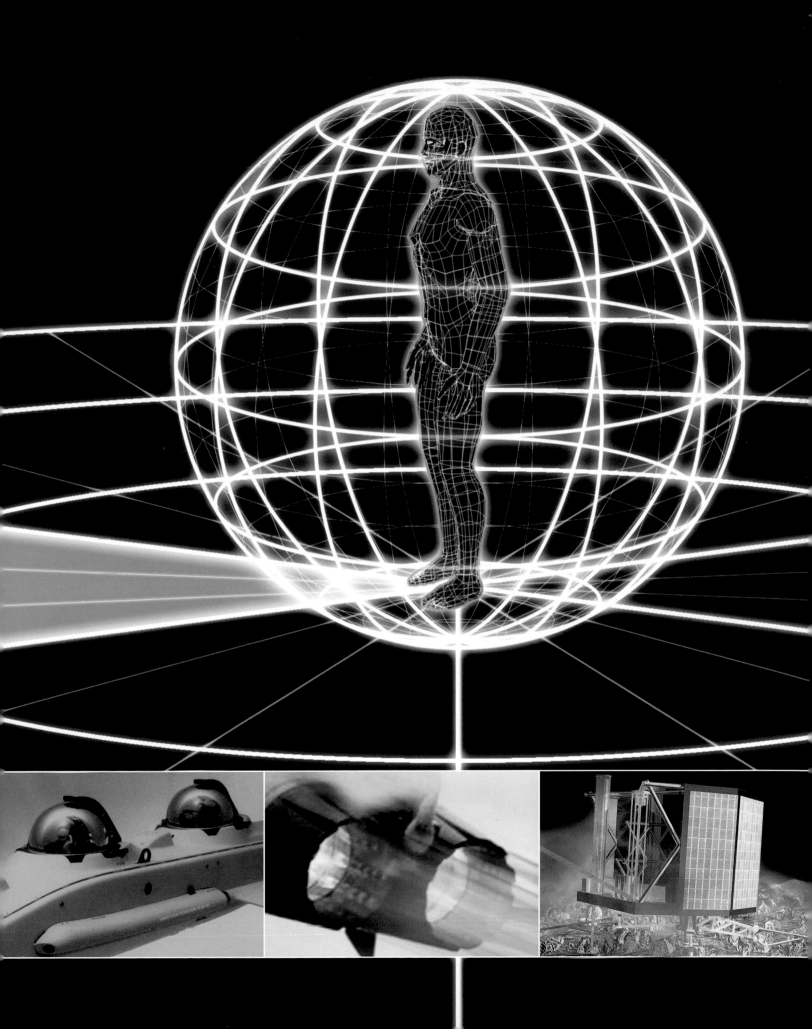

In 1900, the two most important forms of transportation that we use today were in their infancy. The Wright brothers, among others, had begun testing gliders. In 1903, they completed the first powered flight, which lasted just 12 seconds and covered 120 ft (36.5 m). Worldwide, fewer than one in 10,000 people owned a car. Fast-forward a century and the world has been transformed by our devotion to these twin technologies. In 2004, one and a half billion journeys were made by airplane—the equivalent of one flight for every fourth person on the planet. And there are more than 500 million cars on the planet, or one car for every 13 people.

Long before the arrival of the automobile and aircraft, steam engine technology had created its own transport revolution. Until rail networks were developed in the nineteenth century, most people rarely ventured outside their city, town, or even the village where they lived. The fastest it was possible to travel was on horseback. When the first steam train was invented in the eighteenth century, people thought it would be dangerous to travel at a speed greater than 25 mph (40 km/h). By 1916, people were using steam trains to cross continents in speed and comfort. Today, some trains regularly reach speeds of 268 mph (430 km/h).

SPEEDOMETER

The invention of the internal combustion engine, which ran on oil, led directly to the development of the car. This vehicle, more than any other, captured the public imagination with its promise of excitement, speed, and the freedom to travel wherever you chose. By the 1950s, reliable engines could power large planes economically. The Jet Age had arrived and mass overseas travel became a reality. Today, transport for people and goods increases every year, putting more and more pressure on transportation networks. Congestion and safety are becoming serious challenges for the future.

> " In 1900, fewer than one in 10,000 people owned a car. Today, there is one car for every thirteen people on the planet. "

Cutting-edge technology has found its way into all forms of transportation. New developments in engineering, manufacturing, electronics, and computing have had a huge impact on the way we get around. Engines can power vehicles more efficiently, materials are getting stronger and lighter, and essential components have gotten smaller and smarter. Many new cars are fitted with sensors that can identify your precise location using the system of satellites called the Global Positioning System. Other computers control everything from the running of elevators and escalators to rail network signaling.

A majority of vehicles are powered by gasoline, which comes from oil. They produce waste gases that scientists believe are changing the world's climate. Also, world supplies of oil and other fossil fuels will decline as demand keeps growing, so the race is on to find other sources of power. One of the most exciting alternatives is the fuel cell, which uses hydrogen gas and oxygen to make electricity. Fuel-cell cars produce a harmless waste product: water. It is vital that we succeed in the quest for alternative energy if we are to create sustainable transportation and a cleaner future.

MOTORCYCLE

▶▶The fastest motorcycles on the road today can reach speeds of 194 mph (312 km/h) and can accelerate from 0 to 60 mph (100 km/h) in under 3 seconds. ▶▶

▼ **This Ducati** sports motorcycle has a compact engine suspended in a strong, lightweight frame. The engine is more powerful than many car engines, but the motorcycle weighs a fraction of a car's weight. This combination of power and light weight allows motorcycles such as the Ducati to travel extremely fast.

Rear tire can get hotter than boiling water during a race.

Engine shaft spins 175 times a second at top speed.

Carbon-fiber body is five times stronger than steel.

Lightweight alloy wheel

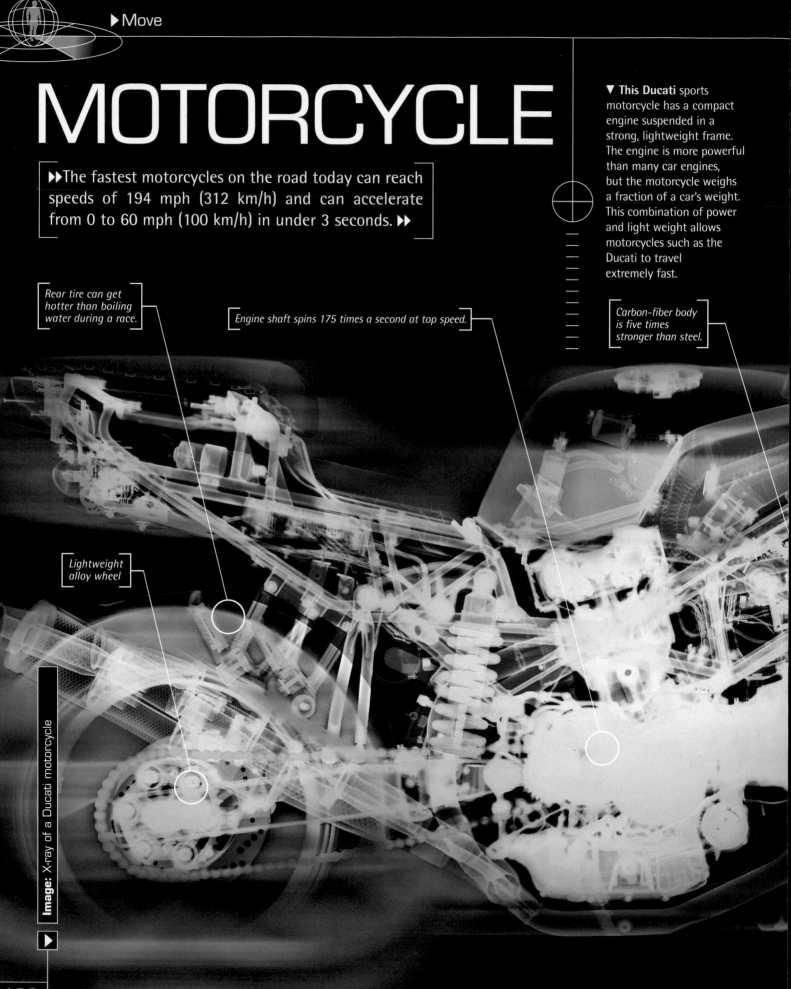

Image: X-ray of a Ducati motorcycle

▶▶ See also: Bike p58, Car engine p130, Gyroscope p245, Wheelchair p138

≫ How do motorcycles balance?

▶When at rest, a motorcycle needs a stand to keep it upright, but when moving, it easily balances on its two wheels. This is because its wheels behave like gyroscopes. A gyroscope is a spinning disc that is very difficult to tilt. When riders go around a corner, they lean into the curve so their weight overcomes the centrifugal (outward-pushing) force that might otherwise tip the motorcycle over. Leaning also lets them corner at high speeds.

Superbike racer leaning into a bend

LCD computer screen displays performance and engine data.

◀ **The handgrip** on the handlebars controls the power of the motorcycle's engine. By twisting the handgrip, more fuel is let into the engine. Burning more fuel makes the engine work faster and produce more power to turn the back wheel. Twisting the handgrip can unleash more than 190 horsepower, equal to the power needed to light about 1,500 100-watt light bulbs.

◀ **Shock absorbers** connect the motorcycle's wheels to its frame. When a wheel hits a bump, a coiled spring around the shock absorber squashes, cushioning the rider from the jolt. The shock absorber then stops the motorcycle from bouncing by slowly pushing its internal piston through a cylinder full of oil.

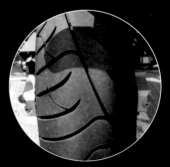

▲ **Motorcycle tires** are made from layers of tough material set in rubber. Additives mixed with the rubber can improve performance. For example, adding silica gives better grip in wet conditions. A tire's tread (grooved surface) also improves traction on wet roads by channeling water out from between the tire and the road.

FUEL-CELL CAR

▶▶ Electric fuel-cell cars are quiet and pollution-free. Originally designed for spacecraft, fuel cells could be the power source of the future as Earth's oil supplies run dry. All they need are supplies of two gases: hydrogen and oxygen. ▶▶

≫ HOW A FUEL CELL WORKS

A fuel cell is a bit like a battery that makes electric power through chemical reactions. Unlike a battery, a fuel cell never goes flat and needs no recharging because the chemical ingredients it contains do not run out. The cell takes in a constant supply of pure hydrogen gas (from a cylinder carried in the car) and oxygen (from the air outside). These react together to make electricity for power and water as a waste product. The electricity is used to drive one or more electric motors, which have far fewer parts and are much quieter than a traditional engine. Fuel cells produce no harmful emissions.

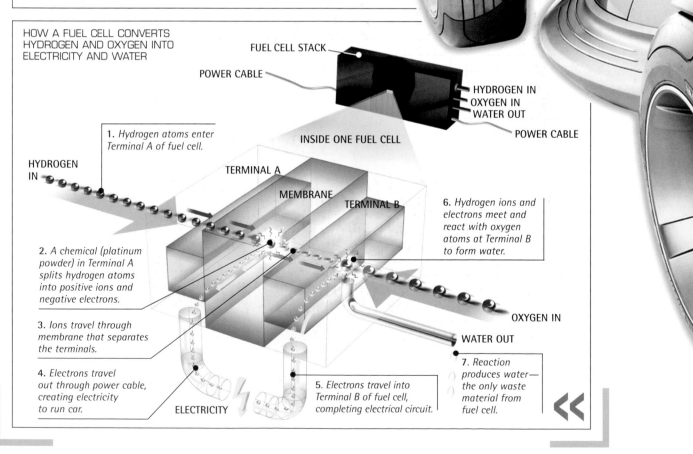

HOW A FUEL CELL CONVERTS
HYDROGEN AND OXYGEN INTO
ELECTRICITY AND WATER

FUEL CELL STACK

POWER CABLE

HYDROGEN IN
OXYGEN IN
WATER OUT

POWER CABLE

INSIDE ONE FUEL CELL

HYDROGEN
IN

TERMINAL A

MEMBRANE

TERMINAL B

1. Hydrogen atoms enter Terminal A of fuel cell.

2. A chemical (platinum powder) in Terminal A splits hydrogen atoms into positive ions and negative electrons.

3. Ions travel through membrane that separates the terminals.

4. Electrons travel out through power cable, creating electricity to run car.

ELECTRICITY

5. Electrons travel into Terminal B of fuel cell, completing electrical circuit.

6. Hydrogen ions and electrons meet and react with oxygen atoms at Terminal B to form water.

OXYGEN IN

WATER OUT

7. Reaction produces water—the only waste material from fuel cell.

≪

Streamlined spoiler cuts air resistance and protects driver.

Driver pod

⌄ Air pollution

▶When cars burn petroleum fuels, they produce waste gases known as exhaust fumes. Of these gases, carbon dioxide adds to global warming, carbon monoxide harms people's health, and sulfur dioxide makes acid rain that harms forests and buildings. Diesel engines also give off microscopic soot particles that harm people's breathing.

Exhaust fumes

Image: Toyota Motor Triathlon Race Car (MTRC)

▲ **This concept car,** made by Toyota, is designed to drive for up to 180 miles (290 km) at up to 97 mph (156 km/h) powered by one stack of hydrogen fuel cells. Cars like this would need to refuel at hydrogen stations, which would supply hydrogen gas instead of gas and diesel.

Stack of hydrogen fuel cells slide in and out of tail section.

Each wheel is driven by separate electric motor for four-wheel drive control.

Exhaust vents in tail release waste water as steam.

▶▶ See also: Battery p94, Car engine p130, Car tower p136, Crash test p134, Electric motor p243

CAR ENGINE

▶▶About 50,000 tiny explosions occur inside a car engine every single minute, turning the chemical energy locked inside fuel into motion that can power the car. ▶▶

▼ **This rear-wheel drive** car transfers power from the cylinders in the engine to the back wheels, using a series of shafts and gears. Changing gears connects gear wheels of different sizes, so that the engine can work faster or slower as the car changes speed.

5. *Rear axle turns back wheels.*

4. *Differential gears use power from driveshaft to turn rear wheel axle.*

3. *Driveshaft rotates, relaying power from gearbox to differential.*

2. *Gearbox takes power from crankshaft and makes driveshaft turn faster or slower.*

1. *Inside engine, cylinders and pistons produce power to turn crankshaft, which is connected to gearbox.*

▶▶ See also: Fuel-cell car p128, Internal combustion engine p245, Jet engine p146

≫ HOW A FOUR-STROKE ENGINE WORKS

Inlet valve lets in air and fuel.

Cylinder

Piston rod moves down.

Crankshaft rotates.

Spark plug ignites fuel.

Raised piston compresses fuel.

Piston rod moves up.

Crankshaft continues to turn.

Ignited fuel produces hot gas.

Piston forced down by expanding gas.

Piston rod moves down again.

Exhaust gas leaves.

Piston rod driven up by rotating crankshaft.

Crankshaft still turning in same direction

Step 1: Intake
The car's power is generated in four continuously repeated steps. First the piston moves down and draws fuel and air into the cylinder through the inlet valve. The lowering of the piston rod turns the crankshaft.

Step 2: Compression
The inlet valve closes. A close-fitting, heavy metal piston slides up inside the cylinder and squashes the fuel–air mixture. This makes it highly explosive. A high electrical voltage makes a tiny, brief spark in the spark plug at the top of the cylinder. The fuel–air mixture explodes and burns, giving off hot gases.

Step 3: Power
The gases expand and push the piston down the cylinder. When the piston rod moves down and back up again, it rotates the heavy metal crankshaft that carries power to the car's gearbox. In this way, the heat created by burning the fuel is converted into mechanical power.

Step 4: Exhaust
The exhaust valve opens. The steady turning of the crankshaft keeps the piston moving. As it drives back upward, it pushes the waste gases out through the exhaust valve, emptying the cylinder. Then the cycle is repeated. A number of cylinders work together to keep the crankshaft turning.

◀◀BACK

The four-stroke gasoline engine was invented in 1876 by German engineer Nikolaus Otto. It was called the Otto cycle in his honor.

Solar cars may replace fuel-powered ones. Solar panels on the car's hood, trunk, and roof convert sunlight into electricity and store it in batteries to power the car.

FORWARD▶▶

PARTS

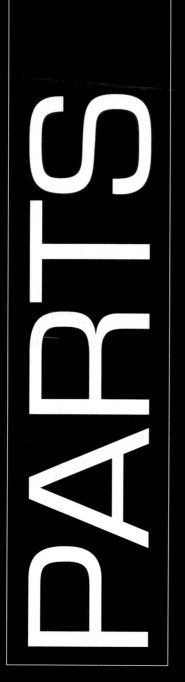

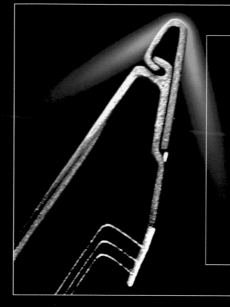

◀◀ Carbon-carbon

This aircraft wing part is made from a carbon-carbon composite (combination of materials). To create this composite, carbon compounds are combined in layers and heat-treated to make them extremely tough. Unlike metals, this material becomes stronger when heated to high temperatures, making it useful for race-car brakes, aircraft, and spacecraft.

▶▶ Kevlar®

Like Lycra® and nylon, Kevlar® is a synthetic (human-made) fiber. Its tightly woven fibers make it five times stronger than steel, which makes it the ideal material for bulletproof vests. It is also used to make bicycle tires, car brake pads, and windsurfing sails, which all rely on strength, long life, and light weight.

Vehicles are now traveling faster and farther than ever before, so their components need to be made stronger, lighter, and more durable. Scientists are constantly developing new materials for this task.

≪ Fiberglass

Developed in the 1940s, fiberglass is the world's best-known composite. This magnified image, taken with a scanning electron microscope, reveals the tiny rod-shaped glass fibers within the material. These fibers provide the material's strength and are held together with a type of plastic called polyester. Fiberglass is heat-resistant, lightweight, and tough, as well as being flexible and durable. It is ideal for making boat hulls, car bodies, and aircraft parts.

⌄ Titanium

These huge jet engine fan blades are made from titanium, a metal found in Earth's crust and also in meteorites. It is as strong as steel, but almost half as light, does not corrode easily, and can tolerate extreme temperatures. It can be combined with other metals, such as aluminum or tin, to make strong alloys. Titanium and its alloys are used to make missiles, spacecraft, boats, and bike frames, which all need to be strong and light.

≪ Testing materials in space

This picture shows a space experiment carried out by NASA. In 1984, a huge cylinder was covered in different materials and taken into space by a NASA Space Shuttle. The materials were exposed to the harshness of space for almost six years. When the cylinder returned to Earth, scientists used its data to see which materials could withstand such extreme conditions, to help NASA to build future spacecraft.

▶▶ See also: Bike p58, Carbon p241, Fabric p60, Fire suit p190, Jet engine p146

CRASH TEST

▶▶ A crash-test dummy is a whole scientific laboratory packed into a plastic body. During a crash test, the dummy records measurements from more than 130 tiny sensors positioned inside it. ▶▶

▶ This crash-test dummy feeds hundreds of measurements to computers as an inflating airbag brings it safely to rest. For over 50 years, dummies have been used to refine seatbelt, airbag, and vehicle design to improve driver and passenger safety.

▶▶ HOW A CRASH-TEST DUMMY WORKS

THE MAIN SENSORS IN A CRASH-TEST DUMMY

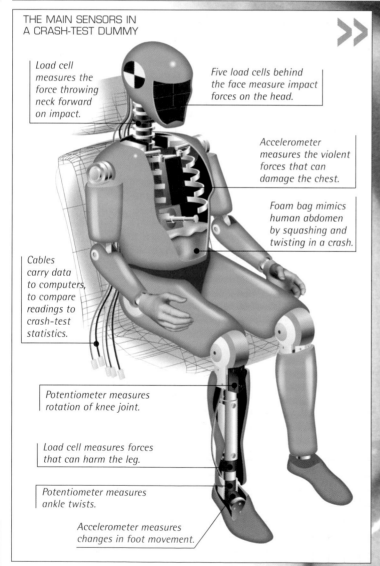

Load cell measures the force throwing neck forward on impact.

Five load cells behind the face measure impact forces on the head.

Accelerometer measures the violent forces that can damage the chest.

Foam bag mimics human abdomen by squashing and twisting in a crash.

Cables carry data to computers, to compare readings to crash-test statistics.

Potentiometer measures rotation of knee joint.

Load cell measures forces that can harm the leg.

Potentiometer measures ankle twists.

Accelerometer measures changes in foot movement.

In a car crash, injuries to the head, chest, and legs are the most likely, so dummies need plenty of sensors in these areas. There are three types of sensors: load cells, accelerometers, and potentiometers. Load cells measure forces using tiny piezoelectric crystals that generate electricity as they stretch or squeeze. Accelerometers contain tiny magnets that slide past each other if the sensor moves, generating bursts of electricity that indicate changes in speed. Potentiometers generate a small voltage that measures how much they twist or turn. Different dummies are made for side impacts and front impacts, with sensors concentrated in specific areas.

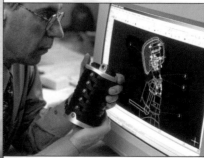

This designer holds the neck of a child-sized dummy as he refines the design on screen. Computer-aided design helps to build dummies of different sizes, ages, and sexes.

Airbag inflates at a speed of up to 200 mph (320 km/h).

Realistic shoulder joint can rotate.

Seatbelt locks and restrains dummy when car's motion changes.

Tough PVC skin covers stainless steel and aluminum body.

⌄ The science of impacts

Aerial view of a car during a crash test

▲ The bigger a car and the faster it moves, the more energy it has. When a car crashes, its sudden stop creates huge forces that can injure the people inside. Cars are specially designed to crumple to release the energy of an impact more slowly. This, combined with airbags and seatbelts, reduces the forces on the occupants and improves their chances of survival.

▶▶ See also: Black box p150, Car engine p130, Car tower p136, Piezoelectricity p248

CAR TOWER

▶▶ In the heart of industrial Germany is the world's largest car factory, producing 3,000 cars a day. Many of them are stored vertically, in a kind of giant vending machine called a car tower. ▶▶

Central mechanism runs two elevators.

≫ HOW A CAR TOWER WORKS

AUTOMATED STORAGE, FROM FACTORY TO TOWER

5. When customer requests car, robotic arm places it back on elevator, which lowers it to the ground.

4. Robotic arms slide car off elevator and into concrete storage pod.

3. Elevator goes up tower to space in stack, located by computer system.

2. Sliding robotic arms remove car from pallet, gripping its four wheels, and place it on elevator.

1. Cars travel on pallets along tracks from factory to tower.

Each elevator can rotate 270°

One of Autostadt's car towers

With around 550 million cars in the world and 40 million new vehicles made each year, finding a place to park can be difficult. The problem is particularly bad at car factories and showrooms, where hundreds of new vehicles need to be stored quickly and safely until customers are ready to pick them up. Volkswagen's car tower solves those problems by rolling three classic inventions—the elevator, the parking ramp, and the forklift truck—into one. As cities become ever more congested, towers like this could soon start replacing urban parking structures.

▶▶ See also: Car engine p130, Fuel-cell car p128

▼ **The two cylindrical car towers** at Autostadt ("Car Town") in Wolfsburg, Germany, have 20 stories, are 154 ft (47 m) high, and can hold 400 vehicles each. The fully automated system delivers direct to a showroom where over 550 new cars are sold each day.

⟱ High-rise stacks in nature

Inside a termite mound

▲ Termite nests, built from mud and chewed wood, are around 20 ft (6 m) high and house a million or more termites—an incredibly efficient use of space. An office building would need to be around 6 miles (10 km) high to hold as many people. This African termite nest has a spiral staircase, allowing the insects easy access to the different levels.

Elevator can haul 2.5 tons at 4½ mph (7 km/h)

20 storage pods per story

Image: inside one of Autostadt's car towers

WHEELCHAIR

▶▶ The acrobatic iBOT™ wheelchair can raise its occupant up to standing height and even climb stairs. Using its powerful four-wheel drive, it can plow through mud and sand and whiz along pavement at 6 mph (10 km/h). ▶▶

▶ **This iBOT™ wheelchair** is in its raised position. From here, the occupant is at standing height and high enough to reach shelves. The chair's special balance mechanism detects when the occupant's center of gravity moves, then shifts the clusters (pairs) of large wheels to compensate and balance the chair safely. When all wheels are on the ground, a joystick steers two smaller front wheels to move the chair.

>> HOW IBOT™ WORKS

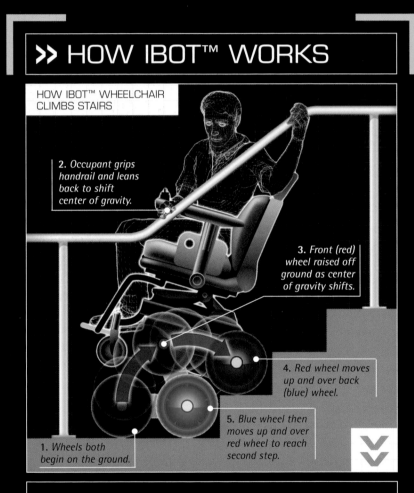

HOW IBOT™ WHEELCHAIR CLIMBS STAIRS

2. *Occupant grips handrail and leans back to shift center of gravity.*

3. *Front (red) wheel raised off ground as center of gravity shifts.*

4. *Red wheel moves up and over back (blue) wheel.*

5. *Blue wheel then moves up and over red wheel to reach second step.*

1. *Wheels both begin on the ground.*

Two small wheels at the front for steering

Balancing mechanism

Wheels stack to give user extra height.

Mechanisms can link wheels in pairs or drive each wheel independently.

It is hard to pull a conventional wheelchair up stairs, because it has to be heaved vertically up each step. A ramp laid up the stairs can make the task easier, because the chair travels up the slope gradually instead of being pulled upward against the force of gravity. The iBOT™ wheelchair climbs stairs another way, using even less effort. Its secret lies in two pairs of large wheels called clusters. As the clusters move up and over one another, the chair rises up the stairs in a series of long, shallow curves. The extra distance each wheel travels helps to reduce the effort needed to climb stairs.

▶▶ See also: Center of gravity p241, Robot helper p118

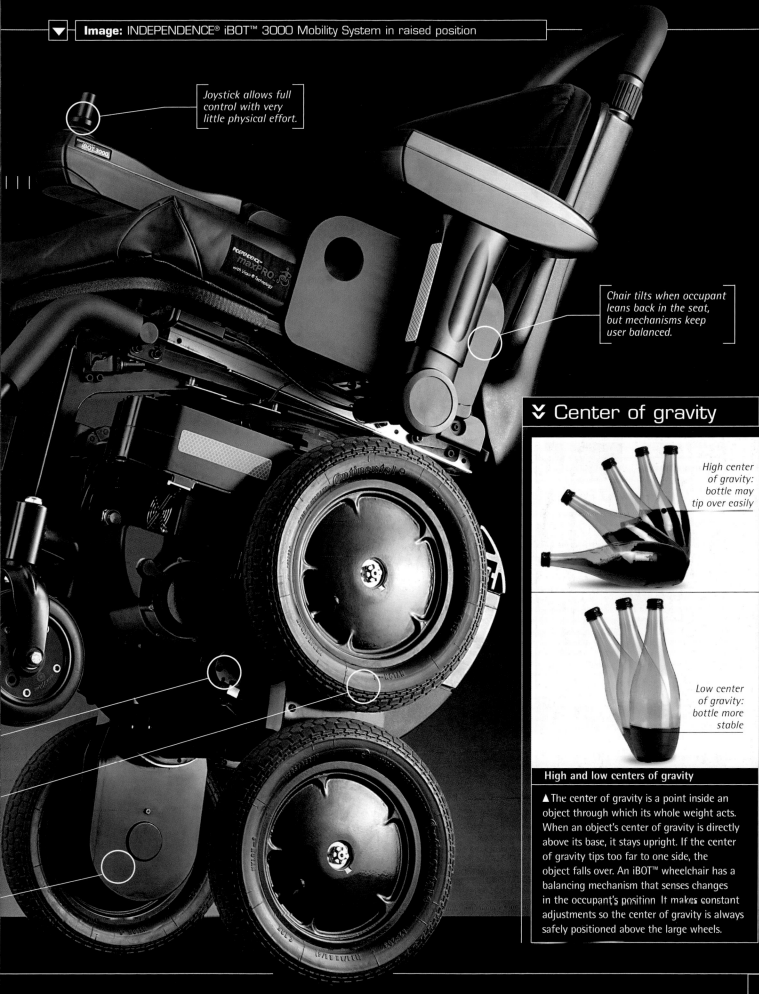

Joystick allows full control with very little physical effort.

Chair tilts when occupant leans back in the seat, but mechanisms keep user balanced.

⌄ Center of gravity

High center of gravity: bottle may tip over easily

Low center of gravity: bottle more stable

High and low centers of gravity

▲ The center of gravity is a point inside an object through which its whole weight acts. When an object's center of gravity is directly above its base, it stays upright. If the center of gravity tips too far to one side, the object falls over. An iBOT™ wheelchair has a balancing mechanism that senses changes in the occupant's position. It makes constant adjustments so the center of gravity is always safely positioned above the large wheels.

>> HOW DEEP FLIGHT AVIATOR WORKS

Deep Flight Aviator is a submersible (mini-submarine) that literally flies through the water. It is made from very light materials that allow it to float naturally. The craft is powered by batteries, which drive its two propellers to move it through the water. As the submersible travels, water flows over the top and bottom of its large, curved wings at different speeds. The more speed the craft builds up, the more downward force is created by the wings. The craft then begins to overcome its natural tendency to float, and starts to dive toward the seabed. To take it back to the surface, the pilot slows the submersible down, so reducing the downward force. To maneuver the craft, the angles of the wings, flaps, and rudders are adjusted.

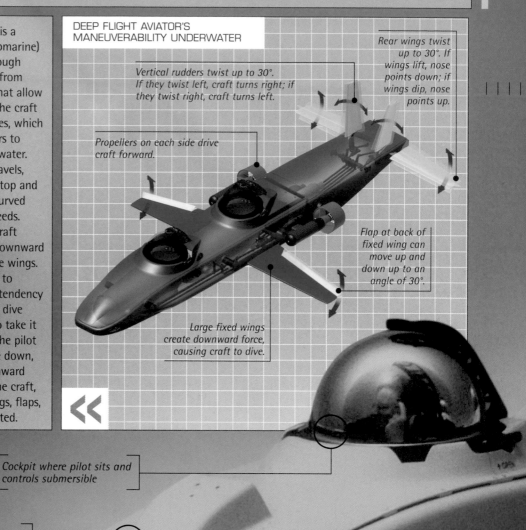

DEEP FLIGHT AVIATOR'S MANEUVERABILITY UNDERWATER

Vertical rudders twist up to 30°. If they twist left, craft turns right; if they twist right, craft turns left.

Rear wings twist up to 30°. If wings lift, nose points down; if wings dip, nose points up.

Propellers on each side drive craft forward.

Flap at back of fixed wing can move up and down up to an angle of 30°.

Large fixed wings create downward force, causing craft to dive.

Cockpit where pilot sits and controls submersible

Body made from strong, lightweight aluminum

SPIRIT of PATRICK

External lead-acid batteries provide about five hours of dive time and are pollution-free.

▶▶ Deep Flight Aviator is a slick submersible that glides through the water. Swift and amazingly agile, it is used to explore the ocean depths and study marine animals. ▶▶

SUBMERSIBLE

⅀ Moving and diving

▶Sharks move through the water in a way similar to Deep Flight Aviator, using their horizontal and vertical fins to maneuver. Other fish control their depth with an organ called a swim bladder. These are filled or emptied with gas if the fish needs to move down or up—conventional submarines also work in this way, filling their tanks with water to dive.

Shark moving through water

▶Deep Flight Aviator's wings are just like an airplane's—only upside down. As the submersible speeds up, water moves more quickly beneath the curved bottom surface of the wings than over the flat upper surface. This lowers the pressure under the wings, producing a downward force that causes the craft to dive through the water.

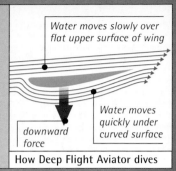

Water moves slowly over flat upper surface of wing

downward force

Water moves quickly under curved surface

How Deep Flight Aviator dives

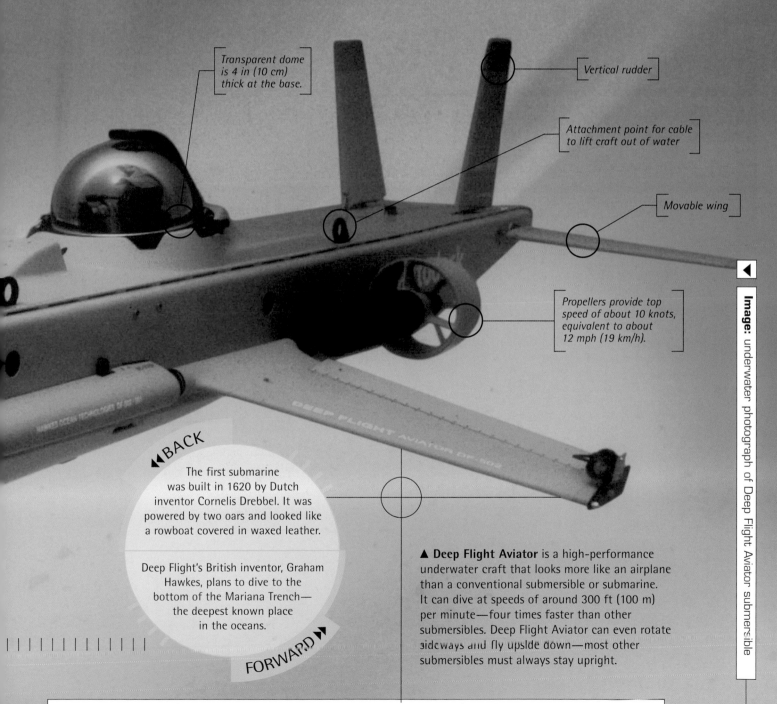

Transparent dome is 4 in (10 cm) thick at the base.

Vertical rudder

Attachment point for cable to lift craft out of water

Movable wing

Propellers provide top speed of about 10 knots, equivalent to about 12 mph (19 km/h).

◀◀BACK

The first submarine was built in 1620 by Dutch inventor Cornelis Drebbel. It was powered by two oars and looked like a rowboat covered in waxed leather.

Deep Flight's British inventor, Graham Hawkes, plans to dive to the bottom of the Mariana Trench— the deepest known place in the oceans.

FORWARD▶▶

▲ **Deep Flight Aviator** is a high-performance underwater craft that looks more like an airplane than a conventional submersible or submarine. It can dive at speeds of around 300 ft (100 m) per minute—four times faster than other submersibles. Deep Flight Aviator can even rotate sideways and fly upside down—most other submersibles must always stay upright.

Image: underwater photograph of Deep Flight Aviator submersible

▶▶ See also: Airfoil p240, Jet engine p146, Osprey p144, Wind tunnel p148

Rotor blade tips spin at 662 ft/s (202 m/s).

Drive-shaft, running through both wings, connects rotors together, so that if one engine fails, the other powers both rotors.

Ten fuel tanks in wings

Image: Bell-Boeing V-22 Osprey

Tail fin provides stability.

4942

MARINES

▲ **Osprey** can take off and land from almost anywhere, even remote parts of the world where there is no airport runway. Its wings and rotors fold inward so that it can be stored easily in a hangar or on board an aircraft carrier. It is one of the most expensive aircraft ever developed: each one costs more than $80 million.

Six fuel tanks in fuselage

Landing wheels fold up into plane shortly after takeoff.

OSPREY

▶▶ Is it a helicopter? Is it a plane? The world's most versatile aircraft, the Osprey can switch from a plane to a helicopter in just 12 seconds. Built for the military, it is also used for rescue missions. ▶▶

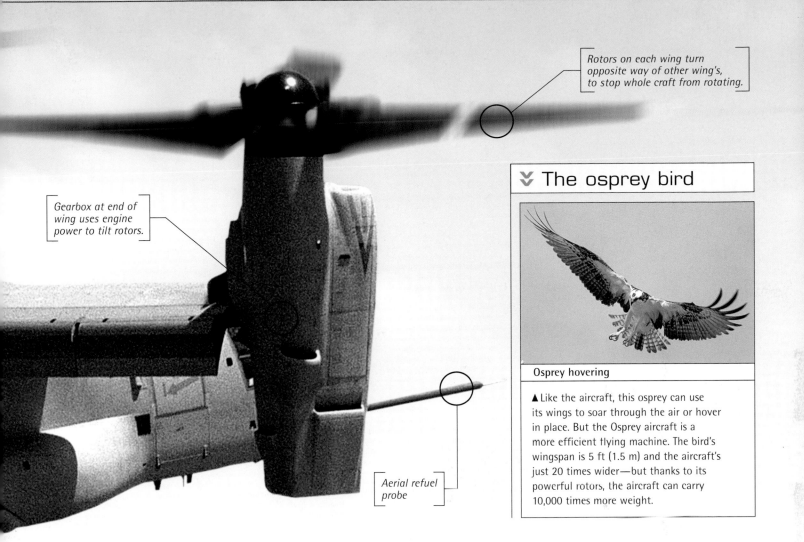

Rotors on each wing turn opposite way of other wing's, to stop whole craft from rotating.

Gearbox at end of wing uses engine power to tilt rotors.

Aerial refuel probe

☇ The osprey bird

Osprey hovering

▲ Like the aircraft, this osprey can use its wings to soar through the air or hover in place. But the Osprey aircraft is a more efficient flying machine. The bird's wingspan is 5 ft (1.5 m) and the aircraft's just 20 times wider—but thanks to its powerful rotors, the aircraft can carry 10,000 times more weight.

≫ HOW THE OSPREY WORKS

In helicopter mode, the two rotors spin above the aircraft, allowing it to take off vertically and hover. The rotors have three blades, each one the length of an average family car, made from a mixture of graphite and fiberglass.

In midair, the engines and rotors tilt forward, converting the Osprey from helicopter to plane. Each wing contains a 6,000-hp engine (about 30 times more powerful than a family car) and a gearbox that powers the rotor and the tilting mechanism.

In airplane mode, Osprey's twin engines power it forward for up to 580 miles (935 km) without refueling. The Osprey can fly twice as fast as a helicopter, at speeds up to 315 mph (507 km/h), carrying 10,000 lb (4,535 kg) of cargo or 24 passengers

▶▶ See also: Airfoil p240, Black box p150, Jet engine p146

JET ENGINE

▶▶ Powerful jet engines speed airplanes forward by blasting a fiery jet of fast-moving gas backward. A large engine can generate as much power as 3,000 cars racing along at top speed. ▶▶

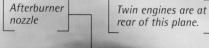

Afterburner nozzle

Twin engines are at rear of this plane.

Jets of fuel ignite when sprayed into exhaust stream.

▲ **This jet engine** gets a short burst of extra power by using an afterburner, which is a ring of pipes that shoots fuel into the exhaust gas. When this fuel burns, it gives the engine around 50 percent more thrust (forward power). Afterburners are used in military jets, such as this one, but because they use so much fuel, they are only switched on for takeoff or to reach supersonic speeds.

⌄ Underwater jet propulsion

▶ This octopus moves itself through the ocean by squirting jets of water from its body. This process uses the same physics as a jet engine and is known as action and reaction. As the water squirts one way (action), it propels the octopus in the opposite direction (reaction). This also occurs if you blow up a balloon and then let go of it. Air rushes out, shooting the balloon in the opposite direction.

Octopus propels itself through the water

◀◀BACK

British engineer Frank Whittle invented the first jet engine in 1930, but in 1939 the first jet flight used an engine made by his German rival, Hans Pabst von Ohain.

Japanese engineers are developing the SuperSonic Transport (SST) plane. It will carry three times more passengers, travel twice as far, yet be no noisier than a normal jet.

FORWARD▶▶

≫ HOW A JET ENGINE WORKS

HOW AIR PASSES THROUGH A
TURBOFAN JET ENGINE

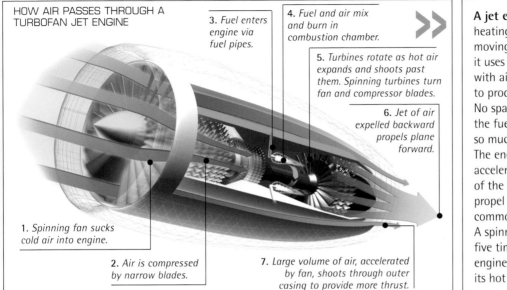

3. *Fuel enters engine via fuel pipes.*

4. *Fuel and air mix and burn in combustion chamber.*

5. *Turbines rotate as hot air expands and shoots past them. Spinning turbines turn fan and compressor blades.*

6. *Jet of air expelled backward propels plane forward.*

1. *Spinning fan sucks cold air into engine.*

2. *Air is compressed by narrow blades.*

7. *Large volume of air, accelerated by fan, shoots through outer casing to provide more thrust.*

A jet engine works by compressing, heating, and speeding up the air moving through it. Like a car engine, it uses internal combustion: fuel burns with air in the combustion chamber to produce energy continuously. No spark is needed to ignite the fuel: the fuel–air mixture is compressed so much that it burns spontaneously. The energy produced heats and accelerates the air, which shoots out of the back to power the engine and propel the plane forward. The most common jet engine is a turbofan. A spinning fan at the front accelerates five times more air through the engine's outer casing than through its hot core, to produce extra thrust.

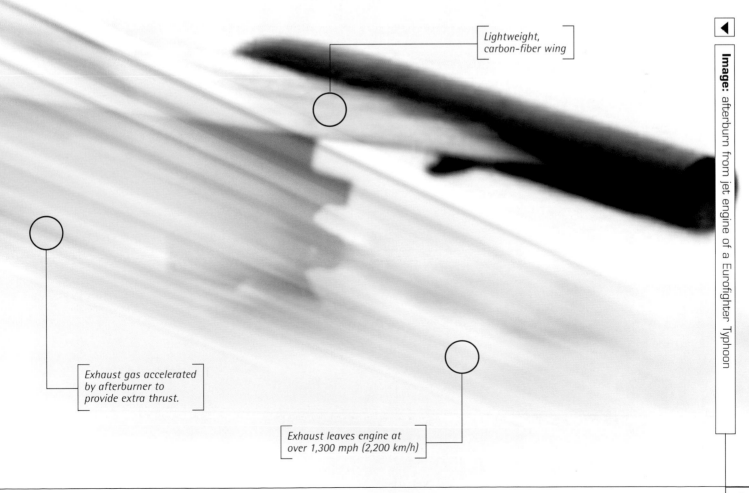

Lightweight, carbon-fiber wing

Exhaust gas accelerated by afterburner to provide extra thrust.

Exhaust leaves engine at over 1,300 mph (2,200 km/h)

Image: afterburn from jet engine of a Eurofighter Typhoon

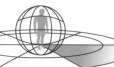

WIND TUNNEL

▶▶ A wind tunnel is a sealed chamber in which airplanes are tested with high-speed air. The wind speed in the tunnel can be ten times faster than the speed of sound. ▶▶

▼ This image shows details of the airflow around a model plane being tested in a wind tunnel. Scientists study how planes react to wind speeds to make sure their structure is robust. As the model plane "flies" at supersonic speeds—faster than the speed of sound—it overtakes the noise made by its own engine and trails shock waves behind it.

Shock waves grow smaller as airstream slows down behind plane.

Shock waves created by tail

Sturdy metal arm holds test model in position.

Shock waves travel outward like ripples spreading across a pond.

Image: Schlieren photograph of airflow around model plane

▶▶ See also: Aerodynamics p240, Jet engine p146, Space Shuttle p156

≫ HOW A WIND TUNNEL WORKS

THE FUNCTIONS OF THE FIVE
SECTIONS OF A WIND TUNNEL

1. Drive section houses huge, spinning fans that generate wind around tunnel.

Closed loop circulates air.

5. Diffuser gradually widens, slowing down the air coming out of the test section.

2. Settling chamber's honeycomb structure straightens slow, turbulent airflow as it passes through.

4. In the test section, sensors measure impact of wind on airplane.

3. Contraction cone squashes slow-moving air into small volume of fast-moving air.

Wind tunnels are used to test how a plane's shape affects its ability to fly. Changes to a plane's design might be made following these tests. Airplanes are streamlined to maximize lift—an upward force that overcomes the plane's weight— and minimize drag—air resistance. The more lift and less drag a plane has, the more efficiently it flies, so that it uses less fuel. Wind tunnel tests are expensive, difficult, and can be dangerous. Even a small wind tunnel needs a huge building to generate the airstream. For supersonic tests, air must travel faster than the speed of sound. In a hypersonic test, when the speed is up to ten times faster still, the air can cool so much that it turns into liquid.

Air hits nose and is deflected around it.

⌄ Computer modeling air turbulence

▶Wind tunnel tests are so difficult to carry out that they are gradually being replaced by a technique called computational fluid dynamics (CFD). This involves using a computer model, based on thousands of complex mathematical equations, that can predict every aspect of an airplane's behavior under different flying conditions.

Computer model of plane test

▶Computer models can explain why an airplane suddenly stalls if the wings tilt too far back. At this stall angle, a wing creates two eye-shaped pockets of turbulence behind it. These disrupt the airflow so the wing no longer creates enough lift to keep the plane airborne—and the plane plummets to the ground.

Airflow over wing

SPACE SHUTTLE

▶▶ The reusable Space Shuttle roars into space using rocket power, but flies back to Earth as gently as a glider. Since the first Space Shuttle *Columbia* took off in 1981, five Space Shuttles have completed more than 100 successful missions. ▶▶

▶ **The Space Shuttle** is designed to carry cargo and to be reused at least 100 times. Behind the cockpit is a huge payload bay for carrying equipment, such as satellites, into space. On this 1995 mission, STS-71, the shuttle *Atlantis* used a specially constructed module to dock with the Russian space station, *Mir*. It also carried spare parts that *Mir* needed for vital repairs.

◀BACK

Before the Space Shuttle was built, most astronauts used to return to Earth in a capsule that splashed down into the sea.

Space Shuttles of the future will have much bigger engines. They will not need separate external booster rockets, so they will be less expensive.

FORWARD▶▶

Flight deck with living areas, beds, kitchen, and toilets beneath

Payload bay

Payload bay doors are opened to prevent orbiter from overheating.

Special docking module connects shuttle and Mir.

▶▶ See also: Parts p132, Satellite p42

Heat-resistant
ceramic tiles

≫ HOW THE SPACE SHUTTLE WORKS

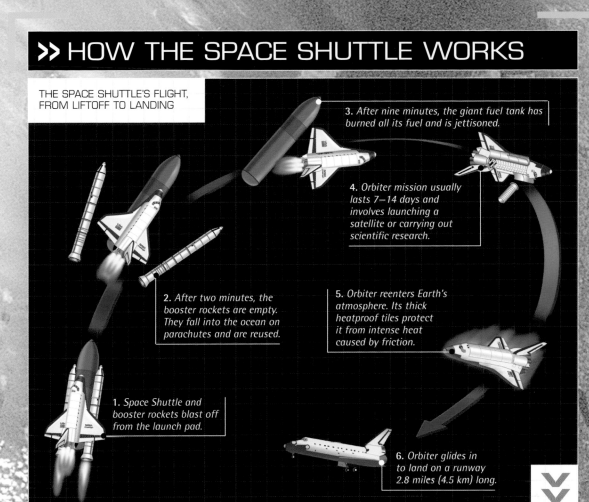

THE SPACE SHUTTLE'S FLIGHT,
FROM LIFTOFF TO LANDING

*3. After nine minutes, the giant fuel tank has
burned all its fuel and is jettisoned.*

*4. Orbiter mission usually
lasts 7–14 days and
involves launching a
satellite or carrying out
scientific research.*

*2. After two minutes, the
booster rockets are empty.
They fall into the ocean on
parachutes and are reused.*

*5. Orbiter reenters Earth's
atmosphere. Its thick
heatproof tiles protect
it from intense heat
caused by friction.*

*1. Space Shuttle and
booster rockets blast off
from the launch pad.*

*6. Orbiter glides in
to land on a runway
2.8 miles (4.5 km) long.*

The orbiter is the planelike, main part of
the Space Shuttle that goes into space and
returns again. It can carry a crew of up to seven
people, including a pilot and mission specialists,
such as scientists, who conduct experiments. At
liftoff, three engines on the orbiter burn liquid
fuel from the huge brown tank underneath. To
reach its orbit, the shuttle uses two of its built-
in engines—the orbital maneuvering system
engines (OMS). These also help to change the
position and speed of orbit.

When returning to Earth, the orbiter slows
down by turning around and firing the OMS
engines in the opposite direction of the flight
direction. Then, the craft turns over so that the
nose and upper side, where the heatproof tiles
are located, hit Earth's upper atmosphere first.
Once in the air, the engines are no longer used
and the shuttle glides back to Earth. It is
traveling at 200 mph (320 km/h) as it comes
in to land: a giant parachute brings it to rest
on a long runway.

SPACE PROBE

▶▶ In a ten-year cosmic adventure, the European space probe Rosetta will chase a comet through space at speeds up to 84,000 mph (135,000 km/h). Rosetta's lander will finally touch down on the comet's surface in 2014. ▶▶

▼ **1. The Rosetta** orbiter blasted off from French Guiana on top of this European Ariane 5 rocket in February 2004. It will finally reach its target, Comet 67P/Churyumov-Gerasimenko, after a hazardous ten-year journey across the solar system. The main Rosetta craft (the orbiter) will then send a smaller craft (the lander) down to the comet's surface.

▼ **3. Rosetta** will be the first spacecraft ever to study the nucleus (rocky center) of a comet. The orbiter will send down its lander to the comet's surface in November 2014. The lander will carry out scientific experiments to reveal the comet's chemical and physical composition, as well as its magnetic and electrical properties.

Comet thought to be made from carbon, hydrogen, oxygen, and nitrogen.

▲ **2. The orbiter,** shown circling the comet in an artist's representation, is a big aluminum box with solar panels like wings, stretching out from either side. It contains the lander and 11 scientific instruments for studying the comet. Like all comets, this one has a heavy, rocky center, called a nucleus, and leaves a long trail of dust and gas in its wake.

›› HOW THE SPACE PROBE WORKS

Comet 67P/Churyumov–Gerasimenko orbits the Sun once every 6.6 years at up to 532 million miles (857 million km) away. No rocket has enough power to send Rosetta this far, so it gains the energy it needs by using the gravity of planets it passes on the way. It travels far enough from each planet not to be pulled into orbit around it. Instead, it is swept along by the planet's gravity and thrown onward at a higher speed. Each planet gives Rosetta a boost that sends it into larger and larger orbits around the Sun until it reaches the path of the comet.

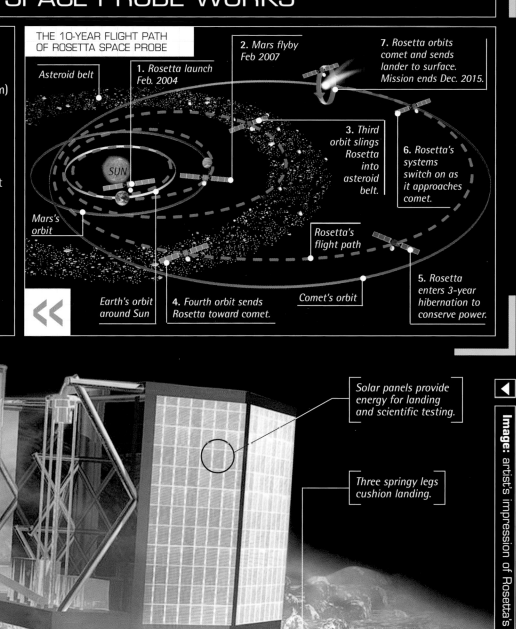

THE 10-YEAR FLIGHT PATH OF ROSETTA SPACE PROBE

Asteroid belt

1. Rosetta launch Feb. 2004

2. Mars flyby Feb 2007

7. Rosetta orbits comet and sends lander to surface. Mission ends Dec. 2015.

3. Third orbit slings Rosetta into asteroid belt.

6. Rosetta's systems switch on as it approaches comet.

SUN

Mars's orbit

Rosetta's flight path

Earth's orbit around Sun

4. Fourth orbit sends Rosetta toward comet.

Comet's orbit

5. Rosetta enters 3-year hibernation to conserve power.

Mechanical arm holds sensors about 3 ft (1 m) away from the lander.

Solar panels provide energy for landing and scientific testing.

Three springy legs cushion landing.

Image: artist's impression of Rosetta's lander on comet surface

Today, we travel farther, faster, and more frequently than ever before. With so many people on the move, both on land and in the air, one of the big challenges for the 21st century is developing the technology to manage our overloaded transportation systems.

Traffic management systems are going to become more important. By 2010 most drivers will rely on in-car satellite systems to guide them around our cities, and direct them to routes where traffic is lowest. These guidances systems may become so intelligent that they will even be driving the cars themselves while we sit back and watch a movie, work, or talk on the phone. Trains will communicate continuously with centralized railroad computers that can coordinate whole networks, and air traffic control developments will use technology-enabling planes to talk directly to computers on the ground.

> **Undersea wonders, such as the wreck of the Titanic, deep sea vents, and even lost cities, will become tourist destinations.**

If current trends continue, by 2020 more than two billion journeys will be made by air annually. To meet this demand, new types of aircraft are being designed, simulated on computers, and tested in wind tunnels. Twin-deck super-jumbos, such as the Airbus A380, will be common within the next few years. These huge airliners will be able to carry more than 500 people. Farther into the future, air taxis that can take off and land on tiny downtown runways will ferry people to and from work, much as ordinary taxis do now. New propulsion technologies have already allowed development of the scramjet, or Supersonic Combustion Ramjet. The scramjet is as powerful as a rocket, but it flies inside Earth's atmosphere rather than in space. This technology may lead to the development of passenger aircraft that can

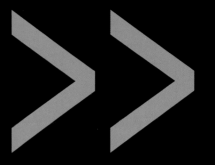

travel from London to Sydney, a distance of 10,553 miles (16,984 km), in less than two hours. Researchers predict that with more development, scramjet speeds could reach 15 times the speed of sound.

The largely uncharted depths of the oceans will be seen as the last true wilderness on our planet. Undersea wonders such as the wreck of the Titanic, deep sea vents, and possibly even lost cities, will become tourist destinations. Paying passengers will fund ocean research and exploration, which will be carried out by a new generation of small, agile submersibles like Deep Flight Aviator.

Space is set to become a travel destination, too. The kind of experience previously available only to astronauts is already within reach of the very wealthy, and it will become cheaper. Tickets will be sold on passenger planes that can travel into space. But flights into space are very damaging to the atmosphere, so in the long run, scientists are considering the possibility of constructing a space elevator in order to ferry goods and passengers in and out of orbit. A super-strong cable, made from a material called a carbon nanotube composite, would connect the elevator from a satellite to a point on Earth near the equator—probably an island specially constructed for the purpose.

WIND TUNNEL

>>WORK

Digital pen >> Laptop >> Motherboard >> Flash stick >>
Virtual keyboard >> Laser printer >> Scanner >> Smart card >>
Radio ID tag >> Robot worker >> Wet welding >> Fire suit >>
Doppler radar

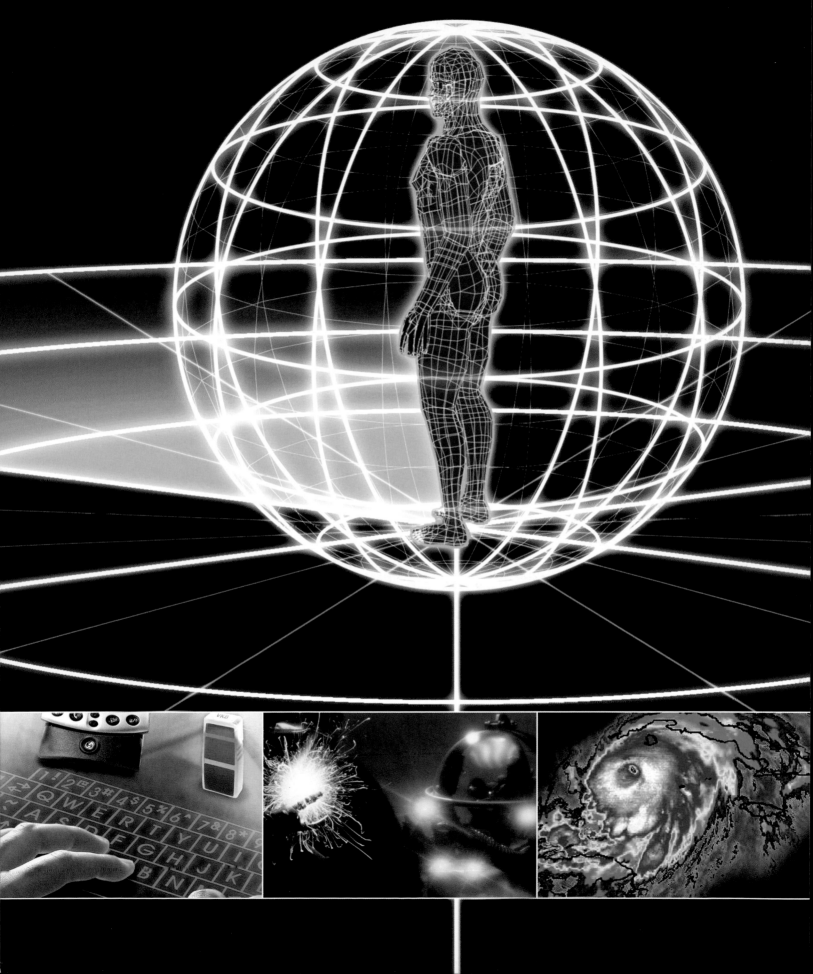

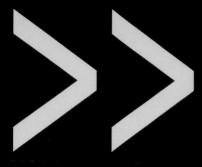

The invention and development of the steam engine in the early 1700s marked the beginning of a huge shift in the way people worked. This new technology was used at first to pump water out of mines. By the end of the century, it was driving factories full of looms producing cotton fabric—the first example of mechanical mass-production. Huge numbers of people left their homes in the country and moved to cities to find work in factories and later in offices.

In the last few decades, computers have changed the way society is organized once again. Any job that can be made routine, or broken down into a series of simple steps, can be taken over by a computer or a robot designed for a specific task, such as spray-painting a car. Robots can also perform the dangerous factory work that people would rather not do, such as handling hot metal plates. Because robots can do most of the repetitive and occasionally risky tasks in factories, factory workers spend less time on the production line. Similarly, in offices, computers process much of the repetitive work, such as calculating figures and printing out documents. Time-saving devices, including laser printers and scanners, have increased productivity. Thanks to the laptop and the cell phone, office workers are less tied to their desks than they

COMPUTER CIRCUIT BOARD

used to be. New technologies such as virtual keyboards, flash sticks, and digital pens have also led to more and more people working from home, working while traveling, or hot-desking—moving from one desk or office to another.

Some jobs can only be done by humans. The decisions that doctors have to make, for example, are too complex and subtle for a computer—diagnosis and treatment of a patient is usually carried out in person. Even so, technology plays a central role in most forms of work. Divers use wet-welding techniques to repair oil rigs and pipes standing deep beneath the ocean. Sailors use satellite navigation to help them pinpoint their exact location. Satellite technology and radar

> **Today, one out of every ten workers on car assembly lines around the world is a robot—massively increasing productivity.**

helps meteorologists predict the weather, which in turn helps farmers who need to know when the sun is going to shine and when it is going to rain. Modern materials such as Kevlar® help protect firefighters inside burning buildings. Forensic scientists use fingerprint scanners to analyze samples taken from crime scenes, while store clerks scan product bar codes to quickly process purchases. Businessmen and women use the number-crunching capabilities of microprocessors to keep track of orders and forecast future market conditions.

One of the reasons people work, of course, is to earn money. Technology has changed the way we access our money, too. The money is mostly invisible, existing as numbers in bank accounts, transferred there directly from the accounts of employers or customers. Sometimes we might go to an ATM and take out our earnings as paper currency, but often we just use a smart card to make speedy, secure transactions.

▶ **The digital pen** contains a tiny digital camera and microchips for storing, processing, and transmitting information. It can be used only with paper on which a grid of tiny dots is printed. Wherever the pen comes into contact with the paper, its camera photographs the pen's position on the grid and stores the dots as a series of coordinates in the memory chip. The data is sent wirelessly to an external device and a replica of what appears on paper is created on screen.

Image: macrophoto of a digital pen writing

DIGITAL PEN

Ink is the same as in an ordinary pen.

Position of pen on the paper is photographed by the camera.

▶▶ The digital pen remembers exactly what you write or draw. You can save ideas, memos, or sketches on the pen until you want to transfer them to a computer for safekeeping or printing. ▶▶

◀◀BACK

The earliest pens date from about 3000 BC. They were just sharpened sticks, used by the ancient Sumerians to scratch their script on clay tablets.

At wireless connection points in coffee shops and train stations, people will pay to download the latest edition of a newspaper onto paper or screens.

FORWARD▼

≫HOW A DIGITAL PEN WORKS

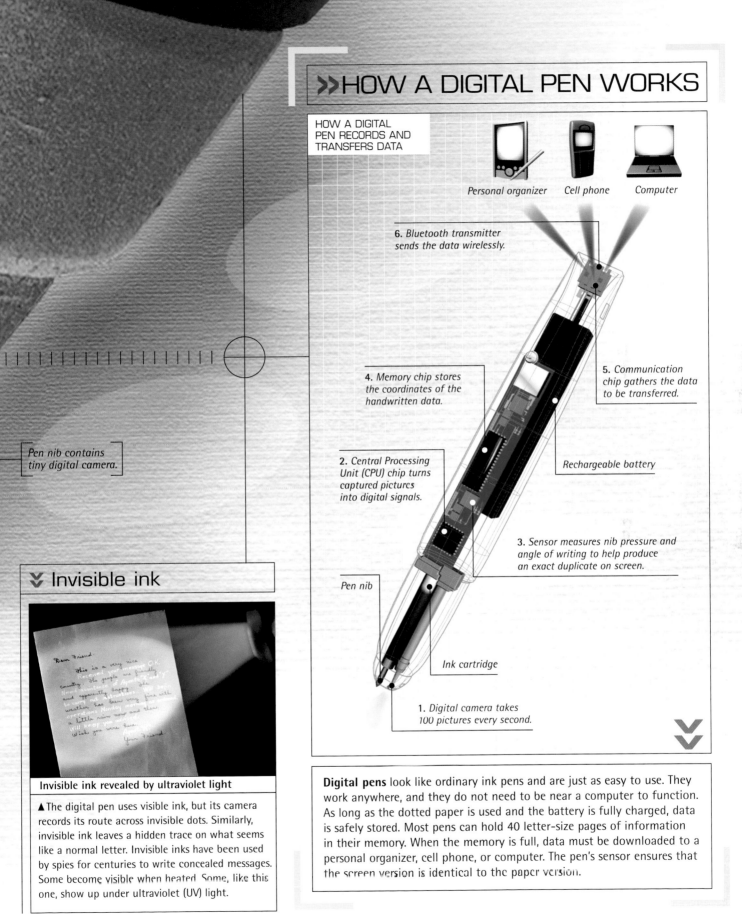

HOW A DIGITAL PEN RECORDS AND TRANSFERS DATA

Personal organizer   *Cell phone*   *Computer*

6. *Bluetooth transmitter sends the data wirelessly.*

4. *Memory chip stores the coordinates of the handwritten data.*

5. *Communication chip gathers the data to be transferred.*

2. *Central Processing Unit (CPU) chip turns captured pictures into digital signals.*

Rechargeable battery

Pen nib contains tiny digital camera.

3. *Sensor measures nib pressure and angle of writing to help produce an exact duplicate on screen.*

Pen nib

Ink cartridge

1. *Digital camera takes 100 pictures every second.*

❯ Invisible ink

Invisible ink revealed by ultraviolet light

▲ The digital pen uses visible ink, but its camera records its route across invisible dots. Similarly, invisible ink leaves a hidden trace on what seems like a normal letter. Invisible inks have been used by spies for centuries to write concealed messages. Some become visible when heated. Some, like this one, show up under ultraviolet (UV) light.

Digital pens look like ordinary ink pens and are just as easy to use. They work anywhere, and they do not need to be near a computer to function. As long as the dotted paper is used and the battery is fully charged, data is safely stored. Most pens can hold 40 letter-size pages of information in their memory. When the memory is full, data must be downloaded to a personal organizer, cell phone, or computer. The pen's sensor ensures that the screen version is identical to the paper version.

▶▶ See also: Bluetooth® p241, Flash stick p172, Laptop p168, Virtual keyboard p174

❱❱ Wearable computer

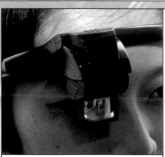

Wearable screen

◀A wearable computer consists of a miniature screen and computer. The screen is worn like a pair of glasses and projects images generated by the computer straight to the wearer's eye. The computer is small enough to fit in a pocket or on a belt. These wearable computers enable technicians to consult manuals while they work on site.

MOTHERBOARD

▶▶ The motherboard is the heart of a computer. As the main circuit board, the motherboard connects the computer's key components and passes on instructions with incredible speed. ▶▶

Image: macro photograph of a computer's motherboard

» HOW A MOTHERBOARD WORKS

THE PROCESS FROM KEYSTROKE TO SCREEN DISPLAY

1. Microprocessor in keyboard detects which key has been pressed and creates scan code to identify it.

2. Central Processing Unit (CPU) receives an interrupt signal telling it to focus on keystroke.

Hard disk holds operating systems and applications to assist CPU when necessary

Motherboard

Random Access Memory (RAM) holds supporting data from hard disk and stores it for CPU to access quickly.

6. Image of new character appears on screen, in the document being typed.

Cooling fan covers the CPU

3. BIOS (permanent memory chip) receives CPU request for scan code as a character (letter, number, or symbol on key pad).

4. CPU receives character and sends it to visual graphics adapter in the form of binary digits (0s and 1s).

5. Visual graphics adapter responds to CPU commands and updates character into an image ready to be displayed on screen.

A computer is made up of hardware and software. Hardware consists of the computer's physical components. These parts store and process information. They include the motherboard, which contains the CPU that does most of the work, and the hard disk. Hardware stores sets of instructions as computer programs, or software. Software lets people connect to the Internet, write letters, or play games.

In 1946, the first digital computer was invented. Electronic Numerical Integrator and Computer (ENIAC) took three years to build and weighed 30 tons. It could do calculations and process 100,000 instructions per second. A modern computer is much smaller and faster, thanks to the invention of the microchip in the 1970s. One tiny chip can now hold many previously separate parts.

Random Access Memory (RAM)

◀ At the center of the motherboard is the CPU, or Central Processing Unit, which is a small microprocessor chip. The CPU performs hundreds of millions of calculations every second. This generates so much heat that the chip needs a fan to keep it cool.

▶▶ See also: Flash stick p172, Laptop p168, Microchip p16, RAM p249

FLASH STICK

▶▶ Packed with useful gadgets, the Swiss Army Knife's latest accessory is a flash stick. It can now carry around photographs, music, documents, or any other data that can be stored digitally. ▶▶

Beam of light from built-in flashlight

Folding scissors

Image: Victorinox's SwissMemory knife

▶ **A flash memory stick** is like a computer's hard disk, only much smaller and more durable. Flash memory does not need a constant power source to retain data, so the flash stick can be carried in a pocket without losing or damaging data.

swissbi
always a bit ahead

Plastic casing contains all components and a battery to operate light.

Keyring

VICTORINOX SWITZERLAND STAINLESS ROSTFREI

Bottle opener

Penknife

File

◄ BACK

In 1891, the Swiss Army Knife was invented for the military by Carl Elsener, a Swiss pocketknife manufacturer. He called it the "officers and sports knife."

An 8-gigabit flash memory chip is being developed that will be able to hold one hour of DVD material or 250 MP3 files.

FORWARD ►►

❯ Stick storage

▶ In the past, businesspeople had to carry their documents, notebooks, and photographs around in briefcases. The lightweight flash stick can carry all this and more. It is small enough to fit inside a pocket and can store 64 megabytes of data, the equivalent of about 9,400 pieces of letter-size paper.

Contents of a briefcase

❯❯ HOW A FLASH STICK WORKS

HOW A FLASH STICK STORES DATA IN BINARY CODE

Ballpoint pen

Flash memory stick can be removed from penknife.

Memory chip stores data.

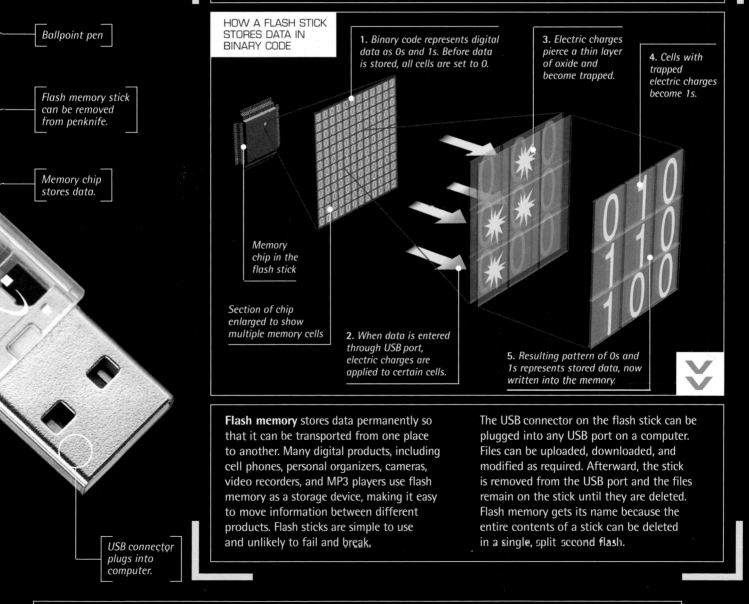

Memory chip in the flash stick

Section of chip enlarged to show multiple memory cells

1. Binary code represents digital data as 0s and 1s. Before data is stored, all cells are set to 0.

2. When data is entered through USB port, electric charges are applied to certain cells.

3. Electric charges pierce a thin layer of oxide and become trapped.

4. Cells with trapped electric charges become 1s.

5. Resulting pattern of 0s and 1s represents stored data, now written into the memory.

USB connector plugs into computer.

Flash memory stores data permanently so that it can be transported from one place to another. Many digital products, including cell phones, personal organizers, cameras, video recorders, and MP3 players use flash memory as a storage device, making it easy to move information between different products. Flash sticks are simple to use and unlikely to fail and break.

The USB connector on the flash stick can be plugged into any USB port on a computer. Files can be uploaded, downloaded, and modified as required. Afterward, the stick is removed from the USB port and the files remain on the stick until they are deleted. Flash memory gets its name because the entire contents of a stick can be deleted in a single, split second flash.

▶▶ See also: Digital technology p243, Laptop p168, Motherboard p170

LASER PRINTER

Toner fused to paper

▲ **This letter "S"** has been printed in toner—a dry, powdery pigment. Laser printing fuses the toner onto paper, using heat and pressure. The particles of toner that make up the letter have been melted and pressed permanently into the paper's porous surface.

◀ BACK

German goldsmith Johannes Gutenberg built Europe's first printing press in 1436. It used metal letters and was the model for presses until the 20th century.

Criminals use laser printers to print forgeries, so scientists have invented printers that add unique "bands" to the paper. The bands identify the printer used to make the forgery.

FORWARD ▶▶

Paper made of fine wood fibers

▶▶ Laser printers shine a powerful beam of light onto a printing drum to create perfect copies of your text or pictures, producing about 45 pages a minute. ▶▶

▲ **Image:** colored SEM of a letter "S"

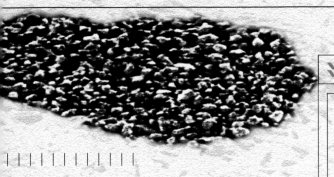

⍦ Toner beads

▶Toner is the dry pigment that laser printers use instead of wet ink. This fine powder consists of tiny plastic beads, each with particles of color attached. Inside the laser printer, negatively charged toner is pulled off first by the positive charge of the drum, then by the stronger positive charge of the paper. When heated by rollers, the beads melt and fuse to the paper, trapping the toner in the wood fibers. Color laser printers use four toners—black, cyan (light blue), magenta (purple-red), and yellow—to create full-color images.

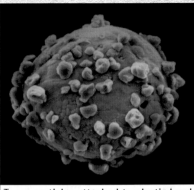

Toner particles attached to plastic bead

▶▶ HOW A LASER PRINTER WORKS

CROSS-SECTION THROUGH
A LASER PRINTER

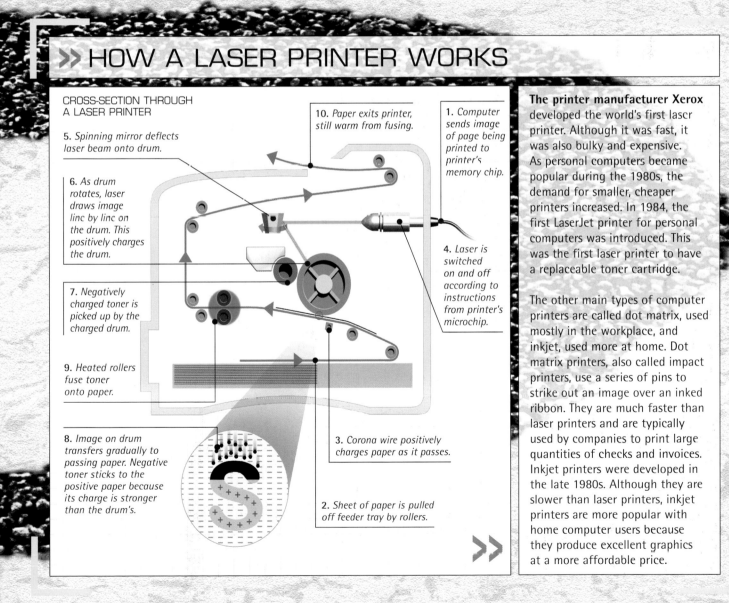

5. *Spinning mirror deflects laser beam onto drum.*

6. *As drum rotates, laser draws image linc by linc on the drum. This positively charges the drum.*

7. *Negatively charged toner is picked up by the charged drum.*

9. *Heated rollers fuse toner onto paper.*

8. *Image on drum transfers gradually to passing paper. Negative toner sticks to the positive paper because its charge is stronger than the drum's.*

10. *Paper exits printer, still warm from fusing.*

1. *Computer sends image of page being printed to printer's memory chip.*

4. *Laser is switched on and off according to instructions from printer's microchip.*

3. *Corona wire positively charges paper as it passes.*

2. *Sheet of paper is pulled off feeder tray by rollers.*

The printer manufacturer Xerox developed the world's first lascr printer. Although it was fast, it was also bulky and expensive. As personal computers became popular during the 1980s, the demand for smaller, cheaper printers increased. In 1984, the first LaserJet printer for personal computers was introduced. This was the first laser printer to have a replaceable toner cartridge.

The other main types of computer printers are called dot matrix, used mostly in the workplace, and inkjet, used more at home. Dot matrix printers, also called impact printers, use a series of pins to strike out an image over an inked ribbon. They are much faster than laser printers and are typically used by companies to print large quantities of checks and invoices. Inkjet printers were developed in the late 1980s. Although they are slower than laser printers, inkjet printers are more popular with home computer users because they produce excellent graphics at a more affordable price.

▶▶ See also: Laser surgery p206, Microchip p16, Scanner p178

SCANNER

▶▶ Any picture or text can be captured as an image by a scanner—from a painting or a family photograph to a legal document. Scanners convert images into digital files, which can be manipulated or printed using a computer. ▶▶

Scanner lid

Image: flatbed scanner beam reading a transparency

Transparency placed face down on scanner

Beam of light scans transparency.

▶▶ See also: Laptop p168, Laser printer p176

▼ **A scanner** uses a beam of light to read the colors of an image or a piece of text. It then converts the information it has received into a digital file, which can be sent to a computer. A photocopier works in a similar way, but it prints multiple copies of the image or text onto paper instead.

Glass plate under which light beam moves

>> HOW A SCANNER WORKS

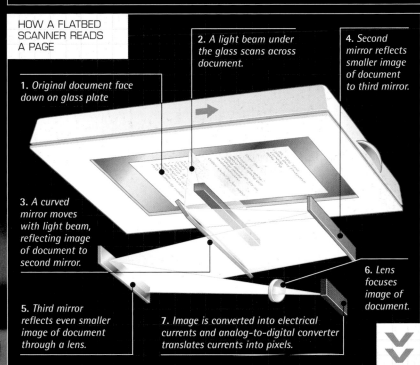

HOW A FLATBED SCANNER READS A PAGE

1. *Original document face down on glass plate*

2. *A light beam under the glass scans across document.*

3. *A curved mirror moves with light beam, reflecting image of document to second mirror.*

4. *Second mirror reflects smaller image of document to third mirror.*

5. *Third mirror reflects even smaller image of document through a lens.*

6. *Lens focuses image of document.*

7. *Image is converted into electrical currents and analog-to-digital converter translates currents into pixels.*

The first scanners, called drum scanners, were developed in about 1957 by the publishing industry to create and print very detailed copies of images or text. These scanners are still used in situations where high quality and color precision is critical, such as pictures of artifacts in museum catalogs. Today, flatbed scanners are used more frequently because, although less precise, they are cheaper and faster. A scanner can form an image of the page, which can be attached to an email and sent to many people at once. To save typing time, Optical Character Recognition (OCR) scanners can extract text from a scan of a page, so it can be edited on word-processing software.

⌄ Automatic mailing system

▶Post offices use Optical Character Recognition (OCR) scanners to help the mail sorting process. The scanner takes an image of a ZIP code and compares it with a list of ZIP codes stored in a table. When the ZIP code is found, a pattern of codemarks is printed on the mail. Phosphor inks are used for these codemarks, since they glow in the dark under ultraviolet (UV) light and routing machines can easily read them, even if the mail is damaged.

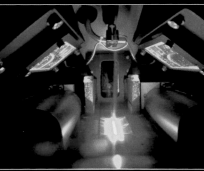

OCR scanner reading a ZIP code

SMART CARD

▶▶ A smart card is a plastic card with an embedded microchip. It can store 32 kilobytes of data, from bank details to medical records, in its memory. The data is encrypted—put into code—for extra security. ▶▶

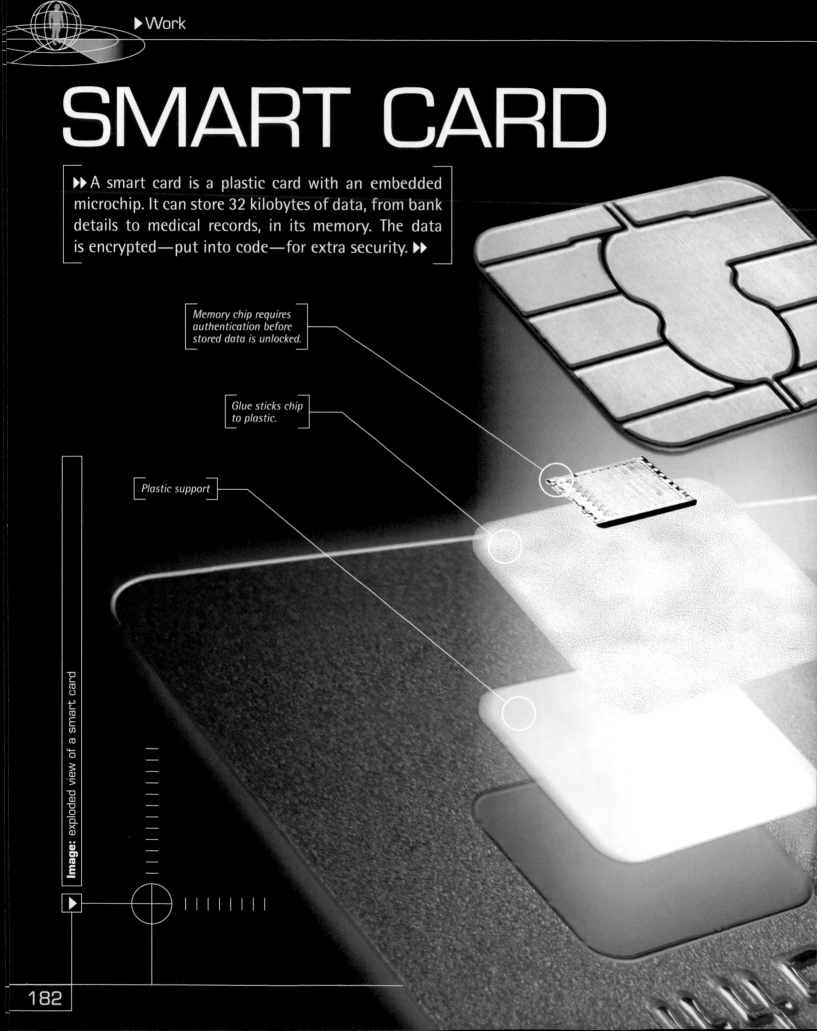

Memory chip requires authentication before stored data is unlocked.

Glue sticks chip to plastic.

Plastic support

Image: exploded view of a smart card

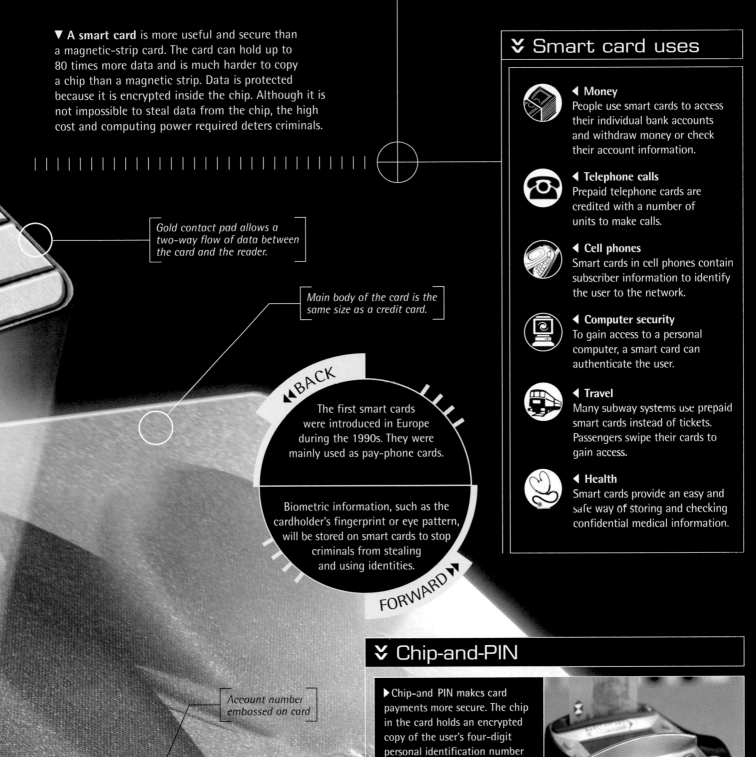

▼ A **smart card** is more useful and secure than a magnetic-strip card. The card can hold up to 80 times more data and is much harder to copy a chip than a magnetic strip. Data is protected because it is encrypted inside the chip. Although it is not impossible to steal data from the chip, the high cost and computing power required deters criminals.

Gold contact pad allows a two-way flow of data between the card and the reader.

Main body of the card is the same size as a credit card.

◀BACK

The first smart cards were introduced in Europe during the 1990s. They were mainly used as pay-phone cards.

Biometric information, such as the cardholder's fingerprint or eye pattern, will be stored on smart cards to stop criminals from stealing and using identities.

FORWARD▶

Account number embossed on card

❮ Smart card uses

◀ **Money**
People use smart cards to access their individual bank accounts and withdraw money or check their account information.

◀ **Telephone calls**
Prepaid telephone cards are credited with a number of units to make calls.

◀ **Cell phones**
Smart cards in cell phones contain subscriber information to identify the user to the network.

◀ **Computer security**
To gain access to a personal computer, a smart card can authenticate the user.

◀ **Travel**
Many subway systems use prepaid smart cards instead of tickets. Passengers swipe their cards to gain access.

◀ **Health**
Smart cards provide an easy and safe way of storing and checking confidential medical information.

❮ Chip-and-PIN

▶Chip-and-PIN makes card payments more secure. The chip in the card holds an encrypted copy of the user's four-digit personal identification number (PIN). By entering the number into a reading device, a user can prove they own the card. This has reduced instances of card fraud; without the PIN, it is almost impossible for a criminal to steal and use another person's card.

Using a chip-and-PIN device

▶▶ See also: Biochip p226, ID p180, Microchip p16

RADIO ID TAG

▶▶ A radio frequency identification tag is a tiny tracking device with a microchip and antenna. Each tag has a unique code to identify the product, person, or animal wearing it. More than 50 million pets and 20 million livestock have already been tagged. ▶▶

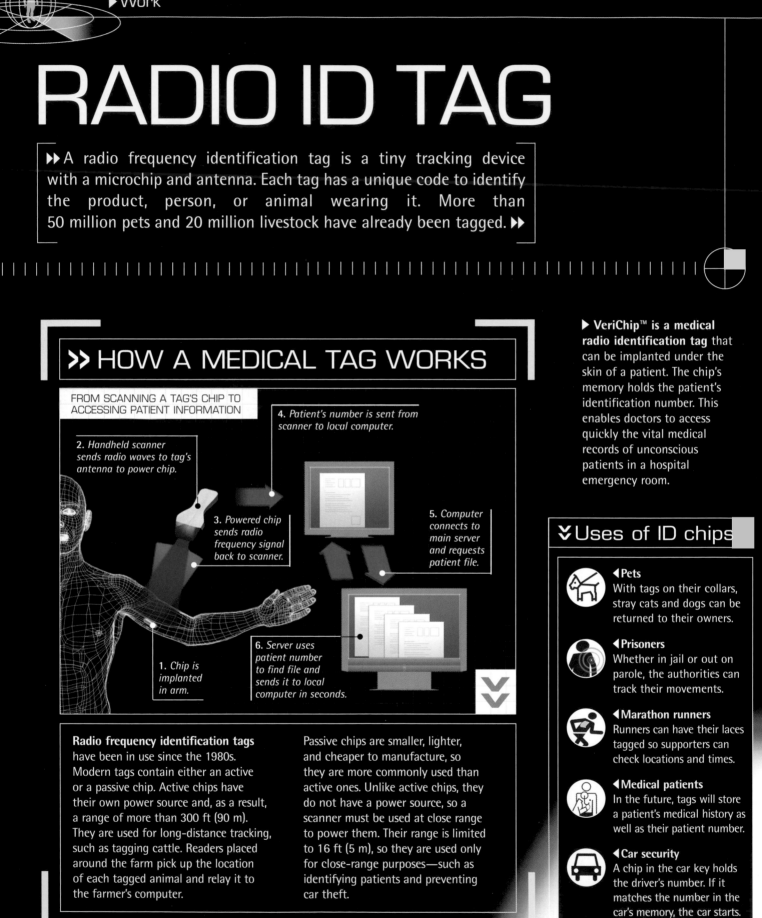

>> HOW A MEDICAL TAG WORKS

FROM SCANNING A TAG'S CHIP TO ACCESSING PATIENT INFORMATION

4. *Patient's number is sent from scanner to local computer.*

2. *Handheld scanner sends radio waves to tag's antenna to power chip.*

3. *Powered chip sends radio frequency signal back to scanner.*

5. *Computer connects to main server and requests patient file.*

1. *Chip is implanted in arm.*

6. *Server uses patient number to find file and sends it to local computer in seconds.*

Radio frequency identification tags have been in use since the 1980s. Modern tags contain either an active or a passive chip. Active chips have their own power source and, as a result, a range of more than 300 ft (90 m). They are used for long-distance tracking, such as tagging cattle. Readers placed around the farm pick up the location of each tagged animal and relay it to the farmer's computer.

Passive chips are smaller, lighter, and cheaper to manufacture, so they are more commonly used than active ones. Unlike active chips, they do not have a power source, so a scanner must be used at close range to power them. Their range is limited to 16 ft (5 m), so they are used only for close-range purposes—such as identifying patients and preventing car theft.

▶ **VeriChip™ is a medical radio identification tag** that can be implanted under the skin of a patient. The chip's memory holds the patient's identification number. This enables doctors to access quickly the vital medical records of unconscious patients in a hospital emergency room.

⌄ Uses of ID chips

◀ **Pets**
With tags on their collars, stray cats and dogs can be returned to their owners.

◀ **Prisoners**
Whether in jail or out on parole, the authorities can track their movements.

◀ **Marathon runners**
Runners can have their laces tagged so supporters can check locations and times.

◀ **Medical patients**
In the future, tags will store a patient's medical history as well as their patient number.

◀ **Car security**
A chip in the car key holds the driver's number. If it matches the number in the car's memory, the car starts.

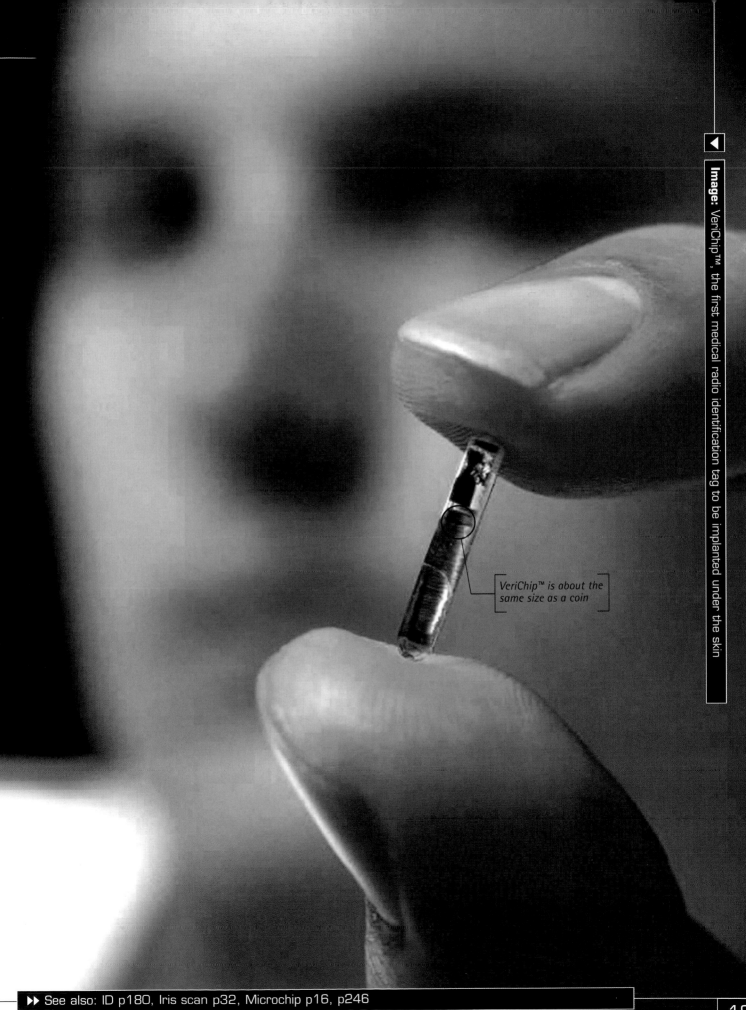

VeriChip™ is about the same size as a coin

▶▶ See also: ID p180, Iris scan p32, Microchip p16, p246

WET WELDING

▶▶ Intense heat of up to 6,300°F (3,500°C) is used to melt and join metals. Wet welding uses a tiny electric arc to generate this extreme heat underwater. ▶▶

▶ **These Deep Rover submersibles** are being used to weld metal underwater. The submersibles are capable of working at depths of up to 3,300 ft (1,000 m)—more than three times deeper than the world-record scuba diving descent of 1,027 ft (313 m). A welder sits inside each submersible and uses the external robotic arms to weld the metal.

Acrylic sphere gives welder a 320° view.

Image: Deep Rover submersibles welding

⌄ Welding on land

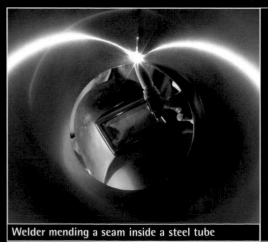

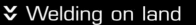
Welder mending a seam inside a steel tube

◀Taking a ship or an oil rig into dry dock for repair is very expensive, but when there is a major crack, it is the only option. Welding on land follows a process similar to welding underwater—the edges of two metals are melted and allowed to solidify together. The sparks and light generated by the electric arc are so intense that the welder must protect the eyes with a safety visor. Visors also give a clear view of how close the welding rod is to the weld.

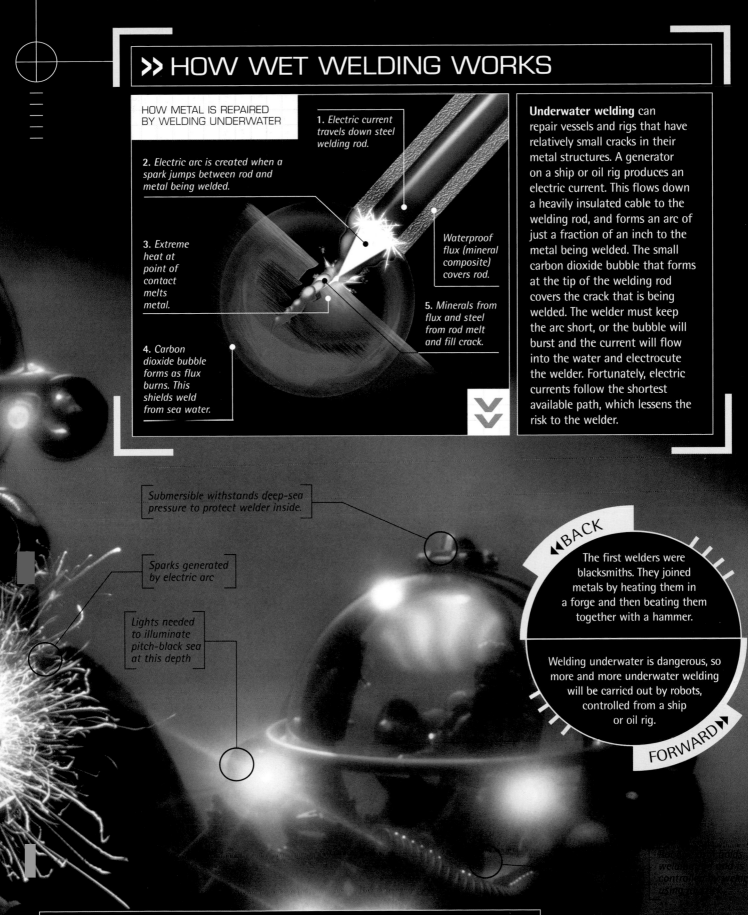

❯❯ HOW WET WELDING WORKS

HOW METAL IS REPAIRED BY WELDING UNDERWATER

1. *Electric current travels down steel welding rod.*

2. *Electric arc is created when a spark jumps between rod and metal being welded.*

3. *Extreme heat at point of contact melts metal.*

4. *Carbon dioxide bubble forms as flux burns. This shields weld from sea water.*

Waterproof flux (mineral composite) covers rod.

5. *Minerals from flux and steel from rod melt and fill crack.*

Underwater welding can repair vessels and rigs that have relatively small cracks in their metal structures. A generator on a ship or oil rig produces an electric current. This flows down a heavily insulated cable to the welding rod, and forms an arc of just a fraction of an inch to the metal being welded. The small carbon dioxide bubble that forms at the tip of the welding rod covers the crack that is being welded. The welder must keep the arc short, or the bubble will burst and the current will flow into the water and electrocute the welder. Fortunately, electric currents follow the shortest available path, which lessens the risk to the welder.

Submersible withstands deep-sea pressure to protect welder inside.

Sparks generated by electric arc

Lights needed to illuminate pitch-black sea at this depth

◀BACK

The first welders were blacksmiths. They joined metals by heating them in a forge and then beating them together with a hammer.

Welding underwater is dangerous, so more and more underwater welding will be carried out by robots, controlled from a ship or oil rig.

FORWARD▶

▶▶ See also: Submersible p142

FIRE SUIT

▶▶ Firefighters depend on their fire suits for protection. They are made of multilayered, synthetic fibers, capable of withstanding temperatures of up to 675°F (360°C). ▶▶

▼ **These two military firefighters** are involved in a practice session to put out fires at airports. Their protective clothing contains the heat-resistant material Nomex®, water-resistant Teflon®, and Kevlar®, which is stronger than steel and stops the suits from ripping or snagging.

Reflective visor reduces glare from the flames.

Aluminum covering reflects heat.

Image: military firefighters putting out a blaze

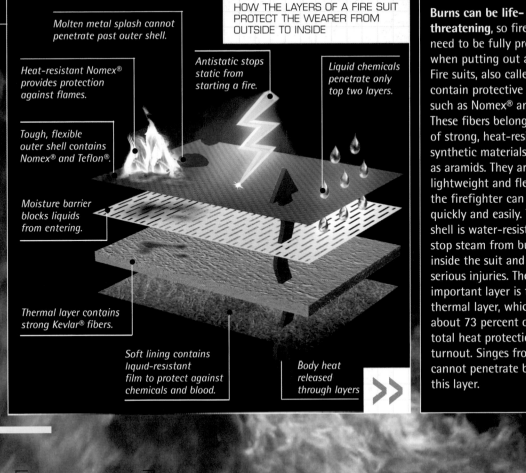

HOW THE LAYERS OF A FIRE SUIT PROTECT THE WEARER FROM OUTSIDE TO INSIDE

Molten metal splash cannot penetrate past outer shell.

Heat-resistant Nomex® provides protection against flames.

Tough, flexible outer shell contains Nomex® and Teflon®.

Moisture barrier blocks liquids from entering.

Thermal layer contains strong Kevlar® fibers.

Soft lining contains liquid-resistant film to protect against chemicals and blood.

Antistatic stops static from starting a fire.

Liquid chemicals penetrate only top two layers.

Body heat released through layers

Burns can be life-threatening, so firefighters need to be fully protected when putting out a blaze. Fire suits, also called turnouts, contain protective fibers such as Nomex® and Teflon®. These fibers belong to a group of strong, heat-resistant, synthetic materials, known as aramids. They are also lightweight and flexible so the firefighter can move quickly and easily. The outer shell is water-resistant—to stop steam from building up inside the suit and causing serious injuries. The most important layer is the thermal layer, which provides about 73 percent of the total heat protection of a turnout. Singes from flames cannot penetrate beyond this layer.

Hose sprays 100 gal (380 liters) of water per minute.

◄◄BACK

The first firefighters, known as vigiles, were introduced by the Roman emperor Augustus in 24 BC.

The next generation of fire suits will be resistant to toxic chemicals and biological warfare agents, such as anthrax.

FORWARD▶▶

▶▶ See also: Crash test p134, Heat p98

GLUES

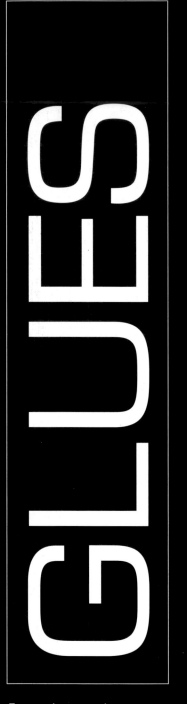

These yellow blobs are bubbles of glue on the adhesive strip of a Post-it® Note. When the note is pressed against a surface, some of the bubbles pop and the glue is released. There are so many bubbles on each strip that a Post-it® Note can be used several times.

V Velcro®
Swiss inventor George de Mestral came up with the idea of Velcro® when he saw prickly seeds, called burrs, stuck to his pants. Under a microscope, the tiny hooks of the burrs clung to the small loops of the fabric. Made of nylon, Velcro® has hooks on one side and loops on the other. When pressed together, the hooks fasten to the loops and form a bond.

For as long as humans have made objects, they have looked for ways to stick materials together. The earliest glues were tar and resin. Today, a wide range of different types of adhesives is in regular use.

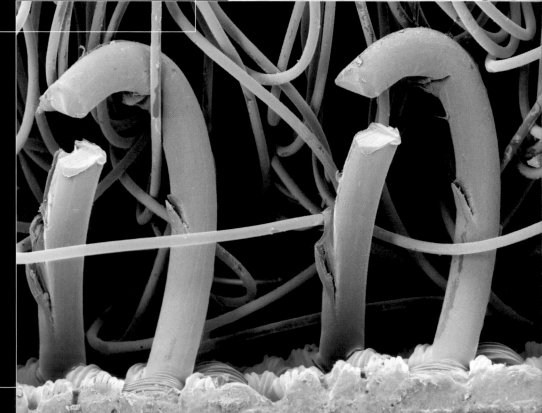

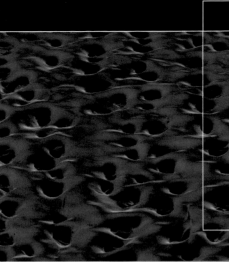

◀◀ Bandage
Adhesive bandages cover and protect most minor wounds and injection sites. Gaps in the glue, shown in black, let the skin breathe. Bandages are sterile and most are individually wrapped. They come in a range of materials, including waterproof and fabric adhesive dressings.

▶▶ Glue
About 4,000 years ago, the Egyptians used animal hides to make glue to stick wood together. Although hide glues are still used, synthetic glues are also available today, such as super glue. Made from a synthetic, acrylic resin, it is far stronger than hide glue.

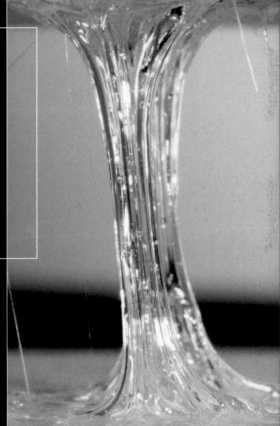

▽▽ Cement
Each year, 1.2 billion tons of cement is produced. Cement is a dry powder that hardens when mixed with water. It is used to bond building materials and is the main ingredient of concrete, together with gravel, water, and sand. As concrete (blue) dries, it hardens to form crystals (brown).

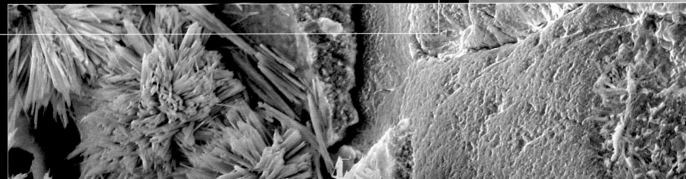

▶▶ See also: Fabric p60

DOPPLER RADAR

▶▶ Doppler radar is used to work out the direction and speed of moving objects. It can predict where a storm will occur. With this advance warning, many lives have been saved. ▶▶

Geographical outline of Cuba

Center of the hurricane, known as "the eye"

▶ **This Doppler radar image** shows Hurricane Ivan heading toward Cuba in September 2004. Ivan's winds reached 165 mph (270 km/h), the sixth-strongest storm ever to hit the Atlantic Ocean. Doppler radar images are used by meteorologists to determine a storm's wind speed, direction, and the amount of rainfall to expect.

⌄ Red shift

Galaxies moving away from us appear redder

▲ The difference in pitch between an object that is moving away from you and one that is moving toward you is due to the Doppler effect. For example, when a car comes toward you, the sound waves made by its engine are bunched up, making it sound higher-pitched. When it moves away, sound waves spread out and the noise is lower-pitched. The Doppler effect also applies to light waves. Astronomers use it to find out whether celestial objects are moving away from or toward Earth. Light from objects moving away appears redder, called red shift, and light from those moving closer appears bluer, called blue shift.

Image: radar image of Hurricane Ivan

◀◀BACK

In 1842, Austrian physicist Christian Doppler devised the term Doppler effect to explain why the whistles of approaching and departing trains sound different.

The next generation of Doppler radar antennae are called phased-array. Phased-array antennae can track more sky and provide sharper images.

FORWARD▶▶

HOW DOPPLER RADAR WORKS

HOW RADIO WAVES ASSESS THE DIRECTION AND SPEED OF A STORM

4. *Movement of rain cloud is from left to right.*

3. *Returning radio waves are further apart as cloud retreats.*

5. *Returning radio waves to second transmitter are close together as cloud advances.*

2. *Radio waves bounce off raindrops and echo back to transmitter.*

1. *First transmitter sends radio waves into the sky.*

Blue and black represent the lightest rainfall

Red represents the heaviest rainfall

Doppler radar is best known for its use in weather forecasting, but it started life as a military technology. The radar was used to detect and track enemy aircraft. Commercial airliners use Doppler radar to avoid a dangerous weather condition known as wind-shear—a sudden, dramatic change in wind direction. Doppler radar "guns" are used by police to record the speed of vehicles. These can also be used in sports to calculate speeds, such as the speed of a tennis ball.

▶▶ See also: Cell phone p18, Digital radio p22, Radio waves p249, Voice recognition p28

Although the invention of the internal combustion engine and the development of the car was the end of the horse-and-carriage industry, it created in its place a whole new industry. New kinds of jobs emerged, from production-line workers to gas station attendants. In a similar way, new industries and jobs, driven by the information technology revolution, are rapidly emerging. Already, the video games industry is bigger than the movie box-office industry. And exciting fields such as nanotechnology, robotics, and new material technology will rapidly expand as the century progresses.

> **As future robots become increasingly agile and intelligent, many more life-threatening jobs will be carried out remotely.**

The ability to perform our jobs more efficiently will rely increasingly on special, so-called smart software. These complex computer programs will make decisions for us using artificial intelligence to learn about our preferences. Smart software will take care of many of the day-to-day, time-consuming tasks—such as prioritizing e-mail, putting through important phone calls while screening others, and automatically updating our schedule.

Artificial intelligence will also drive the development of expert systems. These will draw together all the knowledge of human experts in a particular field, automatically updating themselves with the latest information. Whether you are a doctor, an astronomer, or a journalist, expert systems will guide you through the most complex questions and issues. Voice recognition and digital talking heads on screen will give smart software and expert systems virtual personalities. This will make the way you communicate with the computer a much more user-friendly experience.

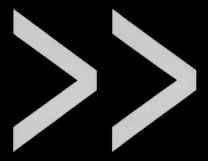

As future robots become increasingly agile and intelligent, many more life-threatening jobs will be carried out remotely. Already, robots are used for bomb disposal and for carrying out tasks inside nuclear reactors where the high radiation levels would harm human beings. Over the next few decades, we will begin to see the use of robots that can be sent into fires to help save lives, and the introduction of robonauts—robots that can perform increasingly complex experiments and other tasks in the hostile environment of space.

This combination of robotics and communications can be used in all kinds of ways. Remote surgery is already a reality, with doctors carrying out operations using robots that may be thousands of miles away. Many other tasks will be done in this way. Instead of having to work in hazardous conditions, skilled operators will control machines for mining, construction, or even exploring other planets from the safety of their offices.

The technology revolution will continue until we can no longer replace human function with technological advancements. However, the drive toward advancing technologies means that employees need training to keep up with these developments in order to stay useful in the workplace.

CONCEPT ARTWORK OF ARTIFICIAL INTELLIGENCE

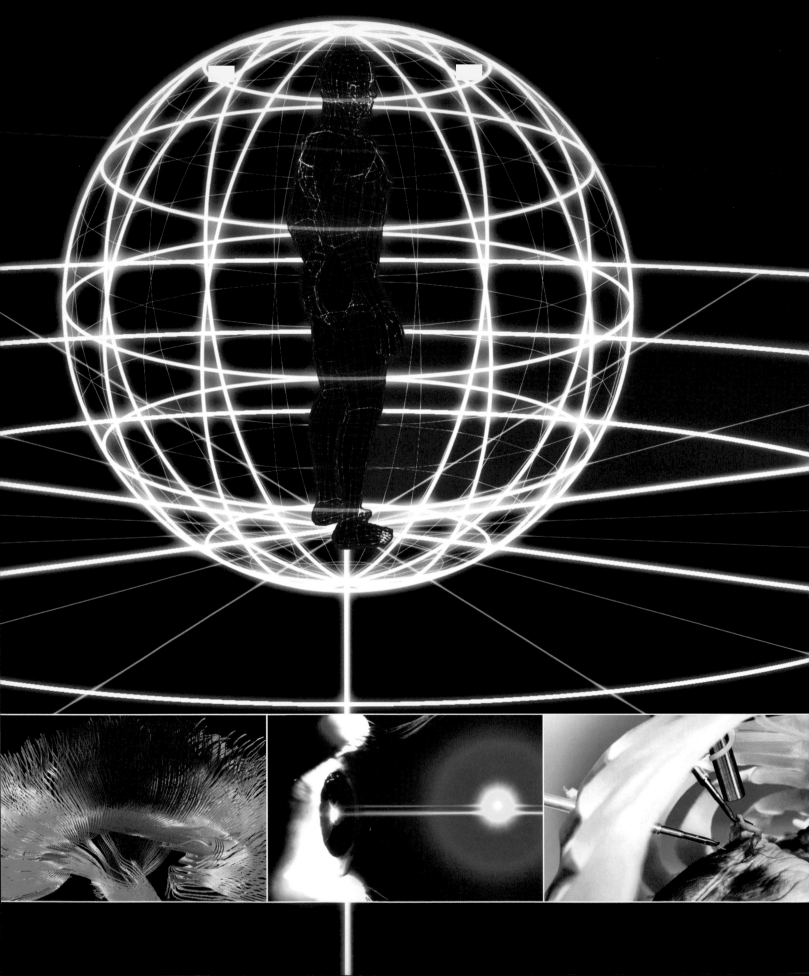

>>SURVIVE

MRI scan >> Laser surgery >> Robot surgery >> Pacemaker >>
Camera capsule >> Bionic limbs >> Skin graft >> Vaccination >>
Antibiotics >> IVF >> Biochip

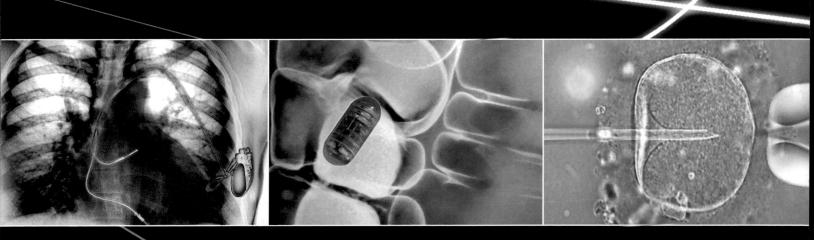

Sometimes the simplest of technologies are the most important. One of these is soap, which has had a major impact on human health and civilization. Soap, in the form that we use today, was invented in the late 1700s. It is made of long molecules that stick to dirt at one end and water at the other, allowing us easily to remove dirt and harmful bacteria from our bodies. This has greatly reduced illness and disease.

A type of soap was used by the ancient Romans. Along with the ancient Greeks, the Romans provided the foundations for modern medicine, developing surgical instruments that are still used today and a more scientific approach to illness. In other ancient cultures, medicine was based on a combination of magic, herbal remedies, and primitive surgery. Illnesses were thought to be caused by evil spirits and treatment was usually carried out by a priest or a magician. In one headache cure, called trepanning, a hole was made in the patient's skull. Some remedies were effective in curing common ailments, but most were hit-or-miss.

The development of the microscope in the 1600s revolutionized medical understanding. This tool, consisting of finely polished curved lenses, led to the discovery of bacteria and blood cells. People began to think of the body as

ELECTRON MICROGRAPH
OF COLD VIRUS

a series of mechanical and chemical processes, no longer an object animated by mysterious spirits. The development of vaccinations in the late 1700s meant that for the first time doctors could combat infectious diseases such as smallpox. Other breakthroughs transformed medicine in the following century. Antiseptics, used to clean wounds and surgical instruments, dramatically reduced the number of deaths from infection. Anesthetics, which made operations free from pain, allowed surgeons to take much more time and care during difficult procedures.

The discovery of X-rays at the end of the nineteenth century provided a way to see through human tissue without surgery and to examine, for example, broken bones. Today, modern scanning techniques such as ultrasound and magnetic resonance imaging (MRI) have given doctors an even greater understanding of the human body. Many other areas of medicine have also been transformed by technology. Robotic aids enable surgeons to carry out extremely complex operations while causing a minimum of damage to the patient. And using highly automated techniques in laboratories and powerful computers, scientist have mapped the 20–25,000 human genes that make up the blueprint for each and every one of us.

Despite the various advances in medicine over the last century, cures have not yet been found for many diseases, ranging from HIV/AIDS to the common cold. The brain also remains largely a mystery to us. Technology, however, is beginning to provide some answers. As scanning techniques become even more sophisticated, scientists are learning even more about the body and understanding how it works in greater detail.

> **Major developments in medical imaging technology mean doctors can see inside the body in incredible detail.**

SCANS

Medical imaging technology allows doctors to look inside the human body without making a single cut. Recent advances in image processing mean doctors can see many internal structures in detailed, three-dimensional (3-D) form.

>> **Full-body MRI**
Unlike X-ray images, MRI (magnetic resonance imaging) scans reveal soft body tissues. As well as the skeleton (yellow), this scan shows the muscles (pink), brain tissue (green), lungs (red), and liver (below the lungs). The scanner detects electromagnetic signals emitted when hydrogen atoms in the body are knocked out of magnetic alignment. These signals are used to create an image on a computer.

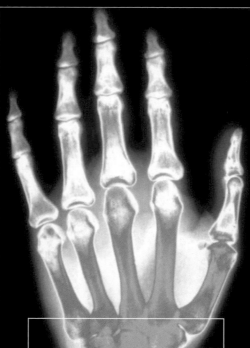

∧ **Hand X-ray**
X-rays reveal hard structures inside the body, such as bones and teeth. This makes them ideal for diagnosing fractures, bone diseases, and tooth decay. They are produced by shining X-rays (a form of electromagnetic radiation) through the body and onto a photographic plate.

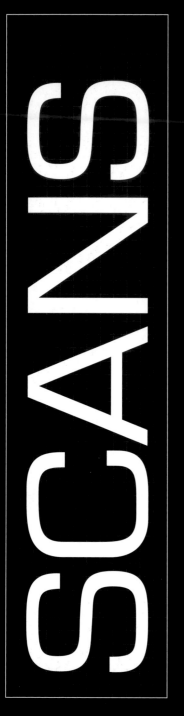

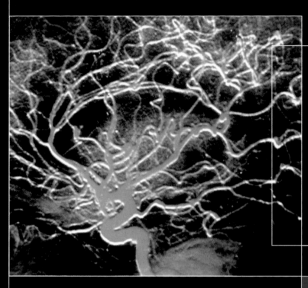

◀◀ Cerebral angiogram
To search for abnormalities in blood vessels, doctors take a rapid series of X-rays after injecting a person with a dye that is radiopaque—opaque to X-rays. In the resulting images, called angiograms or arteriographs, blood vessels stand out brightly. This cerebral angiogram shows the network of blood vessels in a brain (cerebrum). Doctors use angiograms to look for aneurysms—dangerous swellings in blood vessels.

▶▶ CAT scan of pelvis
A CAT (computed axial tomography) or CT scan is a 3-D image compiled by computer from a series of X-rays taken by a machine that rotates around the body. This scan shows the bones of a normal adult pelvis. The pelvis is made of six separate bones that fuse together as you grow. It acts as a bridge between the spine and legs.

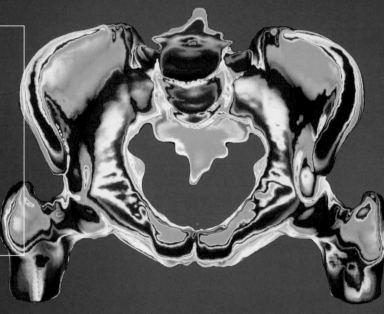

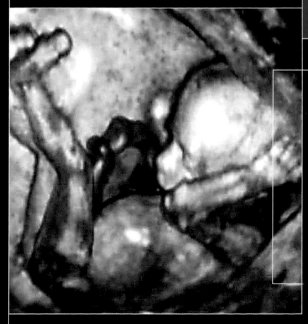

◀◀ Ultrasound
Of all medical imaging technologies, ultrasound scanning poses the least risk to health. That is why it is used to produce images of unborn babies. Ultrasound scanners send high-frequency sound waves through the body. Returning echoes are recorded and used to create an image. Most ultrasound scanners produce a single-slice image, but the latest scanners take multiple slices to produce a 3D image. Unlike other scanners, ultrasound produces a live, moving image on screen.

▶▶ See also: Imaging techniques p10, MRI p204, X-Rays p251

MRI SCAN

▶▶ A magnetic resonance imaging (MRI) scanner uses powerful magnets and radio waves to create images of soft tissues inside the body. The tube-shaped magnet produces a magnetic field up to 40,000 times more powerful than Earth's. ▶▶

▶ **This MRI scan** highlights the major pathways that carry nerve signals through the brain. The colored strands are the brain's main cables, each containing thousands of long, thin fibers. Each fiber is part of one brain cell, and together they form the brain's white matter. They carry billions of electrical signals between brain cells, and between brain and nerve cells.

Image: false-color MRI scan of the brain's nerve pathways

Connections between left and right halves of brain are colored red.

Brain stem connects to spinal cord.

Bottom of brain

Middle of brain

Top of brain

◀ MRI scanners can "slice" through the body, producing images at any depth. To do this, three additional magnets are used. These gradient magnets create variations in the magnetic field along precisely positioned planes through the body. The scanner reads signals from these planes, and a computer processes the signals to create an image.

>> HOW AN MRI SCANNER WORKS

HOW MRI SCANNERS USE MAGNETIC FIELDS AND RADIO WAVES TO BUILD IMAGES OF SOFT BODY TISSUES

These pathways carry signals from eyes to visual center at back of brain.

Connections between front and back of brain are colored green.

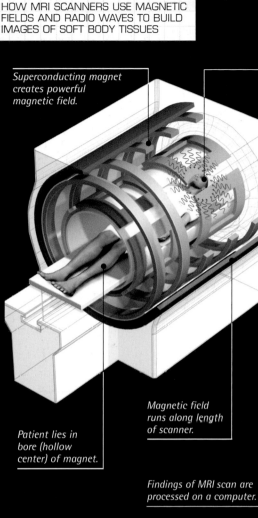

Superconducting magnet creates powerful magnetic field.

Patient lies in bore (hollow center) of magnet.

Magnetic field runs along length of scanner.

Findings of MRI scan are processed on a computer.

Spinal cord transmits information between brain and rest of body.

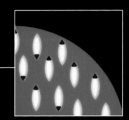

1. Hydrogen atoms in the body are usually randomly ordered, but the powerful magnetic field makes them line up like tiny magnets.

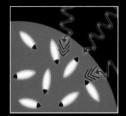

2. A pulse of radio waves produced by the scanner knocks the hydrogen atoms out of their new magnetic alignment.

3. As the radio waves cease, the atoms realign and emit faint radio signals that are detected by a sensor. The sensor sends signals as digital data to a computer.

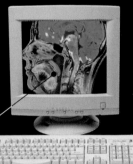

4. Using a complex mathematical process called a Fourier transformation, the computer converts the data into an image. The brightness of the image can be varied by alternating the magnetic field.

Unlike an X-ray, which reveals hard substances like bone and teeth, an MRI scan creates images of soft body tissues. This makes it ideal for detecting abnormal tissues such as tumors and hemorrhages. MRI is the most common technique for scanning brains, but it can be used to scan any soft tissues in the body. The image is built up from faint radio signals emitted by hydrogen atoms, which are found in all body tissues. Since the signals vary from one type of tissue to another, the image produced by the scanner can distinguish between different tissues, revealing details as small as $1/25$ in (1 mm) wide. Although MRI scanners do not produce any harmful radiation, the powerful magnet is hazardous if loose metal objects are present— they are pulled with such force that they hurtle across the room like missiles. The world's first MRI scan took place on July 3, 1977, following seven years of preparation. The image took five hours to produce. Today, it takes seconds to compile an image.

▶▶ See also: Imaging techniques p10, Magnets p246, Scans p202

LASER SURGERY

▶ **The curved surface** of the eye—the cornea—and the lens behind the cornea focus light rays onto the light-sensitive retina deep inside the eye, where an image is produced. If the cornea is slightly misshapen, or thickens over time, sight becomes blurred. Laser eye surgery reshapes the cornea by vaporizing (heating until it turns to vapor) a tiny part of the problem area. The eye's focus is then sharper.

▶▶ People with imperfect vision no longer need to wear glasses or contact lenses. Using the power of a laser to reshape part of the eye, sight can be corrected. ▶▶

❯ Lasers

▼ Most light consists of a mixture of wavelengths. However, a laser is an intense, narrow beam of light that consists of a single wavelength, such as ultraviolet (UV) or infrared. Since lasers were first discovered in 1960, they have found many uses, including guiding missiles, removing tattoos, and reading the data on CDs.

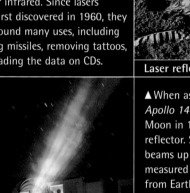

Laser reflector on the Moon

▲ When astronauts from the *Apollo 14* mission landed on the Moon in 1971, they left a laser reflector. Scientists sent laser beams up to the reflector and measured the Moon's distance from Earth to within 1 in (3 cm). They worked out the distance by timing how long it took for the reflected beam to return to Earth.

A laser beam is aimed at the Moon

◀◀ BACK

Before laser eye surgery became widespread, surgeons could correct vision by making a series of spokelike slits in the cornea with a scalpel.

Surgeons may use a strong jet of fluid rather than a blade to cut the cornea flap prior to laser treatment.

FORWARD ▶▶

❯❯ HOW LASER EYE SURGERY WORKS

The cornea's shape is precisely mapped by a computer, which calculates exactly how much tissue needs to be removed. The computer controls the ultraviolet laser to these specifications. A fine knife, or microkeratome, is used to cut a flap in the cornea's surface. The flap is folded aside, and the laser is aimed at the tissue behind. The laser does not penetrate the eye, but gently vaporizes the corneal tissue, making it thinner. The flap is folded back, which helps the eye to heal quickly without stitches. The patient can usually see right away.

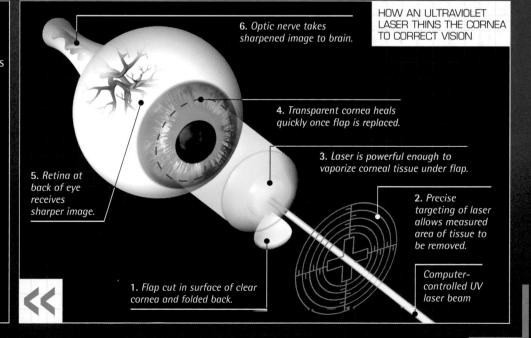

HOW AN ULTRAVIOLET LASER THINS THE CORNEA TO CORRECT VISION

6. *Optic nerve takes sharpened image to brain.*

4. *Transparent cornea heals quickly once flap is replaced.*

3. *Laser is powerful enough to vaporize corneal tissue under flap.*

5. *Retina at back of eye receives sharper image.*

2. *Precise targeting of laser allows measured area of tissue to be removed.*

1. *Flap cut in surface of clear cornea and folded back.*

Computer-controlled UV laser beam

▶▶ See also: Iris scan p32, Laser p246, Laser printer p176

ROBOT SURGERY

▶▶ Robotic arms enter the body through tiny incisions and perform delicate surgical procedures with complete precision. The robot is operated by a surgeon, using a remote-control system. ▶▶

▶ These robotic arms are performing a delicate procedure used in heart surgery on a model of the human chest. The arms pass between the ribs, with no need for a major incision. In 1999, this robot, called Zeus, was used to repair blood vessels on the surface of a beating heart.

◀BACK

Surgical robots were invented in the 1980s. They combined robotic arms with surgical viewing devices called endoscopes.

The high-speed transmission of computer images and data makes it possible for doctors to carry out robot surgery on patients in hospitals thousands of miles away.

FORWARD▶▶

>> HOW ROBOT SURGERY WORKS

◀◀ A surgical robot has two main parts: a robotic arm unit, which is positioned over the patient, and a control console several feet away. During an operation, the surgeon sits at the console, watching the procedure through a magnified viewfinder and guiding the robot arms with his hands. Assistants and an anesthetist may also be present.

▶▶ A camera attached to one of the robot's arms takes images inside the incision and relays them to the magnified viewfinder, which creates sharp, 3-D images. The view is much clearer than is possible with the naked eye. The surgeon's hand movements are translated by sophisticated joysticks into far smaller, precise movements of the robotic arms. The system can eliminate any tremors in the surgeon's hands and improve accuracy.

⌄ Stitching ants

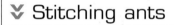
A biting ant sinks its jaws into a fingertip

▲Although surgical procedures are increasingly sophisticated, wounds are still closed using the ancient technology of stitches. Rainforest people in Central America used the jaws of biting ants as tiny clamps to close wounds. Modern stitches are mostly made of synthetic fibers such as nylon or polyester.

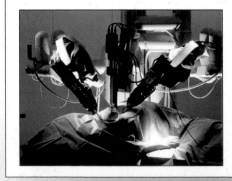

◀◀ The stainless steel robot arms enter the skin through three small incisions, each no wider than the thickness of a pencil. While the camera at the tip of one arm films the operation, other surgical instruments are used to cut, hold, and stitch. When not in use, the arms are rock steady. This reduces the level of trauma for the patient.

▶▶ See also: Camera capsule p212, Robot helper p118, Robot worker p186

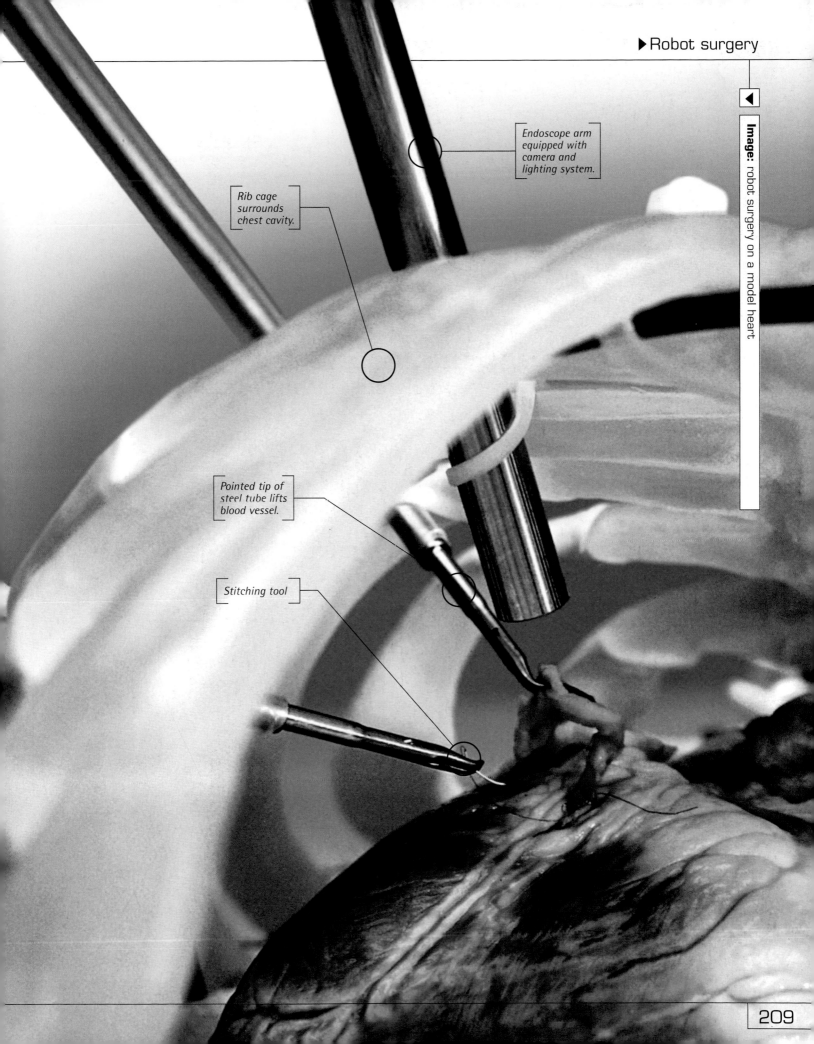

Endoscope arm
equipped with
camera and
lighting system.

Rib cage
surrounds
chest cavity.

Pointed tip of
steel tube lifts
blood vessel.

Stitching tool

Image: false-color X-ray of pacemaker in chest

PACEMAKER

Electric wires enter heart through its major veins.

◀BACK

In 1958, 43-year-old Arne Larsson from Sweden became the first person to receive a pacemaker. He lived to be 86 years old.

Pacemakers will contain sophisticated microprocessors that store details of the patient's medical records and adapt to suit their needs.

FORWARD▶▶

Top electrode makes heart's upper chambers contract.

Heart shown here as red area under rib cage

Bottom electrode stimulates the heart's lower chambers.

▶▶ Implanted in the chest, a pacemaker sends electric signals to stimulate the heart. Most pacemakers act on demand, sending signals only when the heart is not beating normally. ▶▶

❯❯ HOW A PACEMAKER WORKS

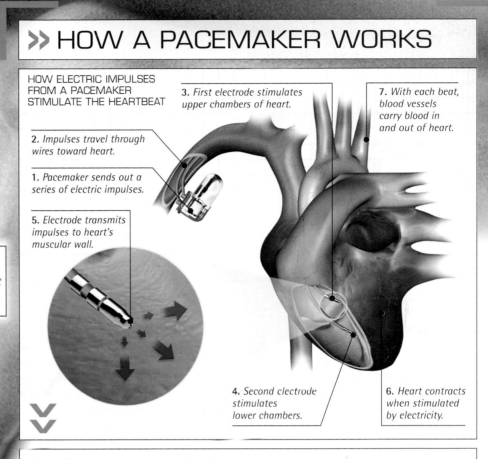

HOW ELECTRIC IMPULSES FROM A PACEMAKER STIMULATE THE HEARTBEAT

3. *First electrode stimulates upper chambers of heart.*

7. *With each beat, blood vessels carry blood in and out of heart.*

2. *Impulses travel through wires toward heart.*

1. *Pacemaker sends out a series of electric impulses.*

5. *Electrode transmits impulses to heart's muscular wall.*

4. *Second electrode stimulates lower chambers.*

6. *Heart contracts when stimulated by electricity.*

Microprocessor control unit monitors heartbeat and controls pacemaker.

A healthy human heart contains its own natural pacemaker: the sinus node. It sends waves through the heart's muscular walls, triggering the contractions that pump blood through the body with each heartbeat. If the sinus node fails to work properly, surgeons can implant an artificial pacemaker. This continually monitors the heart, and when it senses an abnormal heartbeat, it generates a series of electrical impulses that override the sinus node. Some pacemakers vary their output according to need; for example, they can increase the heart rate during exercise.

Lithium battery lasts up to ten years.

◀ **The pacemaker** is surgically implanted under a pocket of skin in the chest. Just 1-2 oz (20-50 g) in weight, it is smaller than a matchbox. It is completely sealed in a waterproof casing to prevent any body fluids from leaking into it. Most pacemakers last about five years before they need to be replaced.

❯ Artificial heart

▶ In 2001, US surgeons installed the world's first self-contained artificial heart in a patient with heart disease. Made of titanium and plastic, the AbioCor heart has a hydraulic motor to pump blood around the body. It is powered by an external battery, carried by the patient. It extends the life expectancy of patients with serious heart disease by a few months.

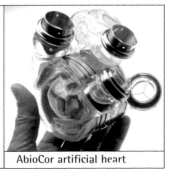

AbioCor artificial heart

▶▶ See also: Battery p94, Robot surgery p208

CAMERA CAPSULE

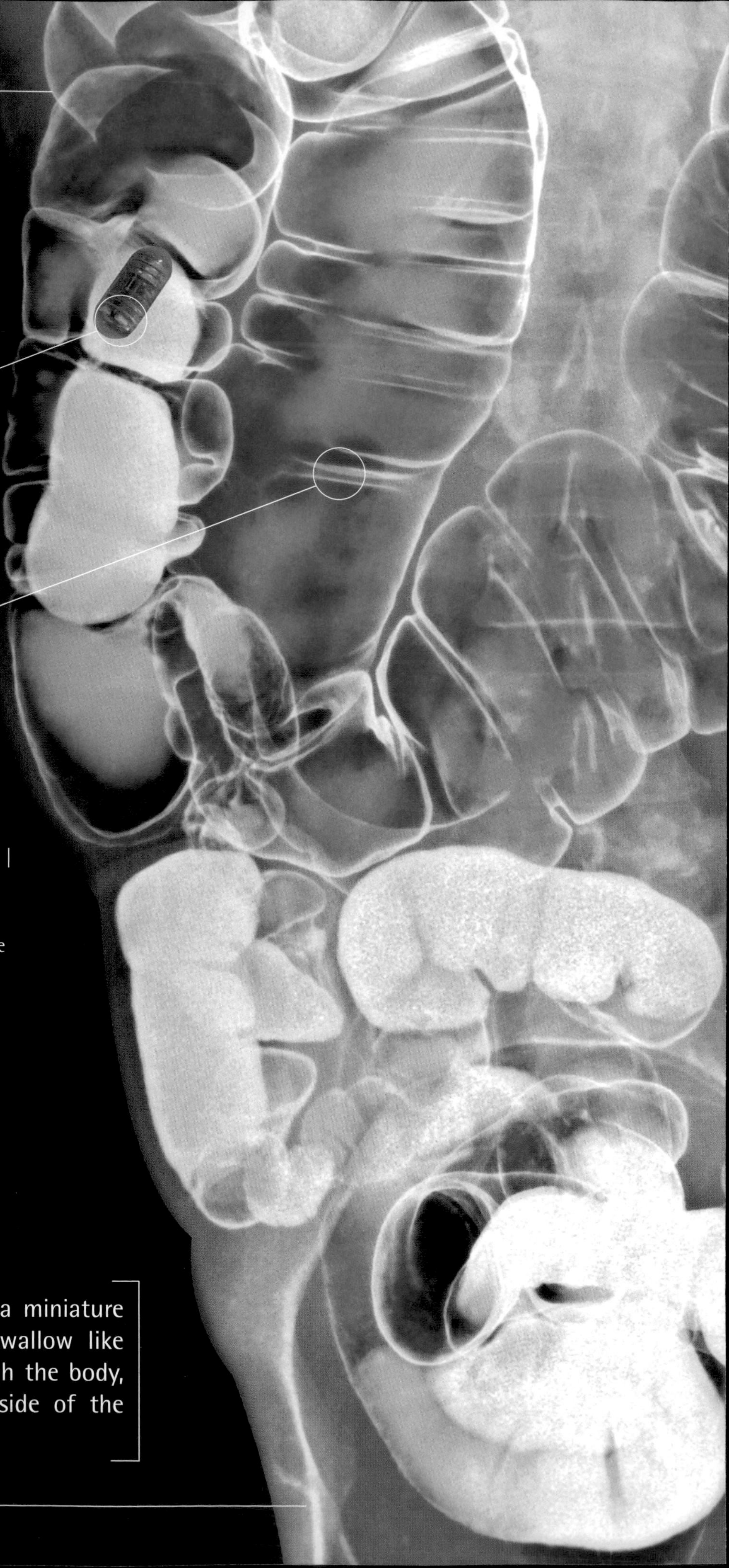

Capsule is 1 in
(30 mm) long and
$1/2$ in (11 mm) wide.

Natural contractions
of the intestine's walls
push the capsule
through the body.

▶ This colored X-ray reveals the
twists and turns of the human
intestines. The camera capsule
takes around 50,000 images
during its seven-hour journey
through the small intestine.
Played back at high speed, the
images produce a half-hour
video of the camera's findings.

▶▶ The camera capsule is a miniature
video camera you can swallow like
a pill. As it passes through the body,
the capsule films the inside of the
small intestine. ▶▶

Image: X-ray of intestines with camera capsule

☒ Endoscopy

▶The viewing device that surgeons normally use to look inside the body is called an endoscope. There are many different types, each suited to viewing a different part of the body. The simplest ones consist of a rigid tube with a lens at one end and a light at the other. The surgeon peers through the lens as though using a microscope.

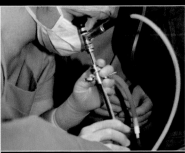

Surgeon looks through an endoscope

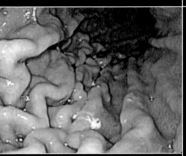

Endoscope view of the stomach

◀More sophisticated endoscopes have a flexible tube and a video camera at the tip, so the surgeon can view images on a screen. Tiny forceps, scissors, or other attachments can be mounted on the tips of endoscopes. This makes it possible to carry out keyhole surgery—operations performed through a small incision in the body.

≫ HOW THE CAMERA CAPSULE WORKS

One of the trickiest parts of the body to examine is the small intestine. It is 21 ft (6 m) in length, and doctors can see only the first third using an endoscope. However, with a camera capsule, the entire length of the small intestine can be filmed in color. The capsule is a miracle of miniaturization, incorporating a digital camera, light source, and radio transmitter in a streamlined package not much bigger than a pill. It passes slowly through the small intestine, taking two pictures every second. The images are transmitted as radio waves to a receiver worn on a belt. The receiver also records the camera's location, so doctors can pinpoint any abnormality

KEY COMPONENTS OF THE CAMERA CAPSULE

Torpedo-shaped waterproof casing

Battery provides power for at least seven hours.

Radio antenna sends images to receiver.

Color image transmitter

Image sensor

Diode illuminates path through intestine.

Wide-angle lens views intestine.

Transparent optical dome covers lens.

▶▶ See also: Camera p62, Fiber optic p244, Radio waves p249, Robot surgery p208

BIONIC LIMBS

▶▶A prosthesis is an artificial replacement for a part of the body. Prosthetic feet allow Paralympic athletes to sprint almost as fast as able-bodied runners. ▶▶

>> HOW A PROSTHETIC FOOT WORKS

HOW A PROSTHETIC RUNNING FOOT ABSORBS SHOCK AND STORES ENERGY

Prosthetic foot on the starting block

Rubber grips on both soles provide equal traction.

Prosthetic foot absorbs shock of impact.

Precision-molded socket provides a tight but comfortable fit.

Prosthetic foot bends as it bears the body's weight.

Prosthetic foot springs back into shape, catapulting runner forward.

Modern prosthetic feet are made from carbon-fiber composite—a combination of carbon-fiber filaments and plastic. This material is very strong and highly resistant to corrosion and stress, yet also lightweight and flexible. Varying the arrangement of carbon fibers in the mold allows designers to change the stiffness of the foot.

The carbon-fiber feet worn by athletes are designed to mimic the natural springiness of the human leg, storing energy as they are compressed and releasing it again as they spring back into shape. For everyday use, smaller, more lifelike prosthetic feet are worn instead. Some designs have the appearance of skin.

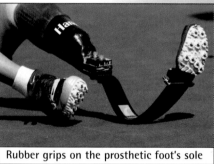

Rubber grips on the prosthetic foot's sole

⌄ Bionic bodies

▶The dream of prosthetics research is to create mechanical (bionic) limbs that the brain can control directly, such as mechanical hands that can pick things up with the dexterity of a normal hand. Prosthetic limbs that respond to movements in a patient's muscles already exist, but connecting a machine to the body's nervous system has yet to be achieved.

Mechanical hand

◀◀BACK
Early prosthetic limbs were made of wood and metal. Major advances in design happened after World War I and II, when many soldiers lost limbs.

Some artificial body parts could become obsolete in the future as scientists develop new ways of growing replacement organs from a person's own cells.

FORWARD▶▶

▶▶ See also: Carbon p241, Skin graft p216, Sneaker p50

▶ **Running on a pair of prosthetic feet,** 17-year-old Oscar Pistorius of South Africa won the gold medal in the 200-meter sprint at the 2004 Paralympics in Athens. He crossed the finish line at 21.97 seconds, smashing the world record for double amputees. His prosthetic feet, called Cheetahs, are custom-made for track and field sports.

Soft liner connects skin with socket of prosthetic foot.

▲ **US athlete** April Holmes won the bronze medal for the long jump at the 2004 Paralympics in Athens. She also set two new world records for her class— single below-knee amputees—in the 100-meter and 200-meter sprints.

Curved carbon-fiber foot springs back.

Traction is provided by rubber grip on sole.

215

CELLS

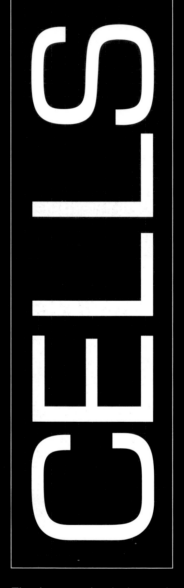

The human body is made of 100 trillion cells, all of which are too small for the naked eye to see. Thanks to the microscope, we can view this miniature world with amazing clarity.

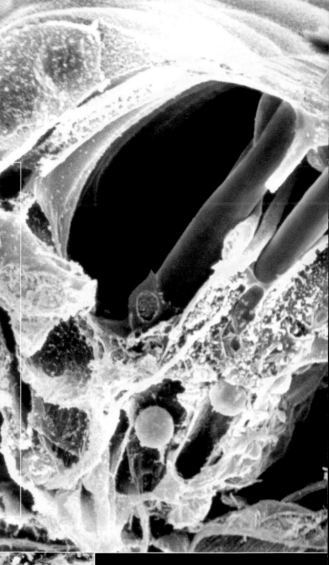

≫ Inner ear

This view through an electron microscope reveals the inner ear's hair cells, which help to give us the sense of sound. Magnified about 1,700 times, the image shows four rows of hair cells, the main bodies of which appear red. Tiny hairs, shown orange, project through a membrane at the top of the picture. When sound waves ripple through the fluid-filled inner ear, this membrane wobbles, tugging the hairs. The movement makes the hair cells generate nerve impulses, which travel to the brain.

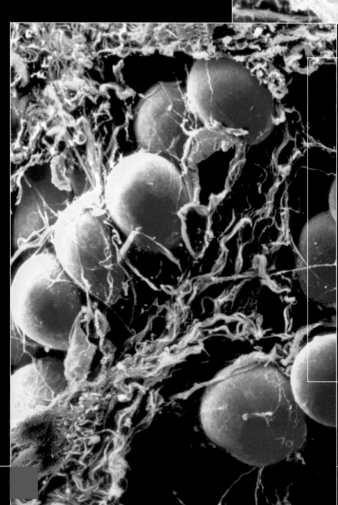

≪ Fat cells

Seen through an electron microscope, these fat cells look like tiny bubbles, surrounded by fibers of connective tissue. Fat cells are among the largest cells in the human body. Each cell contains a single, large globule of fat. Any fat eaten but not used by the body gets stored as fat cells. As well as providing a store of energy, fat cells form an insulating layer below the skin, helping the body retain heat.

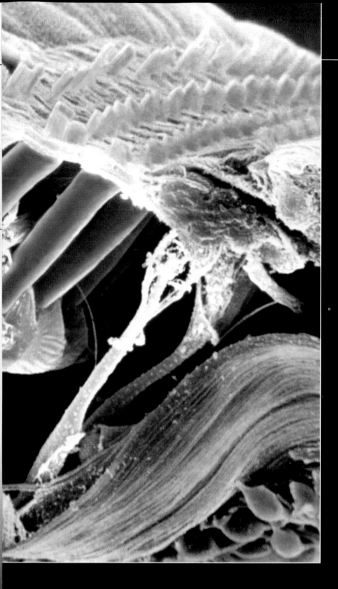

>> Follicle mites

The human face is the natural habitat for the wormlike creatures seen here, magnified 180 times under an electron microscope. These follicle mites live in the tiny shafts where hairs grow, especially eyelashes. Scientists believe most people have these harmless parasites.

V Taste buds

This is a thin slice of the human tongue, magnified 120 times. The large folds are papillae—the tiny bumps on our tongues that feel velvety. In the crevices between them are taste buds. These sensory cells detect the five main tastes—sweet, salty, sour, savory, and bitter.

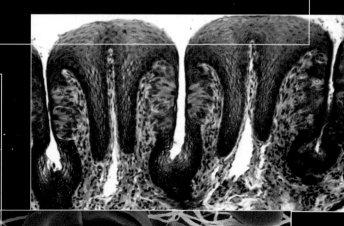

V Blood clot

A drop of blood contains about five million red blood cells. These carry oxygen around the body. Here, red blood cells are tangled up in fibrin, an insoluble protein that forms when a blood vessel is damaged. Fibrin snares moving blood cells so the blood solidifies and plugs the leak.

▶▶ See also: DNA p243, Imaging techniques p10, Vaccination p220

ANTIBIOTICS

▶▶Antibiotics are drugs taken to fight bacteria that have invaded the body. Though poisonous to bacteria, antibiotics are usually harmless to us. Most antibiotics are natural substances made by microorganisms such as fungi.▶▶

◀◀BACK

In 1928, Scottish scientist Alexander Fleming discovered antibiotics by accident, when he noted bacteria dying around *Penicillium* mold on a culture dish.

Although most modern antibiotics are still derived from bacteria and fungi, scientists hope to create new, synthetic antibiotics to fight superbugs.

FORWARD▶▶

▶ **This is the fungus** *Penicillium* magnified 6,000 times. *Penicillium* spreads by producing billions of microscopic spores. Each spore grows into a new patch of mold if it settles in a suitable place. *Penicillium* is the source of the first antibiotic to be discovered: penicillin. The fungus is probably most familiar to people as the dusty blue mold that grows on stale bread and rotting oranges.

>> HOW ANTIBIOTICS WORK

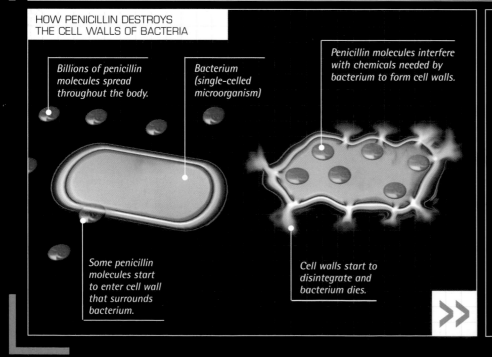

HOW PENICILLIN DESTROYS
THE CELL WALLS OF BACTERIA

Billions of penicillin molecules spread throughout the body.

Bacterium (single-celled microorganism)

Penicillin molecules interfere with chemicals needed by bacterium to form cell walls.

Some penicillin molecules start to enter cell wall that surrounds bacterium.

Cell walls start to disintegrate and bacterium dies.

Antibiotics first became widely used in World War II, when penicillin prevented gangrene and blood poisoning in wounded soldiers. Since then, many more antibiotics have been discovered, leading to cures for hundreds of infectious ailments. Antibiotics attack bacteria in different ways. Penicillin bursts cell walls, but other antibiotics halt cell growth or stop bacteria from multiplying. Some antibiotics, called broad-spectrum antibiotics, attack a range of bacteria. Others target specific types. Surgeons also use antibiotics to keep open wounds from becoming infected during operations. In the past, these operations carried a life-threatening risk of infection.

▶▶ See also: Antibody p240, Bacteria p241, Vaccination p220

⌄ Superbugs

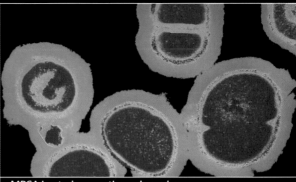

MRSA bacteria seen through a microscope

▲ Bacteria can evolve to become immune to antibiotics. When a person takes an antibiotic, the drug kills most of the bacteria, but a few mutant bacteria may have genes that allow them to survive. These go on to reproduce and spread. Antibiotic-resistant bacteria are sometimes called "superbugs." One superbug is MRSA (methicillin-resistant *Staphylococcus aureus*), which causes infections in wounds. It first appeared in Great Britain in 1961 and has since spread around the world.

Each spore floats in the air, spreading the Penicillium mold.

Branching network of fungus fibers

◀ **Image:** electron microscope view of *Penicillium* fungus

IVF

▶▶ In Vitro Fertilization (IVF) can make it possible for infertile couples to have children. IVF is a technique in which a woman's eggs are fertilized by a man's sperm outside the body and then implanted into the woman's womb to develop normally. ▶▶

Microscopic needle injects a sperm into the egg.

❯❯ HOW IN VITRO FERTILIZATION WORKS

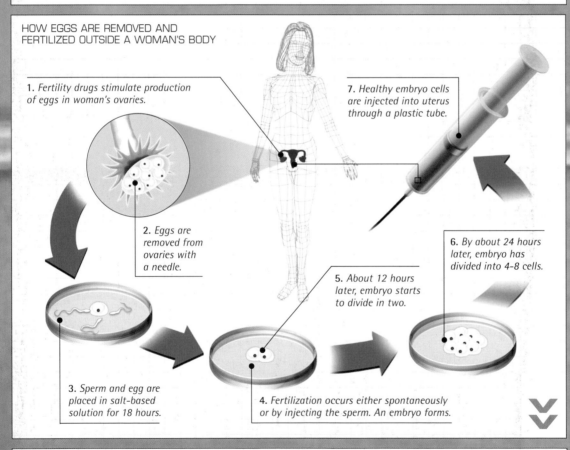

HOW EGGS ARE REMOVED AND FERTILIZED OUTSIDE A WOMAN'S BODY

1. Fertility drugs stimulate production of eggs in woman's ovaries.

7. Healthy embryo cells are injected into uterus through a plastic tube.

2. Eggs are removed from ovaries with a needle.

6. By about 24 hours later, embryo has divided into 4-8 cells.

5. About 12 hours later, embryo starts to divide in two.

3. Sperm and egg are placed in salt-based solution for 18 hours.

4. Fertilization occurs either spontaneously or by injecting the sperm. An embryo forms.

In vitro is Latin for "in glass"—when a couple is unable to conceive babies naturally, an artificial environment must be used, such as a glass test tube or petri dish. Common reasons for infertility include blockage of a woman's fallopian tubes (which carry eggs from the ovaries to the uterus) and a low sperm count in men. The technique has a 20 percent success rate with each attempt, so to improve chances, several embryos are often implanted, but this can lead to multiple pregnancies. IVF has become common in recent decades—one percent of all US children are now born this way. The technique has caused controversy because it involves the creation of human embryos, not all of which survive.

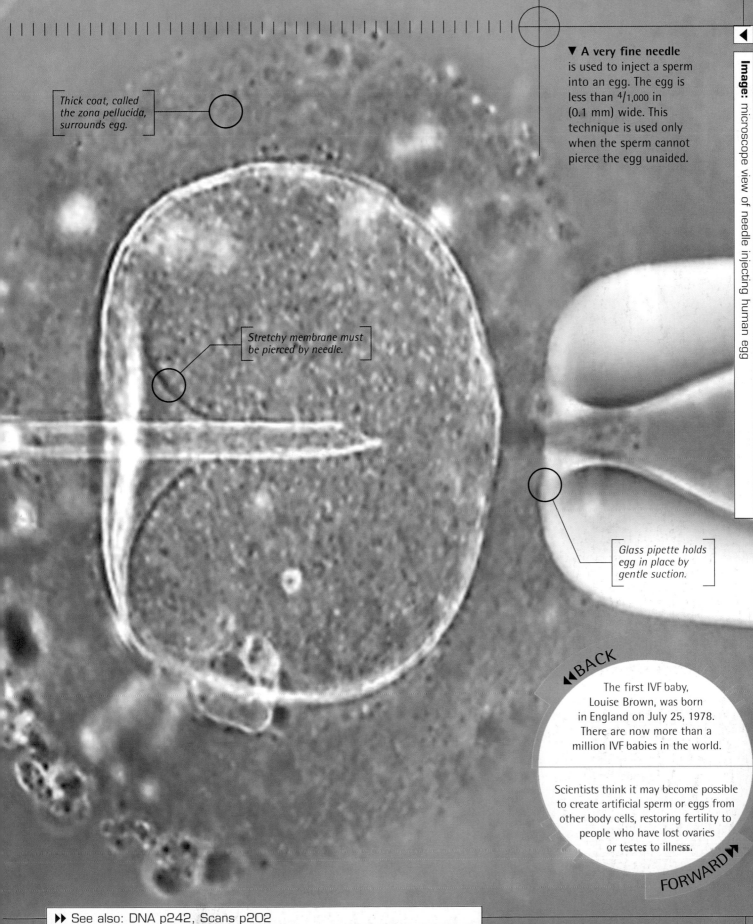

Image: microscope view of needle injecting human egg

Thick coat, called
the zona pellucida,
surrounds egg.

▼ **A very fine needle**
is used to inject a sperm
into an egg. The egg is
less than $^4/_{1,000}$ in
(0.1 mm) wide. This
technique is used only
when the sperm cannot
pierce the egg unaided.

Stretchy membrane must
be pierced by needle.

Glass pipette holds
egg in place by
gentle suction.

◀◀BACK

The first IVF baby,
Louise Brown, was born
in England on July 25, 1978.
There are now more than a
million IVF babies in the world.

Scientists think it may become possible
to create artificial sperm or eggs from
other body cells, restoring fertility to
people who have lost ovaries
or testes to illness.

FORWARD▶

▶▶ See also: DNA p242, Scans p202

BIOCHIP

▶▶ Biochips make it possible to screen a biological sample for thousands of different biochemicals at once. Most biochips are used to test for genes—the inherited instructions, made of DNA, that control the way cells work. Scientists can use biochips to find out which genes are "switched on" inside living cells. ▶▶

▼ **Biochips are** barely larger than postage stamps, yet a single chip can test for thousands of different genes. The surface of the chip bears an array of microscopic dots, each containing DNA from a different gene. Most biochips contain human DNA, which is fixed to the dots of the biochip by high-speed robots at manufacturing plants.

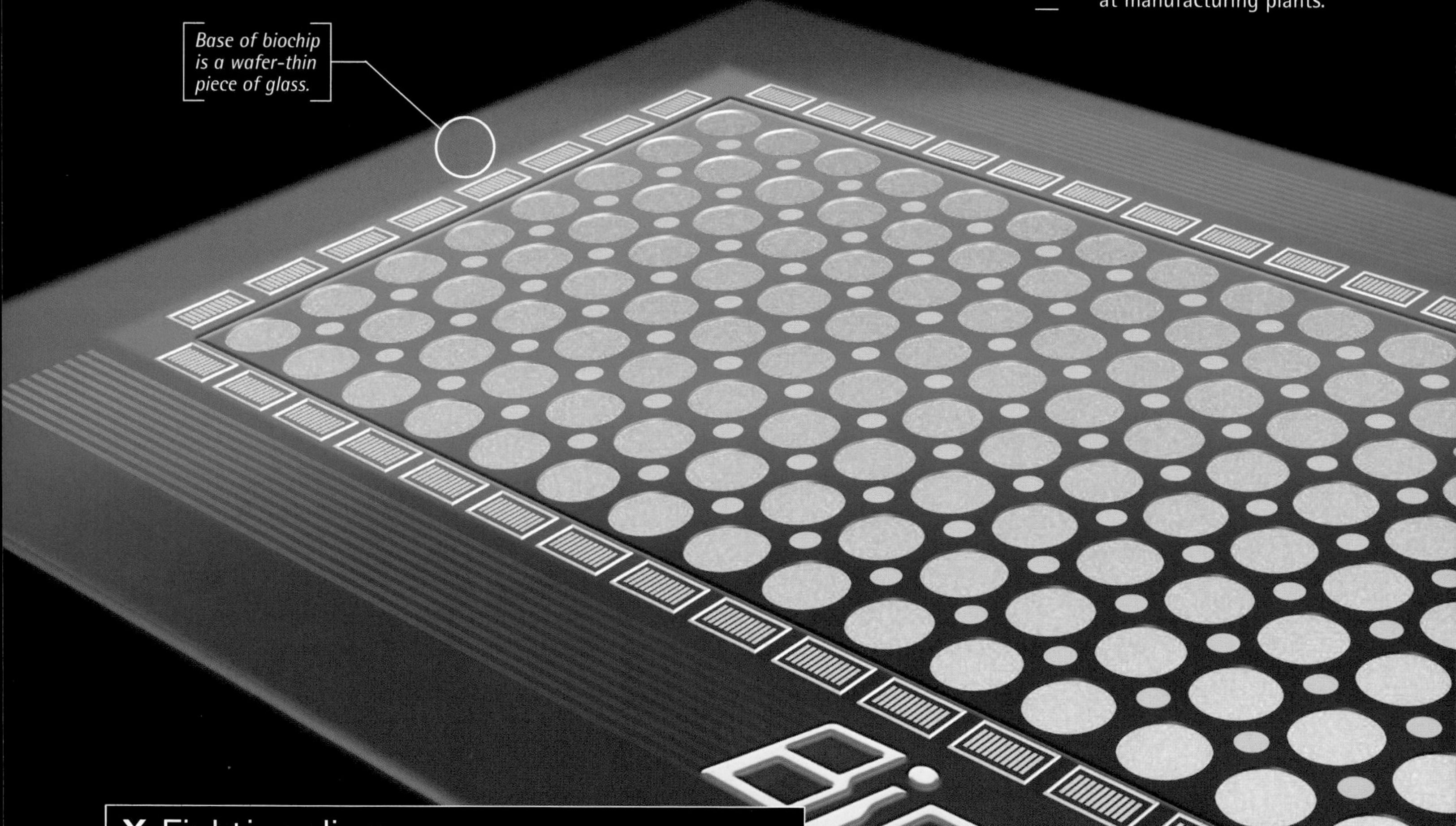

Base of biochip is a wafer-thin piece of glass.
Biochip

¥ Fighting disease

▶ Biochips could help scientists find a cure for malaria. In 2002, scientists created a biochip with genes from the parasite that causes malaria. Using the chip helped them to identify which genes are active at crucial points in the parasite's life cycle. By creating chemicals to block the active genes, scientists hope to create drugs that kill the parasites.

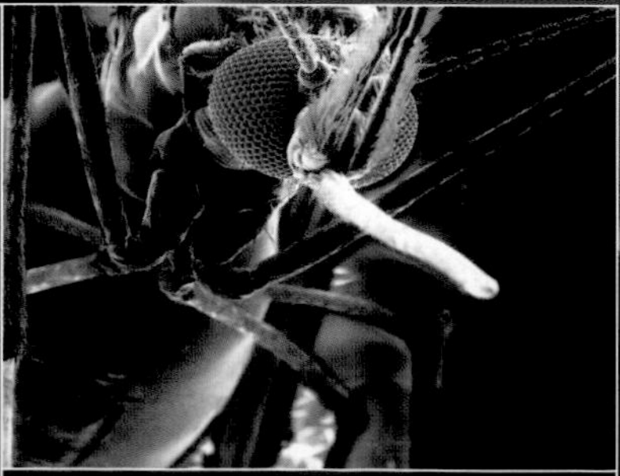

Malaria-carrying mosquito

≫ HOW A BIOCHIP WORKS

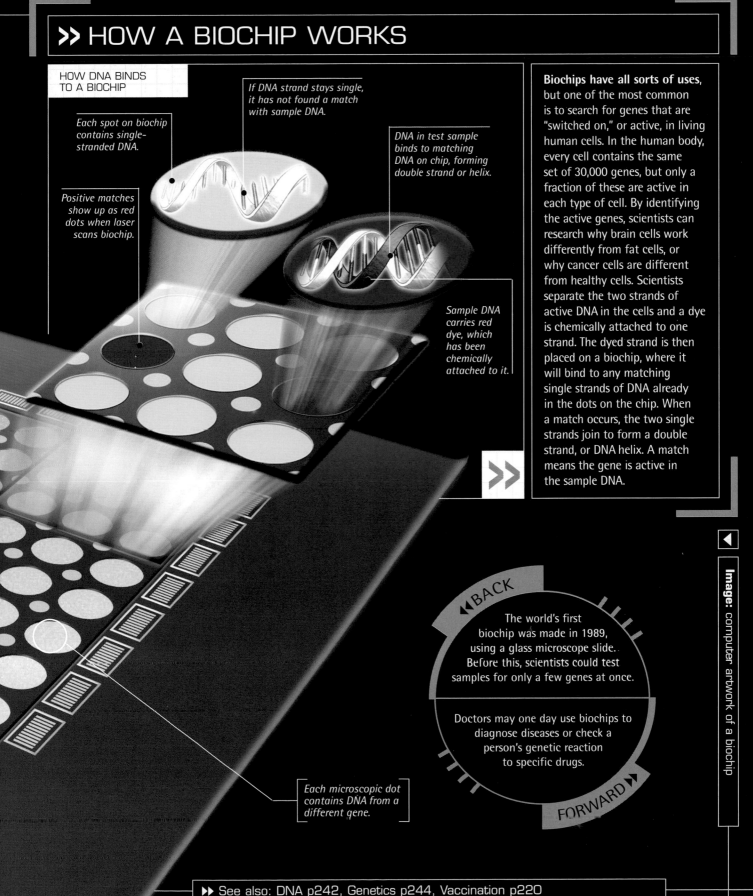

HOW DNA BINDS TO A BIOCHIP

Each spot on biochip contains single-stranded DNA.

If DNA strand stays single, it has not found a match with sample DNA.

DNA in test sample binds to matching DNA on chip, forming double strand or helix.

Positive matches show up as red dots when laser scans biochip.

Sample DNA carries red dye, which has been chemically attached to it.

Each microscopic dot contains DNA from a different gene.

Biochips have all sorts of uses, but one of the most common is to search for genes that are "switched on," or active, in living human cells. In the human body, every cell contains the same set of 30,000 genes, but only a fraction of these are active in each type of cell. By identifying the active genes, scientists can research why brain cells work differently from fat cells, or why cancer cells are different from healthy cells. Scientists separate the two strands of active DNA in the cells and a dye is chemically attached to one strand. The dyed strand is then placed on a biochip, where it will bind to any matching single strands of DNA already in the dots on the chip. When a match occurs, the two single strands join to form a double strand, or DNA helix. A match means the gene is active in the sample DNA.

≫

◄BACK

The world's first biochip was made in 1989, using a glass microscope slide. Before this, scientists could test samples for only a few genes at once.

Doctors may one day use biochips to diagnose diseases or check a person's genetic reaction to specific drugs.

FORWARD▶

Image: computer artwork of a biochip

▶▶ See also: DNA p242, Genetics p244, Vaccination p220

The human body is the most complex machine on the planet. It has about ten thousand billion cells—more cells than there are stars in the visible universe. New technology will have a dramatic effect on our ability to monitor and repair this astonishing mechanism.

Using nanotechnology, the science and technology of manipulating individual atoms and molecules, we may be able to build devices called molecular machines. These miniscule machines, or nanobots (one nanometer is about a million times smaller than a period on this page) may be able to reproduce themselves and perform tasks far beyond the scope of current medical technology. Nanobots could target and destroy cancerous cells one by one without damaging the surrounding healthy tissue, repair damaged cells, and reverse the aging process, or remove harmful plaque from the inner walls of our arteries.

> " Nanorobots may one day travel through the body, armed with chemical weapons, on a mission to destroy bacteria and viruses. "

Micromachines called micro-electro-mechanical systems, or MEMS, may also have a major impact on medical treatment. These use tiny sensors and motors etched onto a wafer of silicon thinner than a human hair. Already found in car air bags to detect movement, they may be used to repair blood vessels by 2020.

Some animals, such as lizard, can regrow a lost tail or leg. Humans, of course, do not have this ability. By taking cells, however, and seeding them on a special scaffolding, it may be possible to regenerate organs such as the liver or heart in the laboratory. By the end of the century, most parts of the body (except for the brain) could be replaced if they become faulty.

Cloning is another technology that offers us new ways of approaching health and medicine. Cloning involves taking genetic material from an adult or embryo cell and fusing it with an egg, which then develops. This technique is called therapeutic cloning. However, the use of human embryos for medical purposes is considered controversial by many. Despite this, cloning continues, and whole organs could be produced from single cells, or damaged cells could be replaced with healthy ones in the future. Cloning could also be used to create genetically modified pigs that would develop organs suitable for human transplants— a technique known as xenotransplantation.

Gene therapy has already successfully treated certain conditions that are caused by our genetic makeup. This technology, which targets and repairs faulty genes, may be used in the future to treat and prevent cancers and diseases such as Alzheimer's, arthritis, and heart disease.

Perhaps the most important new development of all will be something simpler than all these extraordinary new medical technologies—clean water. Millions of lives could be saved each year by ensuring that everyone on the planet has access to clean and safe drinking water. And the technology needed for this? Simple water purification systems.

ARTWORK OF NANOBOT
INJECTING DRUG IN HUMAN CELL

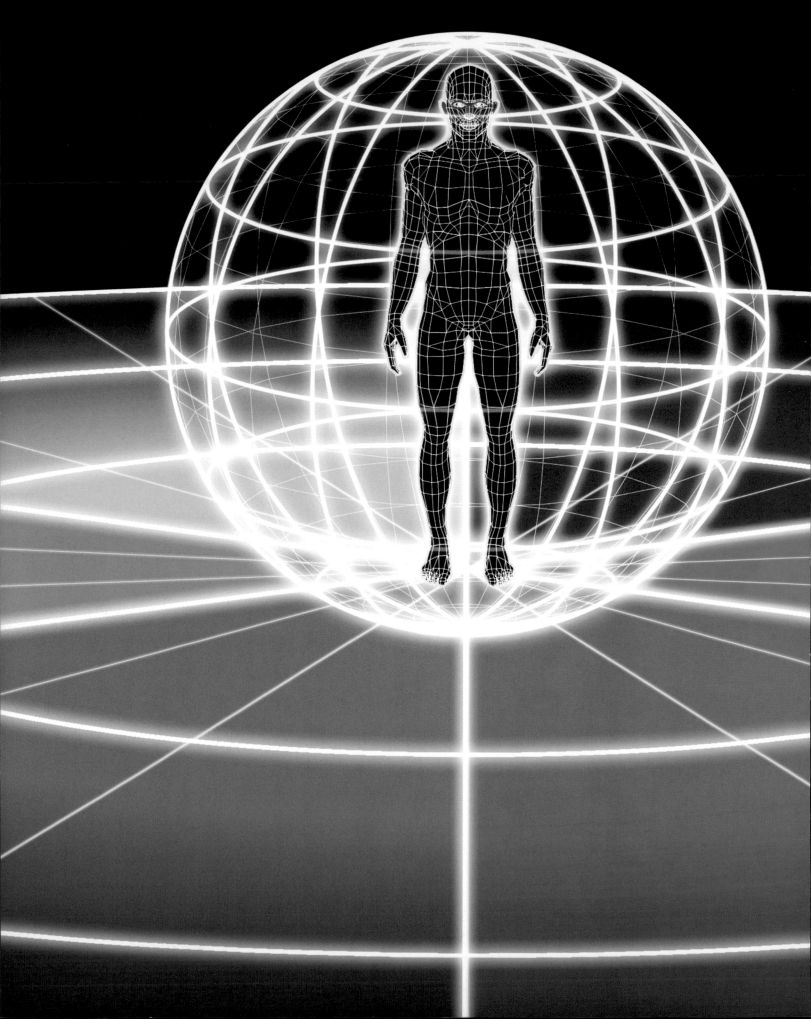

>>REFERENCE

Timeline >> Groundbreakers >> Techno terms >>
Index >> Acknowledgments

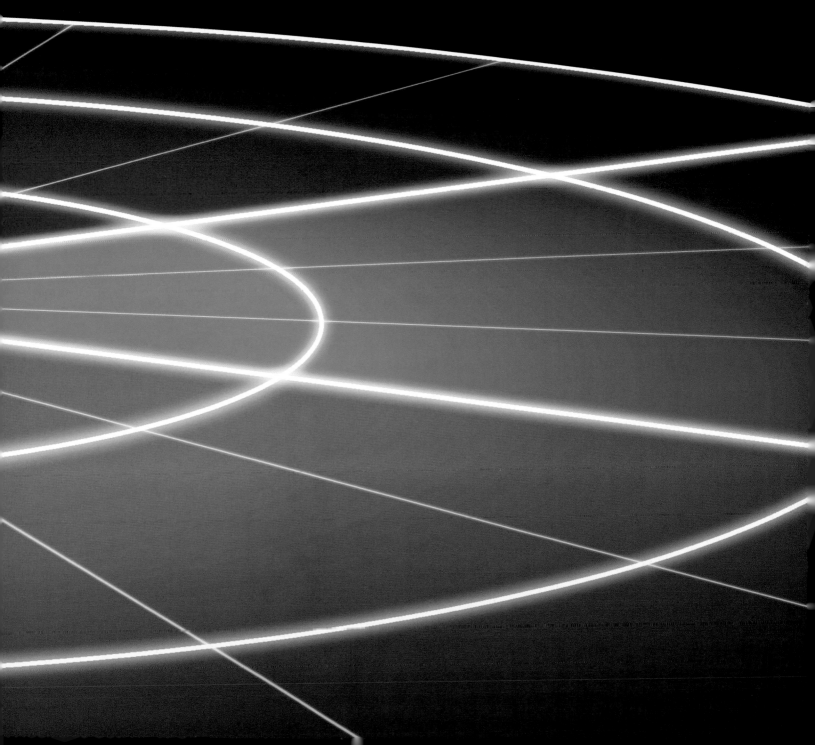

>> c. 3200 BC

Wheels first used for transportation. Ancient clay tablets show they were used on Mesopotamian chariots. A wheel with spokes first appeared in Egypt in about 2000 BC.

>> c. 1350 BC

Decimal numbers first used in China. Rather than inventing a new Chinese character for each number, a decimal system required just ten symbols.

>> 1450

Printing press with movable type invented by German Johannes Gutenberg. Books could now be produced more quickly, making literature accessible to a wider audience.

>> 1642

Mechanical adding machine invented by 19-year-old French mathematician Blaise Pascal. He designed it to help his father calculate sums in his work as a clerk.

>> 1752

Lightning rod invented by American Benjamin Franklin. It protects buildings during storms by transferring the electrical charge of a lightning strike safely to the ground.

>> 1792

Scottish scientist William Murdoch invents gas lighting. After using gas made from coal to light his home, he began manufacturing gas lighting on a commercial scale.

>> 1800

Infrared rays discovered by German astronomer William Herschel. He demonstrated there was a temperature increase just beyond the red end of the visible light spectrum.

>> 1803

Modern atomic theory proposed by English chemist John Dalton. He explained the concept of atoms and described how elements form compounds.

>> 1835

Mechanical computer designed by English mathematician Charles Babbage. It possessed all the essential logical features of the modern computer, such as running programs.

>> 1852

Safety passenger elevator invented by US inventor Elisha Graves Otis. It included a safety device to prevent the passenger car from falling if a cable should snap.

>> 1865

Austrian monk Gregor Mendel publishes his laws of genetic inheritance and the results of his experiments, which explored the inherited characteristics of pea plants.

>> 1876

First practical telephone invented by Scottish-born scientist Alexander Graham Bell. The technology he developed paved the way for electronic sound recording.

>> 1885

First practical car to be powered by an internal combustion engine built by German engineer Karl Benz. The vehicle had three wheels and an open carriage.

>> 1887

First wearable contact lenses invented by German physiologist Adolf Eugen Fick. They were made from heavy brown glass and were first fitted on animals.

>> 1895

Portable motion-picture camera, film processing unit, and projector called the Cinematographe invented by French brothers Auguste and Louis Lumiére.

>> 1895

X-rays discovered by German physicist Wilhelm Röntgen while experimenting with electron beams. A week after his discovery, he took an X-ray photograph of his wife's hand.

>> 1910

First synthetic drug produced by German bacteriologist Paul Ehrlich. He developed 605 different compounds before finding one that could kill a bacterium that caused disease.

>> 1910

First neon light displayed to the public by French engineer Georges Claude. The device was made by applying an electrical discharge to a sealed tube of neon gas.

>> c. AD 1000

First paper money printed in China. It was known as flying money because it was so light it could blow out of a merchant's hand.

>> c. 1280

Mechanical clocks invented in Europe. They used a mechanism called an escapement, which ticks in a steady rhythm, causing gears to move in a series of equal jumps.

>> 1686

Mathematical Principles of Natural Philosophy by English scientist Isaac Newton is published, containing the three laws of motion and his theory of universal gravitation.

>> 1714

First mercury thermometer invented by German physicist Gabriel Fahrenheit. In 1724, he introduced the Fahrenheit temperature scale.

>> 1796

The world's first vaccination created by English physician Edward Jenner. He developed a vaccination for smallpox, a deadly disease that was widespread in the 18th century.

>> 1799

First battery invented by Italian physicist Alessandro Volta. Called the voltaic pile, it was made from thin sheets of copper and zinc separated by moist paper board.

>> 1809

First electric light invented by English chemist Humphry Davy. He used wires to connect a battery to a charcoal strip, which glowed when charged with electricity.

>> 1826

First photograph taken by French inventor Joseph Nicéphore Niepce. The pewter plate he used was exposed to sunlight for eight hours to create the image.

>> 1852

The gyroscope—a spinning wheel set in a movable frame— invented by French physicist Jean Bernard Léon Foucault. Gyroscopes are used in navigational instruments.

>> 1854

Boolean algebra developed by British mathematician George Boole. Microprocessors use the mathematics of Boolean algebra in their calculations.

>> 1879

First four-stroke, piston-cycle, internal combustion engine built by German traveling salesman Nikolaus August Otto. This paved the way for the development of motor vehicles.

>> 1879

First practical electric light bulb developed by US inventor Thomas Alva Edison. Using a carbon filament, this bulb could glow for over 1,500 hours.

>> 1888

German physicist Heinrich Hertz conducts experiments that prove the existence of radio waves. His discoveries led to the development of the radio.

>> 1893

Zipper patented by US inventor Whitcomb Judson. The invention was not an immediate success—it wasn't until the 1920s that the zipper became popular.

>> 1903

First working airplane invented by US brothers and self-taught engineers Orville and Wilbur Wright. The plane stayed in the air for 12 seconds.

>> 1907

First helicopter to achieve free flight while carrying a passenger invented by French bicycle maker Paul Cornu. It flew for 20 seconds and rose 1 ft (0.3 m) above the ground.

>> 1923

Method of flash-freezing food so that it stays fresh invented by Clarence Birdseye, a US businessman. The first frozen vegetables were sold to the public in 1930.

>> 1928

The antibiotic penicillin discovered accidentally by Scottish research assistant Alexander Fleming after he noticed a mold attacking bacteria in a set of culture dishes.

>> 1930

Jet engine independently invented by English engineer Frank Whittle and German airplane designer Hans von Ohain. The first engine was not built until 1937.

>> 1933

Frequency modulation (FM) radio invented by US engineer Edwin Howard Armstrong. FM radio receivers produced a clear sound that is free of static.

>> 1946

Microwave oven invented by US scientist Percy Spencer after he noticed that his chocolate bar melted when he stood near a magnetron of a radar machine.

>> 1947

Transistor invented by Americans John Bardeen, Walter Brattain, and William Shockley at Bell Laboratories, the research arm of telephone company AT&T.

>> 1953

Black box flight recorder invented by Australian aviation scientist David Warren to record voices and instrument readings during flights to help investigate causes of crashes.

>> 1956

Hovercraft—a vehicle that can travel across water supported by a pillow of air—invented by English scientist Christopher Cockerell.

>> 1959

Internal heart pacemaker invented by US scientist Wilson Greatbatch. He also invented a corrosion-free lithium battery to power it.

>> 1960

First working laser built by US physicist Theodore Maiman. Similar devices had been made earlier by other scientists, but none produced visible light.

>> 1967

First successful human heart transplant carried out by South African surgeon Dr. Christiaan Barnard. The 55-year-old recipient lived for 18 days after the operation.

>> 1968

Computer mouse patented by American inventor Douglas Engelbert. He called his invention an "X-Y Position Indicator for a Display System."

>> 1973

Post-it® Notes invented by Art Fry, a researcher at American company 3M. He became frustrated with paper bookmarks falling out of his church hymnbook.

>> 1975

The first laser printer was developed at the Xerox Research Center in the United States, where an engineer developed a way to add laser light power to photocopier technology.

>> 1981

First portable computer, Osborne 1, launched. Designed by the Osborne Computer Corporation, it had two floppy disk drives and a tiny 5-in (13-cm) screen.

>> 1984

Apple Macintosh computer invented. It revolutionized the personal computer with its simple, graphic interface and mouse pointing device.

>> 1990

World Wide Web/Internet protocol (HTTP) and World Wide Web language (HTML) created by British scientist Tim Berners-Lee.

>> 1995

Computer language Java invented by Canadian James Gosling. Java made it possible to connect different computer systems together.

>> 2003

The Human Genome Project, which began in the 1990s, completed. It was an international research effort to sequence and map all human genes.

>> 2003

Infrared Fever Screening System—invented by Singapore Technologies Electronics—used in public buildings to scan for people with a high temperature from a fever.

>> 1938

Ballpoint pen invented by Hungarian Ladislao Biro. He came up with idea after observing how much faster newspaper ink dried compared to fountain pen ink.

>> 1945

The world's first practical digital computer, ENIAC 1, was built. When a moth was discovered to have blown a circuit, the computer bug was invented, too.

>> 1948

Velcro® developed by Swiss inventor George de Mestral. He came up with the idea when burrs caught on his clothes while he was walking his dog.

>> 1953

Double-helix structure of DNA discovered by British and US scientists Francis Crick and James Watson. They were helped by the research of scientist Rosalind Francis.

>> 1957

The first artificial Earth satellite, *Sputnik 1*, launched by the Soviet Union (now Russia). This marked the start of the space race between the Soviet Union and United States.

>> 1958

Microchip separately invented by American scientists Jack Kilby and Robert Noyce. This invention revolutionized computer technology.

>> 1962

First industrial robot invented by Unimation in the United States. The robot was installed at General Motors automobile factory in New Jersey.

>> 1965

Moore's Law developed by US scientist Gordon Moore. The law stated that the number of transistors on a microchip would double every 18 months—and has proved true.

>> 1969

ATM (automatic teller machine) invented by American Don Wetzel. It took $5 million to develop, and the first machine was installed in a bank in New York City.

>> 1971

Microprocessor chip invented by Frederico Faggin, Tcd Hoff, and Stan Mazor at computer firm Intel. They put a computer's central processing unit onto a small microchip.

>> 1979

Walkman® personal stereo invented by Japanese electronics company Sony. It was the first portable music player and came with lightweight headphones.

>> 1981

The first reusable spacecraft, the Space Shuttle, launched by NASA in the United States. *Columbia* returned safely to Earth two days after takeoff.

>> 1985

Windows® operating system for personal computers developed by US company Microsoft. It did not go on sale until two years later.

>> 1986

Disposable cameras introduced by Japanese company Fuji. The camera had film already inside it and was taken whole to the film developing lab.

>> 1995

Standard format for the DVD (Digital Versatile/Video Disc) agreed by all the major electronics firms involved in its invention. The first DVD players went on sale in 1996.

>> 1998

First MP3 player invented. The AMP MP3 Playback Engine was developed by Croatian Tomislav Uzelac of Advanced Multimedia Products.

>> 2004

SonoPrep, a device that can deliver medicine via sound waves rather than injection, invented by bioengineer Robert Langer of the Sontra Medical Corporation.

>> 2004

Translucent concrete developed by Hungarian architect Aron Losonczi. Called LiTraCon, it was made by adding glass fibers to normal concrete mix.

235

Groundbreakers

THOMAS EDISON

CHARLES BABBAGE (1791–1871)

In 1823, British mathematician Charles Babbage designed a machine called a difference engine, which was able to calculate mathematical tables. He went on to propose a device called an analytical engine, which would have the ability to make mathematical decisions as it was calculating. This machine wasn't built, but its design contained many elements that are used in modern computers.

ALEXANDER GRAHAM BELL (1847–1922)

Scottish-born inventor Alexander Graham Bell is best known for his invention of the telephone. In 1875, using the technology of the telegraph, Bell and his assistant, Thomas A. Watson, constructed instruments that could transmit recognizable voicelike sounds over a telegraph wire.

BELL LABORATORIES

Formed as the research and development section of the American Telephone and Telegraph company, (AT&T), Bell Laboratories has become one of the top research institutions in the United States. The transistor, the laser, the solar cell, and communications satellites are among the many technological advances developed at Bell.

TIM BERNERS-LEE (1955–)

British inventor of the World Wide Web, Berners-Lee joined together two technologies—hypertext (a way of displaying documents with automated cross-references) and the Internet. On the World Wide Web, hypertext is viewed using a web browser program, which retrieves web pages from web servers and displays them on a computer. The first website was put online on August 6, 1991.

LADISLAO BIRO (1899–1985)

While working as a journalist, Hungarian-born Biro noticed that newspaper ink dried more quickly than that used in a fountain pen. He tried to use the same ink in a fountain pen, but found that it would not flow into the nib. Working with his brother, Georg, a chemist, he invented the ballpoint pen, in which a ball in a socket picks up ink from a cartridge and deposits it on the paper.

AUGUSTA ADA BYRON KING, COUNTESS OF LOVELACE (1815–1852)

Lovelace became interested in the work of mathematician Charles Babbage and worked with him to improve the design of his analytical engine. She also wrote a plan to program Babbage's machine to solve mathematical problems—making her the first computer programmer.

WALLACE CAROTHERS (1896–1937)

US chemist Wallace Carothers is considered the founder of the science of manufactured polymers. He led the research division of the DuPont chemical company, where his team invented neoprene, a synthetic rubber, and nylon, a synthetic fiber.

JACQUES ALEXANDRE CESAR CHARLES (1746–1823)

French physicist Charles formulated Charles' law, which states that the volume of a gas at constant pressure is proportional to its temperature. This law is fundamental to the operation of any internal combustion engine. For example, heating the air inside a jet engine causes it to expand and rush out of the engine as a fast jet.

GEORGES CLAUDE (1870–1960)

French inventor Georges Claude was the first to apply an electrical discharge to a sealed tube of neon gas to create a neon light.

FRANCIS CRICK (1916–2004) & JAMES WATSON (1928–)

In 1953, English physics graduate Francis Crick and US research fellow James Watson discovered the molecular structure of DNA. They proposed that the DNA molecule consisted of two helical (spiral) chains— a double helix. They theorized that genetic information is passed on through DNA in the genes, which was later demonstrated through the work of other scientists. On the day of their discovery, Francis Crick walked into a local pub and announced: "We have found the secret of life."

WILLIAM CROOKES (1832–1919)

English scientist Crookes experimented with passing electric currents through glass tubes containing gases. The ionized gas in the tube gives out a light—as in a neon sign.

DOROTHY CROWFOOT HODGKIN (1910–1994)

Egyptian-born chemist Dorothy Crowfoot Hodgkin used X-rays to discover the crystal structure of molecules, including penicillin, vitamin B-12, vitamin D, and insulin. This contributed greatly to the development of synthetic versions of these substances, leading to the control of many diseases, such as diabetes.

GOTTLIEB DAIMLER (1834–1900)

German mechanical engineer Gottlieb Daimler was a key figure in the development of the car. He developed the world's first motorcycle in 1885 and the world's first four-wheeled car in 1886.

RUDOLF DIESEL (1858–1913)

French-German engineer Diesel invented an engine that worked using combustion in a cylinder. His pressure-ignited heat engine, the Diesel engine, was the first that proved that fuel could be ignited without a spark.

JAMES DYSON (1947–)

British-born engineer and inventor James Dyson developed a bagless vacuum cleaner—the Dyson Cyclone. It has been manufactured since 1993.

THOMAS EDISON (1847–1931)

US inventor Thomas Edison patented hundreds of inventions in the late 19th and early 20th centuries. He developed the first commercially viable light bulb, invented the phonograph, and refined other inventions, such as motion pictures and typewriters. He famously said: "Genius is one percent inspiration and 99 percent perspiration."

ALBERT EINSTEIN (1879–1955)

German-born physicist Albert Einstein was one of the most influential scientists of the 20th century. He revolutionized our concepts of space and time and developed the theories used to build models of the universe. As well as providing a mathematical description of the random movement of particles, Einstein described the photoelectric effect, in which electrons are emitted when light falls on certain materials. In 1905 he proposed the special theory of relativity, which described the physics of objects moving at constant velocities. The theory contained the equation $E=mc^2$, which explains the relationship between mass and energy. Einstein went on to formulate the general theory of relativity, which explains how gravity works.

EUROPEAN SPACE AGENCY

The European Space Agency (ESA) pools the resources and expertise of many European countries to research space. ESA conducts projects and missions to find out more about Earth and the solar system. It also develops satellite-based technologies. In February 2005, ESA launched the Rosetta space probe, which will land on a comet in 2014.

MICHAEL FARADAY (1791–1867)

English scientist Michael Faraday used electromagnetism to make the first electric motor. He also discovered electromagnetic induction, which laid the foundations for James Clerk Maxwell's understanding of light and Heinrich Hertz's discovery of radio waves. He also invented the transformer. Faraday's momentous discoveries were responsible for the electric generators and motors that power much of the modern world.

ALEXANDER FLEMING (1881–1955)

In 1928, while Scottish scientist Alexander Fleming was working as a research assistant, he discovered a mold growing on a set of culture dishes. The dishes were growing the *Staphylococcus* germ, which causes wounds to become septic. Fleming noticed that germs had stopped developing where the mold was growing. The mold was named penicillin—Fleming had discovered the first antibiotic.

JEAN FOUCAULT (1819–1896)

French physicist Foucault made the first accurate measurement of the speed of light. He also demonstrated Earth's rotation using a long pendulum and invented the gyroscope—a wheel mounted so that it can spin in any direction while its axis continues to point in just one direction.

ROSALIND FRANKLIN (1920–1958)

British scientist Franklin used X-ray crystallography (mapping atoms by looking at an image of a crystal under an X-ray beam) to analyze the DNA molecule. Her research was used by Crick and Watson in their description of the DNA structure. Her contribution to this discovery was not acknowledged during her lifetime.

YURI GAGARIN (1934–1968)

On April 12, 1963, Russian cosmonaut Gagarin became the first human to travel into space. His mission lasted one orbit of Earth.

BILL GATES (1955–)

Gates founded US computer software company Microsoft with school friend Paul Allen in 1975. Today, it is the world's largest software company and its operating systems and programs are used on most computers.

DR. IVAN GETTING (1912–2003)

American Ivan Getting was key in developing Global Positioning System (GPS), a satellite navigational system. It was originally designed for military

purposes, but is now used in cars, boats, planes, computers, and phones.

DR. JOHN GORRIE (1803–1855)

US physician John Gorrie was a pioneer in refrigeration, air conditioning, and the manufacture of ice. He built a refrigerator in 1844, which made ice to cool the air for patients suffering from yellow fever.

WILLIAM GROVE (1811–1896)

In 1839, Welsh lawyer and scientist William Grove invented an electrochemical cell, which he called a gas voltaic cell. It was the forerunner of modern fuel cells.

HEINRICH HERTZ (1847–1894)

German scientist Heinrich Hertz discovered radio waves in 1888, although James Clerk Maxwell had predicted their existence in 1864. Hertz conducted experiments to produce electromagnetic waves and measure their wavelength. The unit of frequency, the hertz, is named after him.

DR. MARCIAN EDWARD "TED" HOFF JR. (1937–)

Ted Hoff was an engineer at Intel Corporation in the United States. In 1971, with his colleagues Frederico Faggin and Stan Mazor, he designed the Intel 4004, a computer-on-a-chip microprocessor. The technology placed a computer's central processing unit (CPU) and memory onto a silicon chip.

JOHN PHILIP HOLLAND (1841–1914)

Irish inventor Holland built the first practical submarine, the *Holland VI* in 1897, which was purchased by the US Navy and renamed the USS *Holland*.

STEVE JOBS (1955–) AND STEVE WOZNIAK (1950–)

Americans Jobs and Wozniak created the first successful personal computer, the Apple I. They built the early models in a garage. Apple, the company they founded, is now one of the biggest computer manufacturers in the world.

ALBERT EINSTEIN

JAMES PRESCOTT JOULE (1818–1889)

While experimenting with paddle wheels, the English physicist James Prescott Joule discovered the mechanical equivalent of heat—the amount of heat generated is precisely related to the amount of mechanical movement. He also demonstrated that different types of energy can be converted from one form to another, and that energy is neither created nor destroyed. The unit of energy, the joule, is named after him.

CHARLES KAO (1933–)

Chinese scientist Charles Kao proposed the possibility of using fibers in telecommunications. This led to the development of optical fibers.

JACK KILBY (1923–) AND ROBERT NOYCE (1927–1990)

Two scientists, unaware of each other's activities, invented integrated circuits at almost the same time. The integrated circuit placed previously separated items, such as transistors, resistors, capacitors, and connecting wire, onto a single crystal, or microchip, made of semiconductor material. Kilby used germanium and Noyce used silicon for the semiconductor material. Jack Kilby also invented the portable calculator in 1967. Robert Noyce went on to found Intel, the company responsible for the invention of the microprocessor.

JOSEPH CARL ROBNETT LICKLIDER (1915–1990)

Licklider was a US psychologist with an interest in computer science. In 1965, he wrote a book called *Libraries of the Future*, in which he outlined his vision of a computer system that could connect the user to "everyday business, industrial, government, and professional information, and perhaps, also to news entertainment, and education." His ideas influenced the development of the Internet.

JOSEPH LISTER (1827–1915)

British physician Joseph Lister noticed that infections in wounds after operations were very common, despite efforts to keep hospitals clean. He began to spray carbolic acid on surgical instruments, wounds, and dressings. This first antiseptic dramatically reduced death rates.

GUGLIELMO MARCONI (1874–1937)

Italian scientist Marconi developed radio communication. In 1895, just seven years after the discovery of radio waves by Heinrich Hertz, Marconi succeeded in transmitting a radio message in Morse code.

JAMES CLERK MAXWELL (1831–1879)

Scottish physicist and mathematician James Clerk Maxwell identified light as part of the electromagnetic spectrum and developed mathematical equations to demonstrate this. His electromagnetic theory of light led directly to Heinrich Hertz's discovery of radio waves and to related advances in science and technology that have transformed the modern world.

GREGOR MENDEL (1822–1884)

Austrian botanist Gregor Mendel is considered the founder of genetics. He experimented with pea plants and noticed that the characteristics of offspring, such as height, exhibited recessive and dominant behavior.

GEORGE DE MESTRAL (1907–1990)

Swiss inventor George de Mestral had the idea for Velcro® in 1948 when he became covered in burrs while walking his dog. He perfected his design, which uses hooks and loops to fasten two pieces of the fabric together, and patented it in 1955.

NATIONAL AERONAUTICS AND SPACE ADMINISTRATION (NASA)

The National Aeronautics and Space Administration (NASA) was formed in the United States in 1958 in reaction to the Soviet Union's launch of the first artificial satellite, *Sputnik 1*. NASA's first high-profile program was Project Mercury, which investigated whether humans could survive in space. In 1969, NASA succeeded in putting the first humans on the Moon. In 1981, NASA launched the Space Shuttle program, building the first reusable spacecraft. It is involved in the construction of the International Space Station and has launched a number of probes to other planets. NASA has played a huge role in the development of satellites, and its technological advances have influenced many areas of modern life.

JOHN VON NEUMANN (1903–1957)

The first electronic computers were not easy to reprogram with new tasks. Hungarian-born Neumann was the first to suggest that a computer's operating program should be stored in its memory. This would allow the rest of the computer to switch quickly from one task to another. All modern computers work in this way.

SIR ISAAC NEWTON (1642–1727)

English physicist and mathematician, Newton studied force and motion and wrote the three laws of motion. He also discovered the law of gravitation, which may have been inspired by seeing an apple fall from a tree. Newton made other important discoveries about light, and developed calculus in mathematics.

HANS OERSTED (1771–1851)

In 1820, Danish physicist Oersted placed a compass needle beside a wire carrying an electric current. The needle moved, showing that an electric current produces a magnetic field. Oersted had discovered electromagnetism, which is used in most modern electrical machines.

HANS JOACHIM PABST VON OHAIN (1911–1998)

In 1935, German scientist Hans-Joachim Pabst von Ohain patented a jet propulsion engine design similar in concept to that of Frank Whittle. In 1939, his design was used to build the first jet-powered airplane.

ELISHA GRAVES OTIS (1811–1861)

In 1852, US inventor Elisha Graves Otis conceived the safety elevator, which uses a ratcheted brake to stop the car from falling if the main cable breaks. Otis demonstrated his invention by standing in an elevator while the cable was cut with an ax.

NIKOLAUS AUGUST OTTO (1832–1891)

Otto was a German engineer who developed the four-stroke internal combustion engine as a power source. In 1876, Otto constructed the prototype of today's car engine.

JOHN R. PIERCE (1910–2002)

John R. Pierce was a research director at Bell Laboratories. He developed the first communications satellite in conjunction with NASA. Named *Telstar 1*, it was launched in 1962.

ROY J. PLUNKETT (1910–1994)

Roy Plunkett was a research chemist at the DuPont chemical company. While working on a refrigerant experiment, Plunkett accidentally discovered one of the best-known and most widely used polymers—Teflon®.

DR. LAWRENCE ROBERTS (1937–)

US scientist Dr. Lawrence Roberts led the team that designed and developed ARPANET—the forerunner of the Internet. While at the Massachusetts Institute of Technology (MIT), he created the first computer-to-computer network. Based on that success, he moved to ARPA, the research arm of the US Department of Defense, where he designed and managed the building of ARPANET. The first four computers were connected in 1969 and by 1973, 23 computers were connected worldwide.

WILHELM RÖNTGEN (1845–1923)

German physicist Röntgen discovered X-rays in 1895. He found that a cathode-ray tube caused barium-coated paper positioned some distance away to glow with light. The tube gave out X-rays, which made the compound glow.

JAMES RUSSELL (1931–)

US scientist James Russell was an avid music fan frustrated by how quickly his vinyl records wore out. He thought a system that could record and replay sounds without physical contact between its parts would prevent the wear and tear, and that the best way to achieve such a system was to use light. From this idea he developed the digital compact disc (CD).

ERNEST RUTHERFORD (1871–1937)

New Zealand physicist Rutherford discovered that an atom is not a solid particle. He realized that an atom has a heavy center, or nucleus, surrounded by electrons. He later discovered the proton, a positively charged particle within the nucleus.

JACOB SCHICK (1878–1937)

US soldier and inventor Jacob Schick developed the electric shaver in the 1920s. He came up with the idea when he had trouble shaving in the freezing conditions of an Alaskan winter.

PERCY SPENCER (1894–1970)

Self-taught American engineer Percy Spencer invented a device to cook food using microwave radiation in 1945. While working on a radar research project, he noticed that a vacuum tube called a magnetron melted a chocolate bar in his pocket. He built a metal box into which he fed microwave energy, and the microwave oven was invented.

COLONEL JOHN PAUL STAPP (1910–1999)

While carrying out crash research for the United States Air Force in the 1940s and 1950s, Colonel Stapp started applying the same research techniques to car crashes. His pioneering work introduced the science of auto crash-testing and the use of crash-test dummies.

VALENTINA TERESHKOVA (1937–)

A former textile worker and amateur parachutist, Russian cosmonaut Tereshkova was the first woman in space. In June 1963, she made 48 orbits of Earth in the *Vostok 6* spacecraft, a flight lasting 71 hours.

WILLIAM THOMSON (LORD KELVIN) (1824–1907)

British mathematician William Thomson researched thermodynamics and developed the concept of absolute zero. With James Prescott Joule, he discovered that gases cool when allowed to expand—the Joule-Thomson effect.

ALAN TURING (1912–1954)

Considered the father of computer science, British mathematician Turing was involved in developing early electronic computers during World War II and wrote code for programming computers.

DR. DAVID WARREN (1925–)

Warren worked at the Aeronautical Research Laboratories in Melbourne, Australia, where he invented the black box flight data recorder in 1953.

FRANK WHITTLE (1907–1996)

English engineer Frank Whittle conceived the idea of the jet engine in 1929, and set about building one. However, the first jet-powered aircraft flew in Germany in 1939. Whittle's own engine was used in an aircraft in 1941, and was the forerunner of the modern jet engine.

WILBUR WRIGHT (1867–1912) AND ORVILLE WRIGHT (1871–1948)

US brothers Wilbur and Orville Wright ran a bicycle shop in Ohio. They also had a great interest in the science of flying and read everything they could on the subject. The brothers built their own wind tunnel to test aerofoils and, on December 17, 1903, Wilbur and Orville Wright made the first sustained, controlled flight in a powered aircraft.

VALENTINA TERESHKOVA

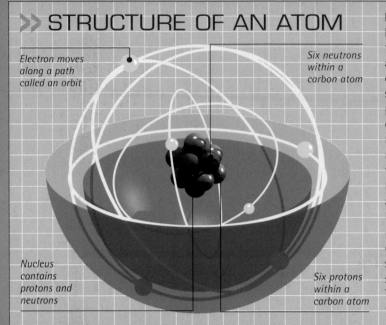

≫ STRUCTURE OF AN ATOM

Electron moves along a path called an orbit

Six neutrons within a carbon atom

Nucleus contains protons and neutrons

Six protons within a carbon atom

Every single thing you can see, hear, feel, smell, and taste is made from microscopic particles called atoms. An atom is itself made up of even smaller particles called subatomic particles. The tightly packed nucleus in the center of each atom contains protons and neutrons. These particles are made up of particles called quarks, which are held together by gluons. Particles called electrons whiz around the atom's nucleus. More than 200 other subatomic particles have been discovered in experiments in which particles are smashed into each other at high speed to create even tinier particles. The machines that are used to do this are called particle accelerators.

Techno terms

A Absorption

Absorption occurs when one substance completely absorbs another, a little like a sponge soaking up water. Absorption also means the taking up of energy such as light. **Mirror p90**

Acceleration

When the velocity (speed) of an object increases, it is accelerating. Acceleration is a change in velocity over a certain amount of time. **Crash test p134, Jet engine p146 Motorcycle p126**

Aerodynamics

Aerodynamics is the study of the motion of gases, particularly air, and the movement of objects in air, for example aircraft. **Bike p58, Soccer p52, Wind tunnel p148**

Airfoil

A structure, such as a wing, which is shaped to give lift as air flows over it. An airfoil is usually curved on top and flat underneath. Its shape causes air passing over a wing to travel faster than the air passing below it. The pressure of the air is reduced as it moves. The faster air moves, the lower its pressure. This is called Bernoulli's effect. It means that the air above the wing has a lower pressure than the air below it. The difference in pressure pushes up the wing and produces lift. The moving air also creates some drag. **Submersible p142, Osprey p144**

Air resistance

Friction, or drag, acting on something that moves through air. **Bike p58, Wind tunnel p148**

Alloy

A mixture of metals or a metal and a nonmetal. Mixing a metal with other metals, or sometimes with another element, such as carbon, results in a substance with more useful properties than the metal alone. Alloying a metal may increase its hardness, strength, and resistance to corrosion. Stainless steel is an example of an alloy. **Motorcycle p126, Parts p132, Robot surgery p208, Vacuum p116, Watch p92**

Amplitude

The height of a peak or trough in a wave, such as an ocean wave or a sound wave. A greater amplitude means that a wave is transferring more energy. For example, a sound wave with a large amplitude is louder than a sound wave with a small amplitude. **DJ decks p76, Guitar p66, Voice recognition p28**

Analog

Analog technology was originally used to broadcast and record sound and images, and to make telephone calls. It transmits sound in the form of continuous electrical signals. **Compact disc p68, Digital radio p22, Motherboard p170, Toys p26**

Antibody

A blood protein that is produced by the body's immune system in response to infection. It recognizes and helps fight infectious agents, such as bacteria and viruses. **Antibiotics p222, Vaccination p220**

Artificial intelligence

The ability of a computer to think and work like a human being. A computer that has some degree of artificial intelligence can assess its own performance, and work out ways to improve it. A computer can be programmed to play a game of chess, for example, but an intelligent computer can learn from each game it plays, so that it is able to play better the next time. **Robot helper p118, Robot worker p186**

Atom

All matter is made up of tiny particles called atoms. An atom is the smallest particle of an element that can exist on its own. There are just over 100 different types of atoms, each of which contains even smaller subatomic particles. Every element has an atomic number, which is based on the number of protons that are contained in the nucleus of its atoms. **MRI scan p204, Neon p34**

Bacteria

Microscopic, single-celled organisms that live in and around us. Some are helpful, but others can cause diseases. **Antibiotics p222**

Bandwidth

The maximum amount of data that can travel along a communications path in a given time, usually measured in bits per second. **Satellite p42, Video link p40**

Binary

Digital technology converts any data that is not already in the form of numerals—such as letters, the parts of an image, and musical notes—into coded numbers. The letter A, for example, becomes 65. These code numbers are then converted into binary numbers, such as 01000001, which is the binary number for 65. The binary code consists of a signal made up of pulses of electricity that are on (1) or off (0). For example, the number 13 becomes the binary code on-on-off-on, because its binary number is 1101. Microchips in a computer process and store these binary signals. **Compact disc p68, Digital radio p22, Flash stick p172, Microchip p16, Motherboard p170, Cell phone p18**

Bit

The word "bit" is short for "binary digit." It is the smallest possible unit

of memory used by a computer. A computer uses electrical signals that are groups of on-off pulses. A group of pulses represents a binary number made up of the numerals 1 and 0. Each numeral in the binary number is called a bit, so 11010011 is an eight-bit number. **Flash stick p172, Microchip p16**

Bluetooth®

Chip technology that enables wireless voice and data connections between a wide range of devices through short-range, digital, two-way radio. **Digital pen p166, Virtual keyboard p174**

Buoyancy

The ability of an object to float in a fluid, such as a liquid or a gas. When a boat is placed in water, the liquid pushes on it with an upward force called upthrust. This occurs because the pressure of the water is greater underneath the boat than at the water's surface. A boat floats if the upthrust is equal to its weight. Solid objects are more buoyant if they have a low density. **Submersible p142**

Byte

When a computer stores data, it converts it into a long sequence of binary numbers. These numbers are changed into signals in binary code. Each number has eight bits and is called a byte. The capacity of a memory unit, such as read-only-memory (RAM) or a disk, is measured by the total number of bytes that it can store. This is given in kilobytes (KB), which each contain 1,024 bytes; in megabytes (MB), which each contain 1,048,576 bytes; and in gigabytes (GB), which contain 1,073,741,824 bytes. **Laptop p168, Microchip p16, Smart card p182**

Carbon

A nonmetallic element that occurs in several forms. For example, diamond is a form of carbon that is a hard crystal, and is used in jewelry and drills. Graphite is a soft, black solid that is used as a lubricant and in pencils. Carbon black is a fine powder used in making rubber. Coke

is a form of carbon used to make steel. Carbon fibers are used to make strong materials, such as reinforced plastic. **Bike p58, Match p86, Motorcycle p126, Parts p132, Bionic Limb p214,**

Center of gravity

The point at which the whole weight of an object is balanced. For example, you can balance a tray of glasses on one hand if you support it directly beneath its center of gravity. The force of gravity pulls equally on all parts of the tray around this point. **Wheelchair p138**

Centrifugal force

In a centrifuge, a container holding a mixture spins around at high speed. This exerts a strong force on the mixture, causing it to separate into its different components. The heavier articles of the mixture move outward because of their greater inertia. There appears to be an outward force, often called centrifugal force, pulling on the particles. **Lift p140, Vacuum p116**

Charge

Each atom has an equal number of negatively charged electrons and positively charged protons, which means that an atom is electrically neutral. If the atoms in an object lose electrons, the object gets a positive charge. The amount of charge depends on how many electrons are gained or lost. **Laser printer p176**

Chemical reaction

In a chemical reaction, the atoms of elements in substances rearrange to form new substances, which contain the same atoms, but in different combinations. For example, when you make toast, a chemical reaction takes place. Bread contains carbohydrate, a compound containing the elements carbon, hydrogen, and oxygen. Heating the bread changes the carbohydrate into black carbon, which forms on the surface of the bread. Water (made of hydrogen and oxygen) also forms and escapes into the air as vapor. **Battery p94, Fireworks p78, Fuel-cell car p128, Match p86**

Color

Our eyes normally detect a range of colors—from red, orange, and yellow, through to green, blue, and violet. We see different colors because each color has a different wavelength of light. Red has the longest wavelength and violet the shortest. Some objects, such as traffic lights, emit (give out) light of a particular color. Other objects appear colored because they absorb some wavelengths and reflect others. Green grass, for example, reflects only green light, and absorbs all other colors. **Fireworks p78, LCD TV p24, Neon p34**

Combustion

Combustion is a chemical reaction between a fuel and oxygen that produces heat and, usually, light. A material that can combust (catch fire or ignite) is said to be flammable. To combust it has to be heated to an ignition temperature. At this point, a chemical reaction starts between the substance and oxygen in the air. This process gives out heat, which keeps the fuel hot enough for combustion to continue until all the material has burned. **Car engine p130, Fireworks p78, Jet engine p146, Match p86**

Compound

A compound is a substance in which the atoms of two or more elements are combined. It contains fixed proportions of elements linked to form molecules, or a larger structure that combines many molecules. The chemical name of a compound shows the elements within it. For example, the chemical name for salt is sodium chloride, showing that it is a compound of sodium and chlorine. A compound's properties may be very different from those of the individual elements it contains. Sodium is a soft metal, and chlorine is a poisonous gas. It is not safe to eat either, yet salt is an important food. **Fuel-cell car p128**

Compression

The action of squashing a substance so that it takes up a smaller space. When a gas is compressed, its pressure increases. When a solid is compressed, forces in the solid react against the compression. These forces are responsible for the strength of a solid. **Car engine p130, Fridge p102, Sneaker p50**

Conduction

The flow of heat through a solid. For example, if a metal bar is heated, the atoms within start to move more quickly. These particles strike others and speed them up, spreading heat energy through the object. A thermal conductor is a material that carries heat in this way. Its conductivity is a measure of the rate at which heat flows. Heat flows easily through materials with a high conductivity, such as metals. **Heat p98**

Conservation of energy

The law of conservation of energy states that the total amount of energy in a system is constant. A system is anything that contains or uses energy. For example, the light and heat produced by a flashlight bulb are equal to the electrical energy produced by the battery. Energy can be neither created nor destroyed; it can only change from one form to another. This law does not apply to the production of nuclear energy, in which mass changes to energy. **Crash test p134, Light bulb p88, Watch p92**

Crystal

A crystal is a solid containing a regular, symmetrical arrangement of particles. Some elements, such as iodine, form crystals. Many compounds form crystals when they leave solutions. For example, if you leave salty water exposed to the air, it forms tiny white crystals of salt as the water evaporates. Most molten compounds also form crystals as they solidify. The process of forming crystals is called crystallization. As a crystal forms, atoms, ions, or molecules link together in a geometric network called a lattice. The crystal grows as more atoms, ions, or molecules join the lattice. The shape of the lattice gives the crystal its particular pattern. **Microchip p16, Mirror p90**

Current

The flow of electric charge through a substance. An electric charge can only flow through a substance that can conduct electricity, such as a copper wire. A charge flows through a wire when an electromotive force, or voltage, drives electrons into the conductor. The electrons are negatively charged, which means that they repel electrons ahead, causing them to jump from one atom to the next. As electrons in the conductor move from atom to atom, the charge is carried along the wire in a flow called an electric current. **Battery p94, Fuel-cell car p128, Wet welding p188**

D Data compression

Any technique used to encode data so that it takes up less storage space. **Iris scan p32, MP3 player p70**

Detergent

Dish soap and laundry powder contain detergents, which are made of chemicals obtained from petroleum. Detergent molecules surround particles of greasy dirt on the surface of a soiled dish or piece of cloth. The molecules carry the particles away from the surface and into the water. **Washing machine p114**

Digital

In communications and computer technology, "digital" refers to a method of encoding data using a binary system made up of zeroes and ones. **Camera p62, Compact disc p68, Digital pen p166, Digital radio p22, Flash stick p172, Iris scan p32, Pet translator p30, Phone p18, Scanner p178, Video link p40**

Digitization

The process of converting analog information into digital format—for example, converting an image into a binary code. **Scanner p178**

DNA (deoxyribonucleic acid)

The chemical within the cells of living things that carries all the information needed to build it and keep it alive. DNA is passed from one generation to the next when living things reproduce. **Biochip p226**

Drag

The natural resistance or friction of the air or water as an aircraft flies or a boat powers forward. Drag increases the faster the craft moves. In order to overcome drag, a craft needs thrust from its engines. A streamlined shape reduces drag. **Bike p58, Fabric p60, Jet engine p146, Submersible p142, Wind tunnel p148**

Efficiency

The measure of how much energy a machine converts into useful work. For example, an efficient light bulb uses most of the electrical energy that it takes in to produce light, rather than heat. **Light bulb p88, Washing machine p114**

Electrical energy

The energy of moving electrons, as in an electrical current that flows through a wire connected to a battery. When we use electricity, electrical energy changes to another form of energy—for example, light in a light bulb or kinetic energy in an electric motor. **Light bulb p88, Neon p34**

Electric motor

A machine that uses electricity to produce movement. It contains a coil of wire, which is suspended in the magnetic field of a magnet or electromagnet. When an electric current flows through the coil, it produces its own magnetic field. The two fields push or pull on each other, causing the coil to rotate and drive the shaft of the motor. **Fuel-cell car p128, Elevator p140, Washing machine p114**

Electrochemistry

The branch of chemistry that involves electricity. Electricity plays a part in all chemical reactions, because atoms contain electrically charged particles. For example, a battery uses a chemical reaction to generate an electric

current. An electrical current can also be used to break up a compound into the individual elements it contains. **Battery p94, Fuel-cell car p128**

Electrode

Any terminal that conducts an electric current into or away from conducting substances in a circuit, such as the anode (positive terminal) or cathode (negative terminal) of a battery. **Battery p94, Fuel-cell car p128, Light bulb p88**

Electrolyte

A nonmetallic substance that conducts an electric current in solution by moving ions (atoms or groups of atoms that carry an electric charge) rather than electrons. **Battery p94, Fuel-cell car p128**

Electromagnet

A form of magnet that works using electricity. It consists of a coil of wire wound around a piece of iron. When an electric current flows through the coil, the iron becomes a magnet. **Headphones p74, Elevator p140**

Electron

A tiny particle that moves in a shell around the nucleus of an atom. Electrons have a negative electric charge. They balance an equal number of protons, which have a positive charge. This makes the whole atom electrically neutral. If an atom gains or loses an electron, the charges are unbalanced and it becomes a charged atom called an ion. **Battery p94, Fuel-cell car p128, Light bulb p88, Neon p34, Solar cell p96**

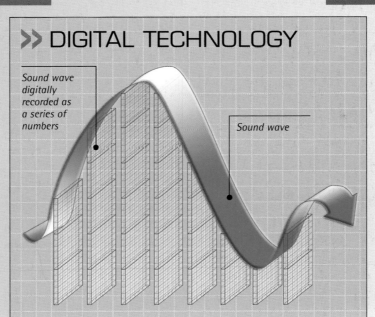

»DIGITAL TECHNOLOGY

Sound wave digitally recorded as a series of numbers

Sound wave

Digital technology can read, write, and store information that is represented in numerical form. For example, music can be digitally recorded. A microphone converts the music into an electric signal, which is measured by a computer thousands of times a second. These measurements are reproduced as a series of numbers in binary code. Each number is a measure of the height of the sound wave at a given point.

Digital technology allows us to electronically store and manipulate data. It can be encrypted for security, or compressed, so large amounts of information can be stored on a tiny digital device. Data can also be transferred between devices, so we can take photos with a cell phone or watch movies on a laptop.

Energy

Energy is the ability to cause an action. There are several different kinds of energy. Whenever anything happens, one kind of energy is present and it changes to another kind. For example, in an electric motor, electrical energy becomes kinetic energy—the energy of movement. **Fireworks p78, Light bulb p88, Neon p34, Racket p54, Watch p92**

F Fiber optic

Light rays are able to pass along a thin glass thread or fiber, called an optical fiber. An outer coating of a different kind of glass reflects the light into the center of the fiber, so that it cannot escape. Fiber optics are used to carry laser light signals along telephone cables. An endoscope is a flexible tube of optical fibers that is inserted into the body. It is used in medicine to produce images of the interior of the body. It carries an image to an eyepiece at the other end. **Fiber optics p20, Camera capsule p212**

Filament

A light bulb contains a piece of thin, coiled tungsten wire called a filament. The filament is heated by an electric current until it gets so hot that it glows white and gives off light. The bulb is filled with a nonreactive gas, such as nitrogen or argon, to prevent the filament from burning out, as it would in air. **Heat p98, Light bulb p88**

Fluorescence

The ability of certain molecules to absorb light at one wavelength and emit (give off) a light at a longer wavelength. Bright fluorescent paints take in light of various colors or invisible ultraviolet rays and emit light of just one color. This light is usually much brighter than normal reflected light. **ID p180, Light bulb p88**

Force

A force can push, pull, twist, turn, stretch, or squeeze an object. A force can cause an object to speed up, slow down, or change direction. When the forces acting on an object are balanced, the object is in equilibrium. **Crash test p134, Racket p54**

Frequency

The regularity with which something happens. It is most often applied to a wave or vibration. A wave's frequency is the number of times its complete cycle occurs each second. Frequency is measured in hertz (Hz). **Digital radio p22, Doppler radar p194, Guitar p66**

Friction

Friction occurs where moving objects or surfaces rub together. It acts against the direction of motion, causing objects to slow down or stop and creating heat. The amount of friction depends on the texture of the surfaces, and the force pressing them together. Rough surfaces create the most friction. **Match p86, Space Shuttle p156**

G Gas

Gas is matter in a form that has no definite shape or volume. Gas particles are spaced far apart. The forces between them are not strong enough to hold them in place, so they move freely and rapidly in all directions. Because gas has no fixed shape or volume, it expands to fill any container it is put into. **Aerosol p112, Fridge p102, Jet engine 146, Neon p34**

Gear

A gear is a pair or series of toothed wheels that are connected so that one wheel turns another. Gears transmit force and motion. The wheels are usually of different sizes and mesh together, or are connected by a chain. A large wheel causes a small wheel to turn with less force, but greater speed. A small wheel makes a large wheel turn with more force, but less speed. Gears can also change the direction of the motion they transmit. **Bike p58, Lock p108, Watch p92**

Gel

A jellylike material composed of a liquid evenly dispersed in a solid. **Aerogel p104, Sneaker p50**

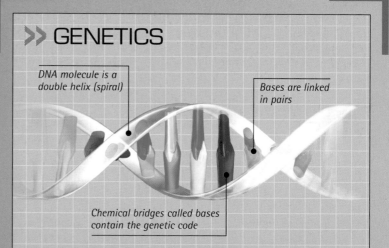

>> GENETICS

DNA molecule is a double helix (spiral)

Bases are linked in pairs

Chemical bridges called bases contain the genetic code

Every form of life is put together by a chemical code. The code is contained in molecules of deoxyribonucleic acid (DNA), which are packed away inside the cells of all living things. The DNA molecule is in the shape of a double helix, linked by chemicals called bases. The chemical code is very complex. The code inside one human cell contains 50,000 to 100,000 separate instructions, called genes, and each one controls a different characteristic. In a cell's nucleus, there are several lengths of DNA. Each one is called a chromosome. DNA works by telling a cell how to make the many different proteins that your cells need to function.

Genetics

Genetics is the study of the way inherited characteristics are passed on in living things. **Biochip p226, IVF p224**

Geostationary satellite

A satellite that circles Earth once every 24 hours, and appears to be fixed in the sky. **Satellite p42**

GPS (Global Positioning System)

GPS is a space-based navigation and positioning system. Receivers on Earth work in conjunction with fixed-orbit satellites to determine a precise location. **Navigation p154**

Gravity

A force of attraction between all objects with mass. All bodies of matter exert a force of gravity, but it is strong only when something has a large mass, such as a planet, moon, or star. Gravity becomes weaker as bodies of matter move farther apart. **Space probe p158**

Gyroscope

A wheel mounted in a ring so that its axis is free to turn in any direction. When spun rapidly, a gyroscope will point in the same direction, no matter which way the ring is turned. Gyroscopes are used as stabilizers to help moving objects balance, and as navigational devices. **Robot helper p118, Satellite p42, Wheelchair p138**

Heat

Heat is a form of energy that makes things hot or cold. All objects, whether hot or cold, possess heat because the particles (atoms and molecules) within them are moving. An object gains heat and becomes hotter the faster its molecules move. When heat is applied to an object, the movement of its particles speeds up. If the molecules slow down, it loses heat and cools. Heat energy always passes from a hotter object to a cooler object. Heat can be produced in many ways, including by friction, combustion, and from electricity. **Aerogel p104, Car engine p130, Fridge p102, Homes p106, Laser printer p176, Match p86, Wet welding p188**

Hypertext

Any text on a web document that contains links to other documents. By clicking on words, phrases, or images in a document, another document is retrieved. **Internet p38**

Image sensor

A light-sensitive device used in scanners, digital cameras, and video cameras that records the brightness of the light that strikes it during an exposure. **Digital camera p62, Scanner p178**

Incandescence

The emission of light by a hot substance. When substances get hot, they become incandescent (glow with light). The color of the light given out depends on how hot the substance is. An object glows red at first, and then yellow and white as it gets hotter. Most household light bulbs contain a thin tungsten filament. When an electric current passes through it, the filament becomes so hot that it gives off a bright white light. **Light bulb p88**

Inertia

Every object has inertia, which causes it to resist a change in its motion. Therefore, a moving object will try to keep moving in a straight line, and a stationary object will try to remain at rest. If you are traveling in a car that stops suddenly, your body's inertia will cause you to keep moving. Wearing a seatbelt contains this movement. Inertia depends on mass—an object with a large mass has a lot of inertia. **Crash test p134**

Infrared ray

When warm and hot objects give off heat by radiation, they produce infrared rays. Remote controls use a weak infrared beam to send signals that operate controls. Thermography uses infrared rays to produce pictures that show the warm and cool parts of an object as different colors. **Imaging techniques p10, Virtual keyboard p174**

Insulator

An insulator is a material that does not conduct heat or electricity well. Insulators include wood, plastics, cork, and air. **Aerogel p104, Homes p106**

Internal combustion engine

A heat engine that burns fuel inside the engine to produce power. A gas is heated and expands. The pressure of the expanding gas moves parts inside the engine, changing the heat energy into kinetic energy (energy of motion). **Car engine p130, Jet engine p146**

Internet

A network of many computers connected via telecommunication networks. The computers communicate using a set of protocols called TCP/IP (Transmission Control Protocol/ Internet Protocol). The Internet provides access to a wide range of resources from all around the world. **Fridge p102, Internet p38, Laptop p168, Links p36, Robot helper p118, Toys p26**

Ion

An ion is an atom, or group of atoms, that carries an electric charge. When atoms gain electrons, they form ions with negative electric charge. These ions are called anions. When atoms lose electrons, they form ions with a positive charge, called cations. Many compounds contain ions joined together by ionic bonds. The electrical charges that attract the ions to each other are very strong, so most ionic bonds are very difficult to break. **Battery p94, Fuel-cell car p128, Neon p34**

Ionization

The formation of ions is called ionization. It occurs when compounds dissolve or melt. A chemical reaction may take place as the ions join up again in new combinations. **Battery p94, Fuel-cell car p128**

J Jet engine

An engine that produces a high-speed jet of air. Most commercial airplanes are powered by jet engines. As the engine burns fuel, a jet of hot air and other gases is forced from the exhaust of the engine, pushing it forward. A turbofan is a jet engine with a large fan at the front. The fan blows air around the gas turbine to join the jet at the rear, increasing the engine's thrust. **Jet engine p146, Space Shuttle p156**

K Kinetic energy

The energy that a particle or object possesses due to its movement or vibration. The faster an object travels, the more kinetic energy it has. It loses its kinetic energy as it slows down. **Crash test p134, Neon p34, Watch p92**

L Laser

A device that produces a beam of high-energy light. Laser stands for "light amplification by stimulated emission of radiation." Inside a laser is a material called a lasing medium. Passing an electric current or light into the medium gives energy to, or excites, its atoms. The excited atoms suddenly release their extra energy and emit (give off) light. One atom emits a light ray, which strikes another atom and causes it to emit another ray, and so on in a cascade of emissions. The waves of light are very concentrated, which means that they move exactly in step. Mirrors reflect the rays, so that the cascade builds up. The light leaves through one of the mirrors, which is partly transparent. Lasers can also emit invisible infrared rays. **Compact disc p68, Fiber optics p20, ID p180, Laser surgery p206, Shaver p110**

LCD (liquid crystal display)

LCD screens use thousands of tiny red, green, and blue filters to create an image. Behind these filters is a layer of liquid crystals. When an electric current is passed through the crystals, they twist or untwist, acting like shutters to allow light to pass through to a transparent screen and form an image. **LCD TV p24, Pet translator p30**

LED (light-emitting diode)

An LED is a diode (an electronic component that can either pass or block an electrical current) that gives out light or infrared rays. They are illuminated by the movement of electrons in a semiconductor material. LEDs are found in many devices. They are often used as warning or safety lights. Remote control units contain LEDs that convert electrical signals into invisible infrared control signals. **Fiber optics p20, Robot helper p118, Virtual keyboard 174**

Light

Light is a form of energy. It travels in waves that have the fastest known speed of anything in the universe. Life on Earth could not exist without light. Our most important source is the Sun, but we can also produce light using electricity. The light you can see is part of a range of electromagnetic radiation. It contains wavelengths that your eyes detect as colors, ranging through the spectrum from red to violet. Light can act either as a wave or as a tiny packet of energy called a photon. **Light bulb p88, Neon p34, Solar cell p96, Virtual keyboard p174**

Luminescence

Luminescence occurs when objects take in energy other than heat and change it into light energy. Luminescent animals, such as glow-worms and fireflies, glow because chemical energy in their bodies changes to light energy. Some television screens contain luminescent materials that light up when struck by a beam of electrons. **Neon p34**

M Magnet

A magnet creates an area around it called a magnetic field, which contains properties that either attract or repel other magnets. A magnet has two poles—a north pole and a south pole. The magnetic force is strongest at each pole. Only certain materials are magnetic. These include some metals, such as steel, iron, nickel, and cobalt; some alloys; and some ceramics. Lodestone is a magnetic mineral made of iron oxide. A permanent magnet is always magnetic, but a temporary magnet can gain and lose its magnetic force. **Guitar p66, Headphones p74, MRI scan p204**

Magnetic field

A magnet only attracts objects when they are within its magnetic field. Two magnets attract or repel each other if their magnetic fields come together. At each point in the field, the magnet exerts a force in a certain direction. These directions follow lines of force, or flux, which loop around the magnet from one pole to the other. A wire carrying an electric current is also surrounded by a magnetic field while the current is flowing. **Guitar p66, MRI scan p204, Sneaker p50**

Microchip

A microchip is an integrated circuit—a complete set of electronic components in one unit. It consists of a single piece of semiconductor, usually silicon, which contains thousands of linked components, such as transistors and diodes. A microchip can carry out many complex actions—so many, in fact, that the circuit of a whole computer may be connected in one chip. **Digital pen p166, Microchip p16, Motherboard p170, Cell phone p18, Racket p54, Radio ID tag p184, Smart card p182**

Microprocessor

A microprocessor is a complete computer on a single tiny chip of silicon. It is the most sophisticated type of microchip. All computers have a central processing unit, or CPU, containing one or more microprocessors. The CPU is the most important part of the computer, and its job is to control the computer, perform tasks, and calculate results. By following the instructions of a program, the CPU processes data and displays the result on the screen. **Games p64, Laptop p168,**

>> INSIDE A COMPUTER

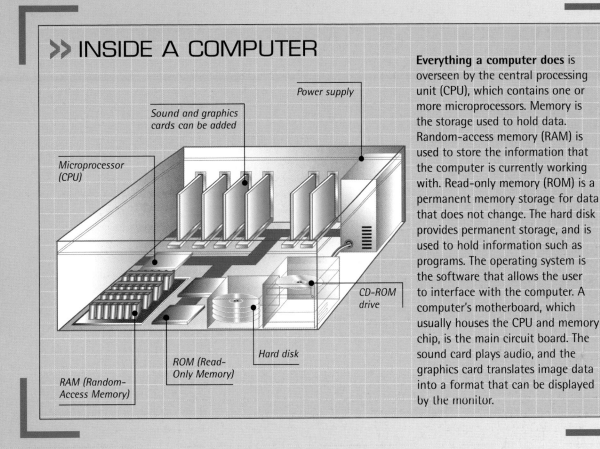

Power supply

Sound and graphics cards can be added

Microprocessor (CPU)

CD-ROM drive

Hard disk

ROM (Read-Only Memory)

RAM (Random-Access Memory)

Everything a computer does is overseen by the central processing unit (CPU), which contains one or more microprocessors. Memory is the storage used to hold data. Random-access memory (RAM) is used to store the information that the computer is currently working with. Read-only memory (ROM) is a permanent memory storage for data that does not change. The hard disk provides permanent storage, and is used to hold information such as programs. The operating system is the software that allows the user to interface with the computer. A computer's motherboard, which usually houses the CPU and memory chip, is the main circuit board. The sound card plays audio, and the graphics card translates image data into a format that can be displayed by the monitor.

Motherboard p170, Smart card p182, Sneaker p50

Microwave
Microwaves are electromagnetic waves with a short wavelength. They are used for telephone and television links. A microwave oven uses microwaves to cook and warm food quickly. A beam of microwaves penetrates the food. The water in the food absorbs the waves and heats up, cooking the food. **Links p36, Microwave p100, Satellite p42**

Molecule
Atoms that have bonded with other atoms are called molecules. These can be formed from atoms of just one element. For example, oxygen molecules are made from two oxygen atoms that have bonded together (O_2). Molecules can also form when atoms of different elements bond. For example, a water molecule has two hydrogen atoms and one oxygen atom (H_2O). Molecules can be very simple, containing just a few atoms, or incredibly complex, containing thousands of connected atoms of different elements. These particles are so tiny that a single drop of water contains more molecules than there are grains of sand on a large beach. **Antibiotics p222, Fabric p60, Microwave p100**

Momentum
The momentum of an object depends on its mass and velocity (speed). The heavier an object and the faster it moves, the greater its momentum, so it is harder for it to stop. This means that an object's momentum changes as it accelerates. Momentum can be transferred between objects. For example, when a moving ball collides with a stationary one, the first ball transfers some of its momentum to the second ball. The total momentum of the two balls is the same as the first ball's momentum before the collision. This is the principle of conservation of momentum. **Crash test p134**

Multiplexing
Multiplexing is the combination of two or more signals from two or more channels to form a single output—for example, transmitting multiple digital television programs through a single digital carrier. **Fiber optics p20**

Noble gases
The elements helium, neon, argon, krypton, xenon, and radon. Noble gases are nonreactive, which means they form very few compounds with other elements. They are also called rare or inert gases. Noble gases make up about one percent of the air and are often used in lighting. **Neon p34**

Optics
Optics is the study of light and the ways in which light rays form images. These images occur when light rays coming from an object are reflected by mirrors and bent, or refracted, as they pass through lenses. **Camera p62, Mirror p90**

K

Kao, Charles *238*
keratin 110
Kevlar® 132
keyboards 171, **174–5**
Kilby, Jack *238*
kinetic energy *246*
Kistler, Steven 105

L

laptop computers **168–9**
lasers 207, *246*
   compact discs (CDs) **68–9**
  holograms 180
  laser printers **176–7**
  surgery **206–7**
LCDs (liquid-crystal displays)
  24–5, *246*
LED (light-emitting diodes)
  88, *246*
Licklider, Joseph Carl Robnett *238*
light *246*
  bioluminescence 35
  fiber optics 21, *244*
  fluorescence 88, 89, 181, *244*
  incandescence 88, 89, *245*
  LED (light-emitting diodes)
    88, *246*
  luminescence *246*
  mirrors 90
  neon lights **34–5**
  optics *247*
  phosphorescence 179, *248*
  photons 90, *248*
  prisms *249*
  red shift 194
  reflections *249*
  refraction *249*
  scanners 178–9
  solar cells **96–7**
  spectrum *250*
  speed of *250*
  virtual keyboards **174–5**
  see also lasers
light bulbs **88–9**, *244*
limbs, bionic **214–15**
Lister, Joseph *238*
lithium 94, 95
locks **108–9**
Lovelace, Countess of *236*
luminescence *246*
Lycra® 61

M

magnetic fields *246*
magnets *243*, *246*
malaria 226
Marconi, Guglielmo 23, *238*
Mariana Trench 143
matches **86–7**
materials: recycling 106–7
  vehicle components **132–3**
Maxwell, James Clerk *238*
medicine
  antibiotics **222–3**

camera capsules 212–13
IVF (in Vitro Fertilization) **224–5**
laser surgery **206–7**
MRI scans **204–5**
pacemakers **210–11**
radio identification tags 184
robot surgery **208–9**
scans **202–3**
skin grafts **216–17**
memory: computers *249*
  digital cameras 63
  flash sticks **172–3**
Mendel, Gregor *238*
Mestral, George de 192, *238*
metals: alloys *240*
  wet welding **188–9**
micromechanisms 109
microchips **16–17**, 171, *246*
  radio identification tags 184–5
  smart cards **182–3**
  in tennis rackets 55
microprocessors 16, 64,
  171, *246–7*
microwaves 37, **100–1**, *247*
mirrors **90–1**
mites, follicle 219
molecules *247*
momentum *247*
Moon 207
motherboards **170–1**, *247*
motion, laws of *248*
motorcycles **126–7**
motors, electric *243*
MP3 players **70–1**
MP4 players 27
MRI (Magnetic Resonance
  Imaging) 202, **204–5**
MRSA 223
multiplexing *247*
music: DJ decks **76–7**
  guitars **66–7**
  headphones **74–5**
  MP3 players **70–1**
  MP4 players 27

N

nanorobots 186
National Aeronautics
  and Space Administration
  (NASA) 133, *238*
navigation 27, **154–5**
neon lights **34–5**
networks: communication **36–7**
  Internet **38–9**
  in nature 39
  neural networks 31
  servers *250*
  transportation **152–3**
Neumann, John von *238*
neural networks 31
Newton, Sir Isaac *238*, *248*
Newton's cradle 93
noble gases *247*
Noyce, Robert *238*

O

oceans **142–3**, 153
octopuses 146
Oersted, Hans *238*
Ohain, Hans Joachim Pabst von *238*
oil pipelines 104
Olympic bicycles **58–9**
optical fibers **20–1**, *244*
optics *247*
oscillation *248*
Osprey **144–5**
Otis, Elisha Graves 141, *239*
Otto, Nikolaus August 131, *239*
ovens, microwave **100–1**
overpasses 152
ozone layer 112

P

pacemakers **210–11**
packets, data *248*
parasites 219, 220
particles, subatomic *240*
passports 181
penicillin 222
pens, digital **166–7**
personal digital assistants (PDAs) 27, 174–5
pets: pet translators **30–1**
  radio identification tags 184
phones *see* telephones
phosphorescence 179, *248*
photography **62–3**, 79
photons 90, *248*
photovoltaic cells 96, *248*
Pierce, John R. *239*
piezoelectricity 55, *248*
pistons *248*
Pistorius, Oscar 215
pixels 24–5, *248–9*
planets, gravity 159
Plunkett, Roy J. *239*
pollution 129
polymers 132
Post-it® Notes 192
pressure *249*
printers, laser **176–7**
prisms *249*
prosthetics **214–15**
protocols *249*, *251*
pulleys *249*

R

rackets, tennis **54–5**
radar 153, **194–5**
radio identification tags **184–5**
radio waves 101, *249*
  digital radio **22–3**
  Doppler radar 195
  MRI scans 205
  satellite navigation 154
  security chips 181
  Wi-Fi cards 26
railroads 153
RAM (random access memory) 171, *249*
razors 110, 111
reactions *249*

recycling, building materials 106–7
red blood cells 219
red shift 194
reflections *249*
refraction *249*
refrigerators **102–3**
remote sensing *249*
roads, overpasses 152
Roberts, Dr. Lawrence *239*
robots: robot helpers **118–19**
  robot workers **186–7**
  surgery **208–9**
  wet welding 189
rockets 78–9, 156, 158
Roentgen, Wilhelm *239*
ROM (read-only memory) *249*
roofs, turf 107
Rosetta space probe **158–9**
routes, transportation **152–3**
running shoes **50–1**
Russell, James *239*
Rutherford, Ernest *239*

S sampling *250*
satellites 37, **42–3**
  geostationary *245*
navigation 27, **154–5**
transponders *251*
saucepans 98
scanners **178–9**
  fingerprint scanners 180
  iris scanning **32–3**
  medical scans **202–3**
  MRI (Magnetic Resonance
    Imaging) **204–5**
Schick, Jacob *239*
Schlieren photography 79
screens, computer 171
security chips 181
semiconductors *250*
sensors *250*
  crash-test dummies 134
  digital cameras 63
  image sensors *245*
  remote sensing *249*
  robots 119
  in running shoes 51
servers *250*
sharks 143
shavers **110–11**
shipping lanes 153
shock absorbers 51, 127
shoes, running **50–1**
showers 98
silicon chips 17
silver, mirrors 91
skateboards 57
skiing, snowdomes 72–3
skin grafts **216–17**
smart cards **182–3**
snowboards **56–7**
snowdomes 72–3
soccer ball **52–3**

software, computers 171
solar power **96–7**, 107,
  131, 159, *248*
sound waves *250*
  amplitude *240*
  compact discs (CDs) **68–9**
  DJ decks **76–7**
  electric guitars 66
  headphones **74–5**
space probes 104, **158–9**
Space Shuttle 42, 133,
  156–7
spectrum *250*
  electromagnetic *250–1*
speed *250*
Spencer, Percy *239*
sperm, IVF (in Vitro
  Fertilization) **224–5**
sports: arenas **72–3**
  Olympic bikes **58–9**
  snowboards **56–7**
  soccer **52–3**
  tennis rackets **54–5**
Stapp, Colonel John Paul *239*
straw, insulation 106
submersibles **142–3**, 188–9
sunlight, solar cells **96–7**
superbugs 223
superglue 193
surfers 57, 72
surgery: laser surgery **206–7**
  robot surgery **208–9**
sweat-absorbing fabrics 61
swim bladder, fish 143
swimsuits 60
Swiss Army Knives **172–3**
synthetic fibers 132

T taste buds 219
TCP/IP (Transmission
  Control Protocol/
Internet Protocol) *251*
telemetry *251*
telephones: cables 37
  cell phones **18–19**, 175
  satellites 37
telescopes, space 91
television **24–5**, 27, 36, 37
tennis rackets **54–5**
Tereshkova, Valentina *239*
termite nests 137
thermograms 98, 99
thermostats 99
Tholos video links **40–1**
Thomson, William *239*
thrust *251*
tires, motorcycles 127
titanium 133
toasters 99
toner, laser printers 177
tongue, taste buds 219
towers, car **136–7**
toys **26–7**, 119

transistors 16, 17, *251*
transponders *251*
transportation: airplanes **144–51**
  cars **128–31**
  elevators **140–1**
  motorcycles **126–7**
  networks **152–3**
  vehicle components **132–3**
turf, artificial 72
turf roofs 107
Turing, Alan *239*

U ultrasound scans 203
ultraviolet rays
  112, *251*
URL (uniform resource
  locator) *251*

V vaccination **220–1**, *251*
vacuum cleaners **116–17**
Velcro® 192
Velodromes 73
vibrations 66–7, *251*
video links **40–1**
virtual keyboards **174–5**
viruses, vaccination 220
vocal cords 29
voice recognition **28–9**, 174
voiceprint technology **30–1**
voltage *251*

W Warren, Dr. David *239*
washing machines **114–15**
watches **92–3**
Watson, James *236*
wave simulators 72
weather forecasting 194–5
Web cams 26
weight 139, 141
welding, wet **188–9**
wheelchairs **138–9**
white blood cells 220–1
Whittle, Frank 146, *239*
wind tunnels 59, **148–9**
wireless Internet (WiFi) 26, 169
World Wide Web 39, *251*
Wozniak, Steve *237*
Wright brothers *239*

X X-rays 202–3, *251*

Z Zip codes 179

DK would like to thank:

Kate Scarborough and Clive Wilson for editorial assistance; Fergus Day and Carey Scott for help writing gallery spreads; Lynn Bresler and Polly Boyd for proofreading; Hilary Bird for the Index; Tim Ridley for photography; Robin Hunter for artwork assistance; Spencer Holbrook for design assistance.

H.R. (Bart) Everett, Robotics Group, SPAWAR Systems Center for advice on Robot helper and Robot worker; Hagen Diesterbeck, adidas-Salomon AG, Intelligent Projects for advice on Sneaker; Colin Crawford and colleagues, PURE Digital for providing a Bug radio, and advice on Digital radio; Emma Halcox, Independence Technology UK for advice on Wheelchair; Karen Hawkes, Graham Hawkes and Adam George Wright at Deep Flight for images and advice; Nicholas Batten, Autostadt for images and advice on Car tower; The Master Locksmiths Association for advice on Lock; Henrietta Pinkham and colleagues, LVMH for images and advice on Watch.

The Publisher would like to thank the following for their kind permission to reproduce these images:

Key:
l=left; r=right; t=top; b=bottom; c=center; A=above; B=below.

Alamy = Alamy Images; DK = DK Images; Getty = Getty Images; Rex = Rex Features; SPL = Science Photo Library

1 Courtesy of Apple Computer, Inc.: X-ray by Gusto. 2-3 Alamy: Stockshot (2); Courtesy of Apple Computer, Inc.: X-ray by Gusto (Background); Courtesy of NEC Corporation, Japan (www.incx.nec.co.jp/robot/): (3); SPL: Du Cane Medical Imaging Ltd (6); Gusto (4); Pasieka (1), (5). 8-9 DK: cl; SPL: GE Medical Systems tcr; Gusto c; NOAA bl; Tom Barrick, Chris Clark, SGHMS br. 10-11 Courtesy of adidas. adidas, the adidas logo and the 3-stripe trade mark are registered trade marks of the adidas-Solomon group, used with permission. The 1 logo and the Interface logo are trade marks of the adidas-Solomon group, used with permission: tc; DK: bc; SPL: Alfred Pasieka cl; Andrew Syred tl; Dr Gary Settles br. 12-13 © The Boeing Company: (6); Corbis: Lawrence Manning (3); Richard Cummins (5); DK: (2); Pure Digital, a division of Imagination Technologies: (1); SPL: Pasieka (4). 14-15 Corbis: George B Diebold. 16-17 Corbis: Charles O'Rear br; Royalty-Free br (insert), cr; National Geographic Image Collection: Bruce Dale l; SPL: Andrew Syred crA, tcl; Dick Luria bcr. 18-19 Courtesy of Motorola: Photography by Kate Bradshaw, Phil Letsu, Louise Thomas; SPL: Cordelia Molloy bc. 20-21 Corbis: Lawrence Manning l; SPL: Ed Young bcr; Maximilian Stock Ltd cr. 22-23 Pure Digital, a division of Imagination Technologies. 24-25 DK: l; Dave King, Courtesy of The Science Museum, London br. 26-27 Alamy: worldthroughthelens tcr; Courtesy of Archos: bl; Corbis: Steve Chenn tl; Courtesy of Garmin (Europe) Ltd: br; SPL: D Roberts c. 28-29 DK: Andy Crawford tr; SPL: CNRI tcr (closed), tcr (open); Hank Morgan l. 30-31 Rex: tr; SPL: Mehau Kulyk tcr; Courtesy of Takara Co., Ltd: l; Courtesy of Japan Acoustic Laboratory r. 32-33 SPL: Mark Maio cl; Mehau Kulyk bcl; Pasieka r. 34-35 Alamy: Phil Degginger crB; Corbis: Richard Cummins l; National Geographic Image Collection: Bill Curtsinger bcr. 36-37 Corbis: Royalty-Free tcr; SPL: John Greim cr; Mike Miller tcl; NCSA, University of Illinois bc. 38-39 Alamy: The Garden Picture Library cB; DK: Will Long and Richard Davies of Oxford Scientific Films br. 40-41 Courtesy of Tholos Systems Communication GmbH. 42-43 © The Boeing Company: t; NASA: (STS41D-36-034) bcl. 44-45 Alamy: IMAGINA The Image Maker. 46-47 Courtesy of adidas. adidas, the adidas logo and the 3-stripe trade mark are registered trade marks of the adidas-Solomon group, used with permission. The 1 logo and the Interface logo are trade marks of the adidas-Solomon group, used with permission: (1);

Courtesy of Apple Computer, Inc.: X-ray by Gusto (6); Courtesy of HEAD: (2); Courtesy of Microsoft: (3); SPL: Dr Jeremy Burgess (5); Gusto (4). 48-49 SPL: Andrew Syred. 50-51 Courtesy of adidas. adidas, the adidas logo and the 3-stripe trade mark are registered trade marks of the adidas-Solomon group, used with permission. The 1 logo and the Interface logo are trade marks of the adidas-Solomon group, used with permission. 52-53 Getty: Adam Pretty l; SPL: Gusto br. 54-55 Courtesy of HEAD; SPL: Lawrence Lawry bcr. 56-57 Alamy: plainpicture tcr; StockShot l; Corbis: David Stoecklein tcrr; Getty: Donald Miralle tr. 58-59 Corbis: Duomo tcr; Mike King crA; Tim de Waele cr; Getty: Stone / Nicholas Pinturas l; Courtesy of University of Sheffield, Sports Engineering Research Group: br. 60-61 SPL: Dr Jeremy Burgess bc, br; Eye of Science cr, tcr; Courtesy of TYR Sport Inc.: tl. 62-63 Courtesy of Fuji. 64-65 The Advertising Archive: tcl; Courtesy of Microsoft: c. 66-67 Alamy: Angie Sharp tcr; SPL: Gusto r. 68-69 SPL: Dr Jeremy Burgess l; Philippe Plailly br. 70-71 Courtesy of Apple Computer, Inc.: bl; X-ray by Gusto r. 72-73 Corbis: Bo Zaunders cl; Pierre Merimee bcl; Getty: Image Bank br; Image Bank / Frans Jansen tcr; Photographer's Choice l; Courtesy of TAG Heuer r. 76-77 Alamy: Redferns Music Picture Library bl; Simon Belcher cB; Getty: Taxi / Mel Yates clB; SPL: Dr Jeremy Burgess crB; Gusto t. 78-79 Corbis: Images.com c; SPL: Dr Gary Settles r. 80-81 SPL: Andrew Syred. 82-83 Courtesy of Dyson: (5); Courtesy of NEC Corporation, Japan (www.incx.nec.co.jp/robot/): (6); SPL: Andrew Syred (3); Gusto (4); Hugh Turvey (2); Courtesy of TAG Heuer: (1). 84-85 Corbis: Richard Hamilton Smith. 86-87 DK: Steve Gorton and Gary Ombler cr; SPL: l; Andrew Syred crA, tr; Scott Camazine / K Visscher crB; Susumu Nishinaga cA, cA. 88-89 SPL: Hugh Turvey t; Lawrence Lawry bcl, clB. 90-91 Alamy: Kim Karpeles tr; SPL: Andrew Syred br. 92-93 SPL: Martyn F Chillmaid tr; Courtesy of TAG Heuer. 94-95 Alamy: f1 online br; SPL: Clive Freeman, The Royal Institution l. 96-97 Corbis: Ecoscene / Chinch Gryniewicz bl; SPL: Bruce Frisch r. 98-99 SPL: Alfred Pasieka cr; Dr Arthur Tucker tl; Gusto br; Hugh Turvey tr; Tony McConnell bcl. 100-101 SPL: Gusto l; Courtesy of NASA/WMAP Science Team: br. 102-103 SPL: Gusto. 104-105 Alamy: Ace Stock Limited cBl; Douglas Armand bcl; Design: Corpo Nove and Mauro Taliani; Development: Grado Zero Espace: bl; Courtesy of Dassault Aviation: cA; Getty: Stone / Greg Pease br; Courtesy NASA/JPL-Caltech: clA, tr. 106-107 Alamy: Marco Regalia tl; Corbis: Morton Beebe tcr; Wolfgang Kaehler cr; SPL: Alan Sirulnikoff cl; Still Pictures: Martha Cooper br. 108-109 Getty: Stone / David Arky c; SPL: Sandia National Laboratories br. 110-111 Alamy: f1 online / Andy Ridder clB; SPL: Andrew Syred b; Eye of Science tcr. 112-113 NASA: Goddard Space Flight Center (GL-2002-002528) bcl; SPL: Dr Gary Settles c. 114-115 Corbis: Brownie Harris bcl; SPL: Gusto r. 116-117 Courtesy of Dyson. 118-119 Corbis: Reuters / Eriko Sugita br; Courtesy of NEC Corporation, Japan (www.incx.nec.co.jp/robot/): c. 120-121 SPL: US Department of Energy. 122-123 European Space Agency: AOES Medialab (6); Courtesy NASA/JPL-Caltech: (PIA82679) (1); Courtesy of Rolls-Royce Group plc: (5); SPL: Dr Gary Settles (3); Gusto (4); Courtesy of Toyota (GB) PLC: (2). 124-125 Corbis: William Whitehurst. 126-127 Alamy: Steven May br; DK: Andy Crawford cr; Courtesy of Ducati: crA, tr; SPL: Gusto l. 128-129 Corbis: Ecoscene / Amanda Gazidis tr; Courtesy of Toyota (GB) PLC: c. 130-131 Jaguar Daimler Heritage Trust. 132-133 NASA: Langley Research Center (EL-1994-00681) bcl; SPL: Bruce Frisch tl; Eye of Science tcr; James King-Holmes br; Sinclair Stammers cl. 134-135 DK: © Mercedes Benz br; Getty: Image Bank / Romilly Lockyer tr; SPL: James King-Holmes bl. 136-137 Courtesy of Autostadt GmbH, Wolfsburg, Germany: bl, c; SPL: Pascal Goetgheluck tr. 138-139 Courtesy of Independence Technology (UK). 140-141 Alamy: Kevin Foy c; Getty: Lonely Planet Images / Jean-Bernard Carillet tr. 142-143 Alamy: Stephen Frink Collection tcr; © 2005 Jay Wade, jaywade.com: Courtesy of Deep Flight Submersibles b. 144-145 ©

Mark Wagner / aviation-images.com: bcr, bcrr, br, t; Corbis: D Robert & Lorri Franz tr. 146-147 Corbis: Stuart Westmorland bcl; Courtesy of Rolls-Royce Group plc: c. 148-149 Corbis: br; SPL: Dr Gary Settles l; NASA bcr. 150-151 Corbis: Reuters / Molly Riley bcr; Sygma / Photopress Washington crB; Courtesy of L-3 Communications, Aviation Recorders: l. 152-153 Alamy: Ace Stock Limited tc; ImageState bcl; Wesley Hitt tcr; Corbis: Sygma / Alain Nogues br; Getty: Stone / Matthew McVay cr. 154-155 Corbis: Sygma / Durand Patrick crB; Getty: Stone / Adrian Neal crA; Courtesy NASA/JPL-Caltech: (PIA02679) c; SPL: Planetary Visions Ltd cl. 156-157 NASA: JSC (STS071-741-004). 158-159 European Space Agency: AOES Medialab cl, r; CNES/ARIANESPACE-Service Optique CSG, 2004 bl. 160-161 Getty: Stone / Louise Bencze. 162-163 Corbis: Roger Ressmeyer (6); DK: (2); SPL: Andrew Syred (1); NOAA (5); Pasieka (3); Courtesy of Victorinox, Switzerland: (4). 164-165 SPL: Tek Image. 166-167 Corbis: Bettmann bcr; SPL: Andrew Syred l. 168-169 Courtesy of Apple Computer, Inc. 170-171 Getty: Junko Kimura tl; SPL: Pasieka c. 172-173 DK: Geoff Dann, Courtesy of Lorraine Electronics Surveillance tr; Courtesy of Victorinox, Switzerland: l. 174-175 Courtesy of Fraunhofer-Gesellschaft, Germany: r; Rex: l. 176-177 SPL: Susumu Nishinaga l; Courtesy of Xerox. Xerox is a Trademark of Corporation: tr. 178-179 Corbis: George B Diebold l; SPL: James Holmes br. 180-181 Corbis: David Pollack tr; Pascal Goetgheluck (www.goetgheluck.com): bcl; SPL: Gusto c; James King-Holmes tcl; Mauro Fermariello br. 182-183 DK: l; Rex: Andrew Dunsmore br. 184-185 Rex: Sipa Press. 186-187 Alamy: Robert Harding Picture Library clA; Image courtesy of Space and Naval Warfare Systems Center, San Diego. 188-189 Corbis: Roger Ressmeyer c; SPL: Colin Cuthbert bl. 190-191 Corbis: George Hall. 192-193 SPL: Astrid & Hanns-Frieder Michler cr; Eye of Science bcl, tcr; Pascal Goetgheluck br; Volker Steger tc. 194-195 SPL: Chris Butler cl; NOAA c. 196-197 SPL: Geoff Tompkinson. 198-199 Rex: (5); SPL: Alfred Pasieka (1); Du Cane Medical Imaging Ltd (2), (3); Tom Barrick, Chris Clark, SGHMS (4); Zephyr (6). 200-201 SPL: A.B. Dowsett. 202-203 SPL: cl, cr; CNRI tcr; GE Medical Systems bcr; Simon Fraser c. 204-205 SPL: Sovereign, ISM bl; Tom Barrick, Chris Clark, SGHMS c. 206-207 Corbis: Roger Ressmeyer cAr; SPL: Alfred Pasieka l; NASA tcr. 208-209 Corbis: Anthony Bannister; Gallo Images blA; Courtesy of Intuitive Surgical, Inc.: cBl, cl; Rex: r; SPL: Peter Menzel bcl. 210-211 Courtesy of Abiomed / Jewish Hospital / University of Louisville: br; SPL: Du Cane Medical Imaging Ltd l. 212-213 SPL: Antonia Reeve tr; David M. Martin, M.D. cr; Du Cane Medical Imaging Ltd l. 214-215 Empics Ltd: European Pres Agency r; Getty: Ker Robertson cl; Phil Cole cr; SPL: James King-Holmes bl. 216-217 SPL: Dr Gopal Murti br; Mauro Fermariello r. 218-219 SPL: Andrew Syred tr; Astrid & Hanns-Frieder Michler crB; Dr Goran Bredberg tc; Steve Gschmeissner bl, br. 220-221 SPL: tr; R. Maisonneuve, Publiphoto Diffusion crB. 222-223 SPL: Dr Jeremy Burgess c; Dr Kari Lounatmaa tr. 224-225 SPL: Zephyr. 226-227 SPL: Alfred Pasieka c; Mona Lisa Production bcl. 228-229 SPL: Roger Harris. 236-237 Corbis: Leonard de Selva l; SPL: Novosti r. 238-239 Corbis: Bettmann r; Rex: 239 l. 240-241 SPL: Volker Steger l, r. 242-243 SPL: Dr Jeremy Burgess l, r. 244-245 SPL: Alfred Pasieka l, r, cBl. 246-247 Courtesy of Apple Computer, Inc.: X-Ray by Gusto l, r. 248-249 SPL: John Greim l, r. 250-251 Courtesy of Apple Computer, Inc.: X-ray by Gusto l, r. Getty: Taxi / Lester Lefkowitz bcr; Pure Digital, a division of Imagination Technologies: bl. 252-253 DK: l, r. 254-255 DK: l, r. 256 DK. **Endpapers:** Courtesy of Apple Computer, Inc.: X-ray by Gusto. **Jacket:** Courtesy of Apple Computer, Inc.: X-ray by Gusto.

FireWire, iPod, and PowerBook are trademarks of Apple Computer, Inc., registered in the US and other countries.

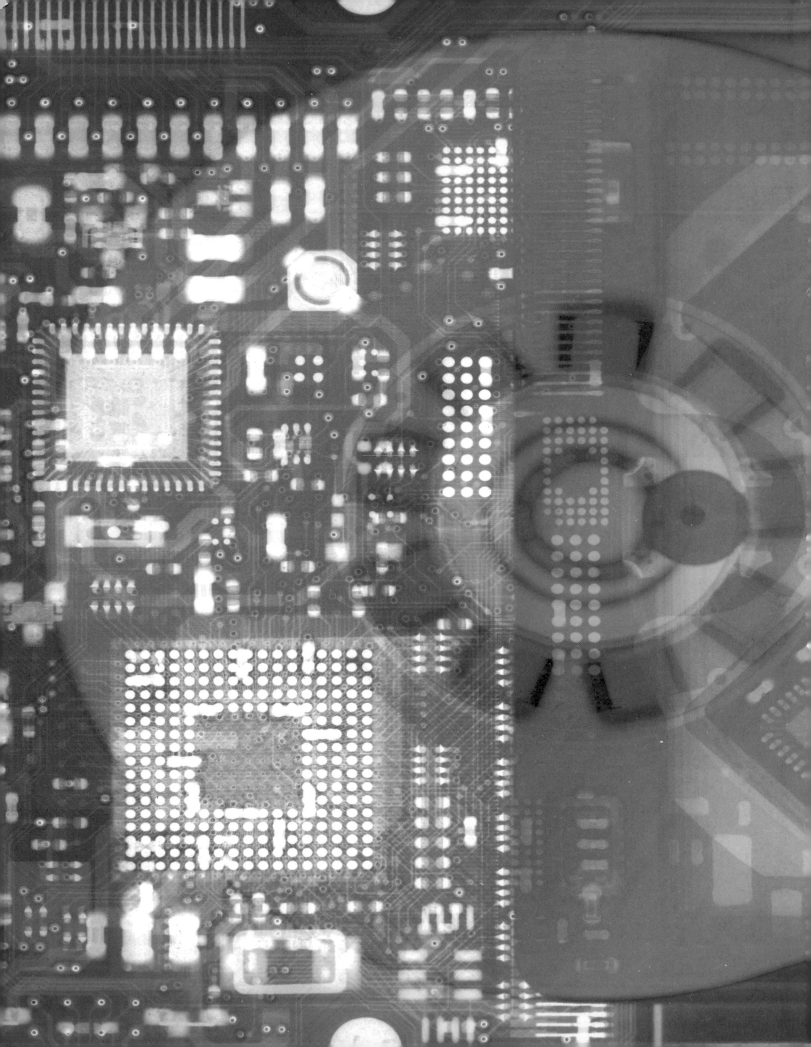